Personal Sustainability

KU-241-055

Transition to sustainability is stuck and academic research has not resulted in significant change so far. A large void in sustainability research and the understanding of sustainable development is an important reason for this. *Personal Sustainability* seeks to address this void, opening up a whole cosmos of sustainable development that has so far been largely unexplored. Mainstream academic, economic and political sustainable development concepts and efforts draw on the macro level and tend to address external, collective and global processes. By contrast, the human, individual, intra- and inter-personal aspects on the micro level are often left unaddressed.

The authors of *Personal Sustainability* invite the reader on a self-reflecting journey into this unexplored inner cosmos of sustainable development, focusing on subjective, mental, emotional, bodily, spiritual and cultural aspects. Although these are intrinsically human aspects they have been systematically ignored by academia. To establish this new field in sustainability research means to leave the common scientific paths and expand the horizon. Together with authors from cultural studies, philosophy, anthropology, psychology, sociology, psychiatry, aesthetics and economics, and supported by contributions from practitioners, this book portrays different approaches to personal sustainability and reflects on their potentials and pitfalls, paving the way to cultures of sustainability.

This book will be of great interest to researchers and students in the field of sustainability and sustainable development, as well as researchers from philosophy, anthropology, psychology, sociology, cultural studies, ethnology, educational research, didactics, aesthetics, economics, business and public administration.

Oliver Parodi, philosopher and engineer, is Managing Director of the KIT-Centre Humans and Technology and Director of the Karlsruhe School of Sustainability at the Karlsruhe Institute of Technology, Germany. His research focus lies in culture and/of sustainability, transdisciplinary sustainability science and personal sustainability.

Kaidi Tamm is a research associate at the Karlsruhe School of Sustainability at the Karlsruhe Institute of Technology, Germany. With a background in culture studies, sociology and political science, her research binds empirical and theoretical approaches and focuses on the participatory and qualitative aspects of sustainability transition.

Routledge Studies in Sustainability

A full list of titles in the series is available at www.routledge.com/Routledge-Studies-in-Sustainability/book-series/RSSTY. Recently published titles:

Sustainability and the Art of Long Term Thinking
Edited by Bernd Klauer, Reiner Manstetten, Thomas Petersen and Johannes Schiller

Cities and Sustainability
A New Approach
Daniel Hoornweg

Transdisciplinary Research and Practice for Sustainability Outcomes
Edited by Dena Fam, Jane Palmer, Chris Riedy and Cynthia Mitchell

A Political Economy of Attention, Mindfulness and Consumerism
Reclaiming the Mindful Commons
Peter Doran

Sustainable Communities and Green Lifestyles
Consumption and Environmentalism
Tendai Chitewere

Aesthetic Sustainability
Product Design and Sustainable Usage
Kristine H. Harper

Stress, Affluence and Sustainable Consumption
Cecilia Solér

Digital Technology and Sustainability
Engaging the Paradox
Edited by Mike Hazas and Lisa P. Nathan

Personal Sustainability
Exploring the Far Side of Sustainable Development
Edited by Oliver Parodi and Kaidi Tamm

Sustainable Modernity
The Nordic Model and Beyond
Edited by Nina Witoszek and Atle Midttun

Personal Sustainability

Exploring the Far Side of
Sustainable Development

**Edited by
Oliver Parodi and
Kaidi Tamm**

Routledge
Taylor & Francis Group

LONDON AND NEW YORK

First published 2018
by Routledge

2 Park Square, Milton Park, Abingdon, Oxfordshire OX14 4RN
52 Vanderbilt Avenue, New York, NY 10017

Routledge is an imprint of the Taylor & Francis Group, an informa business

First issued in paperback 2019

© 2018 selection and editorial matter, Oliver Parodi and Kaidi Tamm;
individual chapters, the contributors

The right of Oliver Parodi and Kaidi Tamm to be identified as the
authors of the editorial material, and of the authors for their individual
chapters, has been asserted in accordance with sections 77 and 78
of the Copyright, Designs and Patents Act 1988.

All rights reserved. No part of this book may be reprinted or
reproduced or utilised in any form or by any electronic, mechanical,
or other means, now known or hereafter invented, including photocopying
and recording, or in any information storage or retrieval system,
without permission in writing from the publishers.

Notice:
Product or corporate names may be trademarks
or registered trademarks, and are used only for identification
and explanation without intent to infringe.

British Library Cataloguing-in-Publication Data
A catalogue record for this book is available from the British Library

Library of Congress Cataloging-in-Publication Data
A catalog record for this book has been requested

ISBN: 978-1-138-06508-6 (hbk)
ISBN: 978-0-367-85302-0 (pbk)

Typeset in Times New Roman
by Florence Production Ltd, Stoodleigh, Devon, UK

Printed in the United Kingdom
by Henry Ling Limited

Contents

List of figures   vii
List of tables   viii
Notes on contributors   ix

1 Personal sustainability: exploring a new field of sustainable
   development   1
   OLIVER PARODI AND KAIDI TAMM

2 Sustainability, culture and personal virtues   18
   REINER MANSTETTEN

3 Psychology of sustainability: psychological resources for
   sustainable lifestyles   33
   MARCEL HUNECKE

4 Care of the self and "Bildung" as condition for and result of
   personal sustainability   51
   MICHAEL NIEHAUS, DIRK SCHMIDT AND SHIRLI HOMBURG

5 Sustainable development: a matter of truth and love   65
   OLIVER PARODI

6 Sustainability in crisis: a perspective of subjective body as
   a 'healing' force   83
   SABIN WENDHACK

7 Developing intra-personal skills as a proactive way to
   personal sustainability: the preventive side of the mental
   health equation   95
   HELENA LASS

8 Inner conflict resolution and self-empowerment as contribution
   for personal sustainability on the case of intentional community
   practices   116
   STELLA VECIANA AND KARIIN OTTMAR

9 Awareness as the new paradigm for personal sustainability:
   a practitioner's perspective on the sustainability transition   136
   INGVAR VILLIDO

10 Reflexivity: exploring the metanarratives of sustainable
   development   151
   KAIDI TAMM

11 Sustainability without the I-sense is nonsense: inner
   'technologies' for a viable future and the inner dimension
   of sustainability   171
   SHELLEY SACKS

12 Personal sustainability: conclusions and perspectives   189
   OLIVER PARODI, SABIN WENDHACK AND KAIDI TAMM

   Index   209

Figures

3.1 Interrelationships between the six psychological resources to foster subjective well-being and sustainable lifestyles   41

8.1 Personal sustainability and alternative sustainable development on the case of community-design practices/methods. Elaborated by Veciana upon Geels Multi-level perspective (2002: 1263)   117

8.2 Forum situation in Sieben Linden ecovillage, 2015. Photographer: Satoshi Hirsch   122

Tables

3.1 Strategies for leading a good life and the associated psychological resources, functions for personal sustainability and positive emotions   38

3.2 Domains of application for the support of the psychological resources for sustainable lifestyles   43

10.1 Dualistic development perspectives of civil society and governance   157

11.1 The four phases of Earth Forum and its capacity-building processes   182

Notes on contributors

Shirli Homburg is a Senior Developer at SAP (Content-as-a-Service, Energy & Natural Resources Industries, EHS & Sustainability Products) and a former consultant in SCC (Scientific Consulting Company). She specialises in toxicology, ecotoxicology and regulatory affairs and is Member of Res et Verba – The Sustainability Network.

Marcel Hunecke is Professor for General Psychology, Organisational and Environmental Psychology at the University of Applied Science and Arts in Dortmund, Germany. His research focuses on strategies to foster sustainable lifestyles, mobility psychology and methods of transdisciplinary research.

Helena Lass is a practicing psychiatrist with a medical degree from Tartu University, Estonia and a founding partner at Wellness Orbit. She specialises in proactive education for mental wellness, intra-personal skills and prevention in mental health.

Reiner Manstetten is a member of the Department of Philosophy at Heidelberg University, Germany. His research focuses on ethics, ecological economy, as well as on the philosophical foundation of economics. A core area of his interest is philosophical mystics. He is an assigned Zen teacher and teaches Zen and Christian Contemplation.

Michael Niehaus has operated his own philosophical practice since 2000 in Dortmund, Germany. He is CEO of the German Professional Association for Philosophical Practice and associate board member of the International Society for Philosophical Practice. He is a professional in research and consulting and a member of Res et Verba – The Sustainability Network.

Kariin Ottmar is a graduated psychologist and long-term ecovillager. She's a trainer and facilitator of courses and events on community building, personal growth and sustainability with long-term experience. She works as a consultant, mediator and supervisor for community-led sustainable projects and as a researcher for the ecovillage movement.

Oliver Parodi, philosopher and engineer, is Managing Director of the KIT-Centre Humans and Technology and Director of the Karlsruhe School of

Sustainability at the Karlsruhe Institute of Technology, Germany. His research focus lies in culture and/of sustainability, transdisciplinary sustainability science and personal sustainability.

Shelley Sacks is Professor of Social Sculpture at Oxford Brookes University, Director of the Social Sculpture Research Unit and cultural activism practitioner. Key research projects 'Lab for New Knowledge and an Eco-Social Future' and 'Earth Forum' explore the role of imagination in transformation, ecological citizenship and paradigm shift in practice.

Dirk Schmidt is Founder and Coordinator of Res et Verba – The Sustainability Network. His work and research focus on cultures of sustainability in organisations, leadership, consulting as well as in professional services.

Kaidi Tamm is a Research Associate at the Karlsruhe School of Sustainability at the Karlsruhe Institute of Technology, Germany. With a background in culture studies, sociology and political science, her research binds empirical and theoretical approaches and focuses on the participatory and qualitative aspects of sustainability transition.

Stella Veciana teaches "Transdisciplinary Realworld Laboratories" at the Institute for Ethics and Transdisciplinary Sustainability Research at Leuphana University, Lüneburg. Her research focuses on Transition Research, Higher Education for Sustainability, Community-Based Participatory Research and Methods, and Artistic Research. She is a member of the Federation of German Scientists, Berlin.

Ingvar Villido is an awareness teacher, Kriya Yoga Acharya and the head of the adult education company Human LLC. His awareness-based The Art of Conscious Change course series combines yogic and scientific knowledge. He is also the founder of the Lilleoru community and ecovillage in Estonia.

Sabin Wendhack graduated in philosophy, economy and economic engineering and works as a software engineer. Also practicing as body therapist, her main research interest is the relationship of the individual to the world, particularly experienced from a perspective of subjective body.

We, the editors, want to thank Sabin Wendhack for her great and precious support in co-editing this book. More than once you were a knight in shining armour.

1 Personal sustainability

Exploring a new field of sustainable development

Oliver Parodi and Kaidi Tamm

What could "personal sustainability" mean? At first, it is the working title for a new and emerging field of sustainability research and action that covers all kind of human aspects. Among others, personal, intra- and inter-personal, psychological, anthropological, philosophical, aesthetic and perceptive aspects of sustainable development are addressed. The formation process of this book started an international research expedition towards an understanding of the field of personal sustainability, with the aim of drawing a preliminary map of the research field. To enable a deeper insight into the aspects that contribute or hinder personal sustainability, we invited both researchers and practitioners active in different areas of the broad topic of sustainable development to contribute as authors to our expedition and create landmarks by formulating their perspectives on various human aspects of sustainable development. So, this book as a whole delivers an overview and initially answers what personal sustainability is about and provides a starting point for further discussion.

First, we want to outline our way to "personal sustainability" and why we think that something like personal sustainability is very important for the theoretical discussion of sustainable development and furthermore for its implementation and realisation.

Towards personal sustainability

In the course of the editors' sustainability research and as a result of cooperation on various disciplinary and transdisciplinary sustainability projects over the last 15 years, we've become aware that in the scientific discourse on sustainable development as well as in the societal, technical and political efforts aiming at sustainable development, a big part of the puzzle is still missing. Or, to put it another way: one half of the sustainability universe is still mainly unrecognised and unexplored.

We can approach this unrecognised half from different sides. Theories, texts, projects and approaches of sustainable development normally mention and address only the *collective* side, such as political decisions, scientific findings, technical solutions, legal regulations, economic mechanisms and so on, but not the *individual*, the *personal* side. In terms of scale, the field of sustainable development extends across the *macro level* (e.g. earth system, climate change, worldwide financial and commodity flows) and *meso* level (e.g. regional processes, milieus, sustainable lifestyles and consumption patterns) but does not really encompass the *micro* level including the individual, intra- and inter-personal aspects.

Furthermore, the discussion addresses sustainable development in terms of an object or points at objects of sustainable (or unsustainable) development. However, it does not consider the conscious and acting subject of sustainable development, the human being perceiving and pointing at these objects. In discussions about sustainable development for example, the ecological backpack or the ecological footprint are mentioned, measured and discussed – but not those responsible for it. It is us as human beings who leave the footprint or wear the backpack. Somehow the human being and us as individuals are missing in the theories of, considerations on and endeavours for sustainable development. Human beings are almost systematically excluded.

Additionally, sustainable development is normally discussed as a matter of the *outer world*, the world surrounding us human beings but not as a matter of our *inner* world. Discussing sustainable development we talk about the *environment*, environmental damage and protection, but not about the world inside us, our very own landscapes, structures and 'inner ecosystems'. Up to now, sustainable development addresses the transformation of infrastructures, economic systems and societies but not the transformation of individuals. It deals with economic and social patterns and problems but not with emotional and psychic ones. Biodiversity is mentioned but not our subjective body. The way we make sense of the world, including perception and interpretation processes, (individual) experiences, thoughts, emotional patterns, psychic structures, awareness etc. are not taken into account when striving for sustainable development.

To summarise, stepping back and looking at the sustainable development universe from the abovementioned perspectives, half of it, respectively several halves of it, are not really addressed yet: the personal side, the micro level, the conscious and acting subject and the inner human world are not taken into account so far. These halves are what personal sustainability and this book are about.

We, you and I, are missing. This is like reckoning without one's host – and our efforts for a sustainable development will remain incomplete, insufficient and ultimately might fail.

The need for a broader and increased understanding of the human role in sustainable development processes became evident to us, as well as the need for research covering a larger depth of the human issues and dimensions that directly influence sustainable development processes. So far we have found surprisingly little systematic study on the topic.

Furthermore, dealing with sustainability research for years has led us to the conclusion that the scientific discourses on the problems and syndromes of an unsustainable world, as well as the solutions that have been suggested and pursued in order to foster sustainable development, are often, to a high degree, superficial. Looking at and dealing with sustainable development from an ecological, economic and social dimension – or even from an institutional, cultural, political, procedural, etc. dimension – is necessary and the right thing to do, but at the end of the day it is not sufficient as an answer to the global unsustainability we face and it will not be enough to make the shift and allow the transition to a sustainable future.

The chapters of this book try to provide more detailed answers from various perspectives to the question of why sustainability discourse needs completion as suggested. The allegory of an 'iceberg' might illustrate the dimension of the hidden and unnoticed sphere in a good way: looking at unsustainable development as a combination of ecological, economic and social problems shows the tip of the iceberg above the surface (of our collective, scientific and political awareness). But nine-tenths of the problem are still hidden and unknown, beneath the surface of our collective shared awareness. For us, the hidden nine-tenths of (un)sustainability are a matter of culture, which means that they underlie and shape the upper part of the iceberg, i.e. the social, economic and ecological problems (and also the sustainable efforts and solutions proposed). In order to get a more reasonable and appropriate view of sustainable (non-)development, we have to step back, broaden the horizon and dive deeper into our cultural patterns, cultural and human history. Culture and also cultural change takes place through the interplay between the collective and the individual. Getting access to the necessary cultural change linked to sustainable development in a more appropriate way would mean to bring the individual, the personal side of sustainable development into the spotlight more than ever.

The Malthusian diagnosis broadly known since the 1970s as the "limits to growth" line of reasoning is in a way very simple and has been confirmed over and over again (Meadows *et al.* 1972, Turner, Alexander 2014): we as humankind live beyond our global limits and are heading for catastrophe. The United Nations' answer for turning the disastrous diagnosis into a positive programmatic for "our common future" is: "sustainable development" means a "development that meets the needs of the present without compromising the ability of future generations to meet their own needs" (WCED 1987: 41). That is simple, too, and, one could think, in a way very basic and natural. Every mother, father or grandparent is familiar with this 'programmatic'. So, the interesting question concerning sustainable development is: why did we need a global group of experts convened by the United Nations to determine what should be obvious for every human being: to care for our children and grandchildren?

So, there is something going really wrong in our modern times and it is apparently hard to grasp. We propose that one reason for that is that the unsustainable cultural patterns are embedded in our contemporary modern way of life so deeply that they are to an extent normal, popular, ubiquitous and natural. That makes them neither easy to detect nor easy to change. Many of these cultural patterns leading to unsustainability can be traced back hundreds or thousands of years in our cultural and human history and nowadays infuse not only all continents and areas of life – but also us as individuals, persons and human beings as well as our self-perception and self-conception and what it means to be "human" at all.

Following the meaning of culture and cultural change as interplay between collective and individual, we are convinced that a sustainability transition that will succeed in the long run cannot take place as a mere transformation of society but will necessarily imply a transformation of us as persons. In consequence, personal sustainability is concerned with the human being, its personal, intra-personal, mental and perception patterns, thoughts, emotions, habits, the subjective body and our self-conceptions that are closely linked to an unsustainable or sustainable development.

To foster the transformation to sustainability – the last reason for dealing with personal sustainability that will be mentioned here – there is a need to bridge the gap between theory and practice, knowing and living, and thinking and acting. This is needed to move sustainable development as a concept and idea forward into life, towards lived cultures of sustainability. Therefore it is necessary to bring the concepts and ideas of sustainable development closer to the people. That would also suggest to extend and refine the discussions and concepts of sustainable development so that they become much more human, vivid and personal.

What is meant by sustainable development?

Before going deeper into the field of "personal sustainability" we have to explain and clarify our understanding of "sustainable development",[1] especially because the following chapters refer to and are based on this concept and the respective discourses.

Although there are different interpretations of this concept in the following texts, we and all the authors basically refer to a concept intentionally created in the 1980s to convey a specific multi-dimensional development model aiming to balance the ecological, social and economic interests and achieve inter-generational and intra-generational equity on the global scale. The classical sustainable development definition stems from the World Commission on Environment and Development's (WCED) 1987 report "Our Common Future" and ties together the concern for the carrying capacity of natural systems with the social challenges faced by humanity by balancing the three development dimensions (WCED 1987).

The editors' understanding of sustainable development is close to the "Integrated Concept of Sustainable Development" (Kopfmüller et al. 2001, Schultz et al. 2008), which is based on the Brundtland Report and integrates and reflects the international discourse of the following decades. As a concept, it adds the cultural dimension and overcomes the common separation of the (three or more) sustainable development dimensions or pillars. It considers both sufficiency as well as efficiency requirements to fit into the natural limits to growth and leans towards the strong rather than the weak sustainability stance.

However, by introducing personal sustainability as a missing part of sustainable development and sustainability research, we exceed the content of this integrated concept addressing human, personal and inner aspects.

Sustainable development and personal sustainability

Through the chapters of this book we argue that the mainstream concepts and understandings of sustainable development are not sufficient to realise a viable sustainable future and to transform our unsustainable cultures into cultures of sustainability. By using the concept of "personal sustainability" we want to widen the understanding of sustainable development as a guiding principle. Therefore, we base personal sustainability on a common understanding of sustainable development as described in the section above. Personal sustainability is not meant as an alternative to sustainable development, but as an essential extension, complementary to the common understanding(s) of sustainable development focusing on collective, quantitative, outer and macro/meso-level aspects. As we said above, relevant keys to sustainability transition lie in the realm of personal and human aspects. Employing "personal sustainability", we want to explore the ability to live in a way that is sustainable for oneself and one's surroundings. That includes a qualitative view on the inner situation of a person, the inner conditions shaping their lived experiences, their perception and their scope of action.

According to our approach, inner and outer sustainability are not separate, but interconnected dimensions. The aspects influencing personal sustainability include a set of primarily outer characteristics such as physical health or natural beauty, as well as inner features such as consciousness, spiritual, cultural and worldview-related aspects or a sense of well-being. The inner features further include perceptions, bodily experiences, as well as thoughts and values, needs and wishes, emotional and habitual patterns. In individual cases and different circumstances, the inner needs and qualities that support personal sustainability can differ. Furthermore, personal sustainability helps to avoid setting humans apart from the rest of the world and purporting the human being (as individual) as not part of the sustainability game.

Not having established a consistent theory of personal sustainability yet, in the first instance we consider the relations between personal sustainability and sustainable development in three ways:

1   Personal sustainability as a *part* of sustainable development: personal sustainability is a necessary and so far under-researched part of sustainable development that helps to complement the current discourse with human aspects. Including this dimension in the sustainable development concept broadens the perspective and opens up new ways of approaching, understanding and realising sustainable development.

2   Personal sustainability as a *condition* for sustainable development – knowing more about the conditions and obstacles for achieving personal sustainability – is one of the preconditions for a successful realisation of the outer sustainable development. An outer sustainable development transformation is not fully realisable without an inner transformation; a collective transformation is not realisable without an individual transformation. Leaving the personal aspects aside constitutes a part of the reason for the slow progress of the sustainability transformation.

3   Personal sustainability as an independent *goal* of sustainable development: if we consider sustainable development as a process leading towards a more sustainable world, personal sustainability can be seen as one of the goals of sustainable development. It is important to understand personal sustainability as an *independent* goal of sustainable development, as it would contradict the idea to use it as an instrument for 'sustainability' purposes or achieving utilitarian aims. That means it has to be considered a value in itself. In the end, only that makes sure that the human being cannot be instrumentalised and will not lose their autonomy and freedom in the name of sustainability.

Considering these three relations might be useful to clarify the connections between sustainable development and personal sustainability.

The term and history of "personal sustainability"

The term "personal sustainability" (German: "Personale Nachhaltigkeit") was invented in 2008 in the course of the formation of the School of Sustainability[2] (SoS) at the Karlsruhe Institute of Technology (KIT) as a search term and working title for new ways of understanding, teaching and practicing sustainable development. The quest for such new ways was driven by the increasing unease and concern about ongoing unsustainable development, be it globally or locally, including the negative and unhealthy side-effects of our modern, industrialised, technological and knowledge-based societies – which can be very personal, concrete and painful. It was also driven by the perception that the available answers and solutions of the sustainable development discourse and endeavours fall short and are insufficient.

The concrete starting point of the quest for our SoS team were the following questions: What has yoga got to do with sustainable development? (How) can we bring together the elaborated scientific-ethical ideas of sustainable development with yoga as an age-old eastern tradition, philosophy and way of life?[3] (How) can yoga contribute to a sustainable world? Quickly the quest was extended, a sustainable development for mind, body and soul as well as for societies, nations and humanity was in demand – and more questions arose.

We started a lecture series, carrying out research and self-experiments, we invited experts and, in 2009, we held a workshop with pioneers of sustainable development in different areas of action: managers in leading positions in worldwide companies, a university rector, leaders of sustainability institutes at universities, philosophers, politicians and students. During this workshop it became clear that the quest for personal sustainability would be a highly worthwhile and nearly revolutionary endeavour, but at the same time extremely difficult to achieve. We would have to bridge gaps between science and eastern philosophy, mind, body and soul, science and individual experiences, theory and practice, brainstorming and 'brain-silencing', etc. – categorical gaps, gorges that were shaped long ago in human history and that have deepened over time. Now, after 10 years of dealing with personal sustainability we have successfully built several provisional bridges, but not more. It takes more than a team of five to ten persons – rather 5,000 to 10,000 – and more time to build solid bridges over these wide and deep gorges.

Why did we choose the term "*personal* sustainability"? First of all we want to address something new and different in the sustainability cosmos, therefore we needed a term that was not used yet. The term "personal sustainability" fits but is not meant that highly selected as "*ecological* sustainability" or "*economic* sustainability". As a search term it points at the other, the mostly unexplored side of the sustainability universe, at the omitted halves mentioned above and therefore at a wide range of (unexplored) topics. It would have been possible and partly suitable to call the endeavour "individual sustainability", "subjective, "inner", "human", "micro", "self" or "subjective bodily sustainability" as well – but we chose "personal sustainability", as all other terms have a limited perspective, too, and have their own theoretical discourses and philosophical backgrounds. In the end, "personal" seemed for us the most open and less directing term, and it includes human, subjective, individual, micro and inner aspects. In consequence, we want to explicitly include all the aforementioned terms and possible discourses around them into the research field of personal sustainability. This also applies for similar endeavours and terms such as "inner transition", "inner change" and "personal development" if they are addressed in the context of a sustainable development.

With the term "personal" we associate a lived personal sustainability, as in the end sustainability is not only a question of theory and science but one of a collectively and commonly shared transformation. So personal sustainability in a way is more than a scientific endeavour (and as individual experience and transformation process it could never be scientific). Thus, we have not chosen a term that refers back to or corresponds with a scientific discipline directly, in the way that "*ecological*" or "*economic* sustainability" do. For example, even if we include psychological aspects, it's not a "psychological sustainability" we are heading for. That (term) would fall too short.

Furthermore, with recourse to the term "person", we want to address and highlight the acting, responsible, conscious and self-aware, free and, in a broad understanding, political human being – that can act and live according to (or 'in harmony with') a sustainable development or not, that is free to transform itself according to a sustainable development or not.

Last but not least, through a reinterpretation of a (contested) etymologic root of "person" i.e. the Latin term "per-sonare" (English "to sound through"), we want to point out the following: In "personal sustainability", allegorically the future of a collectively shared, lived and vivid culture of sustainability sounds through, not very loud and clear currently, but if you are mindful and silent while reading this book it will definitely be perceptible. We hope you will hear this 'sound of the future' and respond to it, so that the calls for change and a sustainable future will grow louder and discursively clearer.

Similar approaches

Prior use of the term "personal sustainability"

Even if personal sustainability is not introduced as a research field and categorical and programmatic part of sustainable development by others so far, there are some authors who have used the term "personal sustainability" in their research in different contexts.

Some authors have used the term as an utilitarian concept dealing with the usefulness of people to society for as long as possible. For example, the idea that one should use one's whole lifespan in a meaningful way, including the last 25–30 years after retiring when people tend to also withdraw from social life and engagement and become 'useless' has been described as "personal sustainability" by Bill Berkowitz. He considers personal sustainability in this sense as something everybody can do to contribute to the well-being of society (Berkowitz 1996). In a somewhat similar manner, "personal sustainability" has been used in the area of human resources management. In this context, investing in "human capital", e.g. by providing stress reduction or training for employees, is discussed as a requirement for achieving more sustainable working conditions (see e.g. Filinkov *et al*. 2011). These reductionist and somewhat economic approaches are not in line with our understanding of "personal sustainability" – our understanding at least goes far beyond this utilitarian approach.

In a similar manner to our understanding, the concept has been used in the sense of what individuals can do to contribute to the achievement of external sustainability aims, e.g. more sustainable or green behaviour (see e.g. Jakubowitz 2002, Leibson-Hawkins 2005, Degenhardt 2007, Bilharz 2009). Focusing on the person and personality, Rebecca Collins used the term to describe sustainability of persons and sustainable development as part of the development of a personality (Collins 2015), which is very akin to our approach.

Contributions to "personal sustainability" from various fields not using the term

There are endeavours that strive to widen the scope of ideas and concepts of sustainable development by something similar to personal sustainability but do not use the term.

In the sphere of the ecological movement and community building, for example, there are strong efforts to bring together ecology and personality, as well as communal and individual sustainable development, and this not only in theory but also in practice (e.g. Kunze 2009). The Global Ecovillage Network with its United Nations (UN)-endorsed international Ecovillage Design Education programme and a series of four books covering socially, ecologically and economically sustainable alternatives as well as worldview aspects (Joubert, Alfred 2007, Dawson *et al*. 2010, Mare, Lindegger 2011, Harland, Keepin 2012) also need to be mentioned here.

Another sphere where ideas of a personal sustainability have gained ground are the (overlapping) fields of human resource management, organisation management and leadership in the context of or aiming for sustainable development. Two different ways of joining *sustainability* and *leadership* into one concept prevail. There is *sustainable leadership* in the meaning of how leadership could continue in a sustained manner to achieve its goals, and *leadership for sustainability*, encompassing ways to ensure a leadership that is directed towards sustainability (Marshall *et al.* 2011). Leadership for sustainability theory goes by different names, including corporate social responsibility, environmental leadership, ethical leadership, distributed and servant leadership.

Environmental psychology has been a well-established and broad discipline, or better an interdisciplinary research field, for decades. With its focus on the interplay between individuals and their surroundings and its value and motivation orientation, it addresses the person and their inner world. In consequence, there is a major intersection of the fields of environmental psychology and personal sustainability. Environmental psychology with its (research) aim of solving complex environmental problems in the pursuit of individual well-being within a societal or cultural context can contribute to personal sustainability to a high degree. On the other hand, these research approaches address a large number of different topics as well.

Other scientific research endeavours such as *human ecology, social-ecological research* or *social psychology* touch on and can contribute to personal sustainability and have to be mentioned here. *Deep ecology*, introduced by Arne Naess in the early 1970s (Naess, Glasser 2005) and *ecopsychology* (Roszak *et al.* 1995) are approaches that are in many ways similar to personal sustainability. They broaden horizons, leave the conventional purview of science, address the human being in a more holistic way (including a spiritual dimension), put them in a wider context, and try to stop and change an eco-destructive way of life. However, deep ecology refers to and builds a certain philosophy and draws the picture of a specific way of life. In contrast to that we want to propose a much wider concept of personal sustainability and would not agree to all assumptions made by and assertions growing on the philosophy of deep ecology.

In the fields of the arts, respectively at the interface between arts and sciences, there are approaches to sustainability dealing with inner human aspects such as the "imaginal work in the inner atelier" or the "Earth Forum" (Shelley Sacks, see Chapter 11) or Hildegard Kurt's works "*Growing! Concerning the Spiritual in Sustainability*" (Kurt 2010, own translation) and "*The New Muse: An Attempt to Future Viability*" (Kurt 2017, own translation) for example. Sacks' and Kurt's works refer to artists such as Wassily Kandinsky or Joseph Beuys. Because arts have no restrictions of inter-subjectivity or general truths (like science has), they often deal with inner, spiritual and very personal aspects and are very culture sensitive, therefore they are a rich field of inspiration for personal sustainability.

In studies dedicated to the cultural dimension of sustainability or in sustainability research focusing on cultural aspects or cultural change, sometimes personal aspects are mentioned – partly intended and often in passing (see e.g. Krainer,

Trattnigg 2007, Banse *et al.* 2011, Holz, Stoltenberg 2011, Parodi 2011, Parodi *et al.* 2011, Parodi 2015, Routledge 2017). However, there is no systematic collection and reappraisal of personal or individual aspects in the research field of culture and sustainability.

Recently, singular and scattered approaches (even if small), which are very close to personal sustainability, but named differently, are occurring and increasingly entering the scientific discourse of sustainable development. For example in 2017 at the International Sustainability Transition conference in Sweden a dialogue session "Exploring the Role of Inner Change in Sustainability Transition" took place, organised by an international group of sustainability scientists interested in "inner transition" (IST 2017).

More and more, sustainability researchers all over the world are addressing the topic of personal sustainability within their work. They are focusing, for example, on well-being and the needs of people in the context of sustainable development (Rauschmayer *et al.* 2012), arguing for *Mindfulness in Sustainability Science, Practice and Teaching* (Wamsler *et al.* 2017) or *Mindfulness and Sustainable Consumption* (Fischer *et al.* 2017), dealing with *Spirituality and Sustainability: New Horizons and Exemplary Approaches* (Dhiman, Marques 2016), or arguing for the relevance of "interiority for sustainable urban development" (Woiwode 2016) – just to mention some of a growing number of works.

Aims and approaches of the book

With this book we want to illustrate that one half of the sustainability cosmos is almost unexplored by now. We recommend "personal sustainability" as the name for this unexplored half and introduce it as an important and emerging field of sustainability research. We would like to outline its possible contributions to a better understanding of (un)sustainable development and its potential to support a transition to sustainability, heading for a future culture of sustainability.

Looking at the abovementioned similar approaches, we conceive "personal sustainability" at first as a collecting basin and melting pot for all kinds of approaches covering human, personal and inner aspects of sustainable development. So far these approaches are – compared to the amount of classical sustainability research – very rare, and what is more, very sparse. One can find works in the field of aesthetics dealing with personal sustainability topics or in human ecology, cultural studies, ecopsychology or organisation management. Each of them remains a peripheral phenomenon in its research field. However, gathered together across the various disciplines, it becomes obvious that there are many and important approaches. So, the first landmarks, the first dots on the map of the unrecognised half of the sustainability cosmos become visible and slowly you can imagine the vast expanse of the terra incognita.

And what is more, by collecting different 'personal' approaches of various disciplines and research fields and bringing them together under the heading "personal sustainability", references between these approaches become apparent. Thus, it's not only about creating a map of solitary points but also showing similarities, differences, overlaps and possible interactions of the approaches. By doing so a better, consistent and shared understanding of personal sustainability can grow, and by and by a theory of personal sustainability can emerge.

Before hastily 'defining' personal sustainability, we find it necessary to open up a spectrum of different approaches. Therefore, we have invited authors from different disciplines and backgrounds with both theoretical and practitioners' contributions to write for this book. As a result, this volume aims to start mapping the new field and research sphere of personal sustainability by describing a few landmarks more in detail.

In preparation for this book the editors also supervised three transdisciplinary research seminars on personal sustainability at the Karlsruhe Institute of Technology from 2015 to 2017 (KSN 2017). Some of the authors included in this book also presented their perspectives there. During this time we have noticed that there is increasing interest in personal sustainability. However, in the irregular meetings at transition or sustainability conferences or in virtual groups of likeminded researchers and practitioners it became apparent that the scope and approaches are so diverse that a step forward was needed in order to establish a field of research bundling and to host this interest. This book aims to make this step forward, as we expect this field of research to gain importance in the coming decades and wish to facilitate its emergence.

As we suspect that there is a link between personal sustainability and the difficulties we face regarding the transition to sustainable development, this book aims to illustrate this relation and state the need for further research in the field of personal sustainability as it can be expected to support and facilitate the transition to sustainability.

Regarding the transition towards sustainable development, this book shows that personal sustainability, while being of high importance itself, also serves as an intermediate step towards a related topic: culture(s) of sustainability. While personal sustainability deals with the inner situation of the individual, the personal 'space' of sustainability, at the same time it has to be addressed and followed together, in relation to each other and the world. However, the possibility to relate to each other and to the world requires the access to oneself and the proper 'inner space' as a precondition. Knowledge, orientation and habit regarding this inner space provide personal sustainability that is the precondition to engage in common and connected development processes towards a viable future. Therefore, preparing these grounds, with this book we also want to pave the way for a subsequent book on the emerging topic of culture(s) of sustainability.

Our effort and attempt as editors of this book start from the basis of sustainability sciences. First of all we address the *scientific* discourse about sustainable development and aim at widening the scientific understanding of sustainable development. However, if you want and try to do this in a deep and significant manner, you have to leave the solid ground of the established scientific discourse (about sustainable development), leave the well-known theories and ways of thinking and have a look at other topics and on different grounds. We did and do so by leaving established sustainability sciences in a transdisciplinary and philosophical manner, but not with the aim of creating an alternative to science but to broaden and complement (sustainability) science. What may happen by searching for personal sustainability is that the ways sciences are practiced nowadays, along with their paradigms, become questionable and might have to be revised. But even that is not unusual for the practice and evolution of sciences (e.g. Kuhn 1962).

The transdisciplinary research journey of the book towards and beyond the borders and also the constraints of common science shows that the fundamental terms of science, e.g. "truth", "knowledge" and "reasoning" are not sufficient to handle the topic in an adequate and satisfying way, in order to answer the questions and support transformation. Terms such as "perception", "connectedness", "awareness" and "love" are employed, providing behind their unscientific image the potential to further access the subject in question. In consequence, this book aims to question the suitability of common sciences' approaches and tools for this particular subject and invite the reader to extend thinking in a way that allows a more wholesome human sustainable development.

As already said, this book invites the reader to take part in a research expedition to the far side of sustainable development. As this far side is the *personal* or the *inner* side of the human being, the approaches in this book are most of all self-reflexive ones. So the reader is asked to attend this journey in a self-reflexive and self-exploring way, too. If you are curious and want to engage yourself, *you* could be subject of this research expedition, too. Perhaps joining this journey with the authors might give you new insights into yourself, your inner world and how to deal with sustainability personally.

Content of the book

The chapters included in this volume were chosen, on the one hand, to fill the gaps in sustainability research and sustainable development and, on the other hand, to show the variety of topics and perspectives in the research field of personal sustainability. By presenting the chosen chapters the landscape of personal sustainability is mapped and the frontiers – what should belong to the research area of personal sustainability and what not? – are opened to discussion.

The transdisciplinary approach includes the different types of knowledge and experiences as mutually and equally relevant contributions to the field. Accordingly the contributors have different backgrounds, include both researchers and practitioners, and are active in fields ranging from economics, psychology, psychiatry, culture studies, sociology and philosophy to health consultation, "Bildung",[4] body therapy and aesthetics.

Personal sustainability implies the question of the adequate conception of man. So we start our (self-reflexive) journey through the field of personal sustainability with a philosophical reflection on the different conceptions of man corresponding to sustainable or unsustainable development. Preparing this, Reiner Manstetten, a philosopher, economist and contemplation teacher, leads us through basic considerations about nature, culture, liberty and the good life in the context of sustainable development and in recourse to ancient Greek philosophy. To overcome a "homo non-sustinens", he draws a detailed picture of a "homo sustinens" along with his or her personal virtues of will, insight and receptivity. He mentions the respective aesthetical education and spiritual practice. According to Manstetten, "if humanity does its utmost there is sound reason for hope for a sustainable good life" in the future.

Psychology surely is a discipline that is able to contribute much to an inner personal sustainability in particular and to sustainable development in general. Marcel Hunecke, organisational and environmental psychologist, focuses, in his chapter "Towards a psychology of sustainability", on specific mental resources necessary for sustainable development. He argues that within the context of cultural transformation towards a sustainable post-growth society, people should and can be supported in developing their own internal psychological resources to ensure subjective well-being independent of material wealth. Based on positive psychology, environmental psychology, socio-ecological research and resource-oriented counselling, six psychological resources are identified, which can support this cultural transformation.

Next, Michael Niehaus, Dirk Schmidt and Shirli Homburg show us (practiced) philosophy as an art of life. Based on the lessons from ancient philosophy, they describe the ability for self-care, self-guidance and self-knowledge as the foundation for the good life, leading to personal sustainability. Therefore self-receptive, self-reflective and self-productive aspects, as well as social, prospective and preventive ones are considered essential. By asking (us) a couple of specific self-reflecting questions, the authors show how to bring personal sustainability into everyday life. Furthermore they put Bildung and personal sustainability in a reciprocal relationship, and argue that Bildung is the further context and that self-care is a specific 'technique' of Bildung. Both are considered conditions for and results of personal sustainability.

Sustainable development is a matter of truth and love, states Oliver Parodi, sustainability researcher, and a transition from unsustainable to sustainable culture(s) will fail if not both aspects are lived – and mentioned in theory and practice of personal sustainability. Starting from a very human and everyday perspective on the connections of truth, fear and love to sustainable development, he later puts sustainable development, truth and love in the context of human history and the evolution of consciousness. How we deal with the world is an expression of our relatedness. Referring to a typology of human-world-relationships, he shows categorically different qualities of human relations to the world. The appearance of "sustainable development" is a clear hint for a (collective) dawning shift to a new type of relationship, an "I-We relation". Therefore, a realised sustainable development and a future culture of sustainability mean a categorically new quality of life and being human.

Starting from the "subjective body", Sabin Wendhack, body therapist and philosopher, diagnoses "Sustainability in crisis" and proposes "a perspective of subjective body as "healing" force". In her chapter, she outlines that the crisis of sustainability is connected to the missing intensity and quality of the relation of the individual to the world. In order to address the crisis and find an answer to it, that would have more likely the quality of 'healing' than that of a 'solution', it is necessary to take into account the situation where contact between a person and the world takes place: the subjective body. Referring to Sigmund Freud and Martin Buber, "healing" can be described as a process of integrating experience into the own self, thereby overcoming disruption and enlarging the own potential to relate to the world. By such personal transformation processes towards sustainability, taking place in the subjective body, caring for others and the world will become a subjective necessity.

Psychiatrist Helena Lass discusses the relevance of developing intra-personal skills as a proactive way to individual resilience. She argues that mental health diseases are steadily gaining the status of an epidemic and stresses the relevance of an efficient preventive approach to mental health. Lass suggests that intra-personal health depends in the first place on the extent to which one is aware of the different functions of one's being. Second, it depends on the skills for operating with different functional fractions in the inner world. Considering this, unsustainable personal conditions can be transferred to sustainable ones. In its argumentation the chapter refers to an explorative case study of ten individuals with mild psychological complaints conducted by the author.

As researchers and practitioners of community-design methods Stella Veciana and Kariin Ottmar discuss "Inner conflict resolution and self-empowerment as contribution for personal sustainability on the case of intentional community practices". Intentional communities are particularly relevant in their pioneering path towards innovative sustainable lifestyles following an integrative approach of sustainable development. From a socio-cultural perspective their innovative methods nurture intra-personal growth processes based on a matured conflict culture and a peaceful coexistence culture in regards to both human and natural systems. The main aim of this chapter is to explore the impact of four selected community-design methods on competences for personal sustainability as practiced in intentional communities.

Ingvar Villido, yoga and awareness teacher, states that unsustainability is very often a result of following automatic habit patterns. There are different ways to achieve a more sustainable development. The usual way includes regulations, control mechanisms and is very (inner) resource intensive. This chapter explores alternatives based on increased use of awareness as the key to personal and societal sustainability. He suggests that individuals, communities and societies can function sustainably in the long run only when the amount of automatic emotional and mental complexes disconnecting us from the surrounding reality are reduced and substituted with action with awareness. Being aware always includes becoming aware of the present. Awareness of awareness constitutes the new paradigm offering a new, more sustainable way of living.

The following chapter discusses the role of metanarratives in personal and communal sustainability crises. Kaidi Tamm, social and cultural scientist, shows how metanarratives, with their often-unquestioned normative power, are shaping the individual and collective attitudes as well as peoples' perception of the best development path. Narratives as a basic human way of making sense of the world are inevitable, but becoming more aware of the underlying mental patterns building up metanarratives, often creating unsustainable instead of sustainable solutions, helps to build a reflexive basis necessary for enabling transformations towards well-informed and broad-based personal and societal sustainability.

"Sustainability without the I-sense is nonsense". We need "inner 'technologies' for a viable future and the inner dimension of sustainability". Artist and social sculpture expert Shelley Sacks explores the connection between inner work and outer action in the shaping of a humane and ecologically viable future. This includes a redefinition of the "aesthetic" as all that enlivens our being, in contrast to the "anaesthetic" as all that numbs us. In contrast to (outer) technologies "inner technologies", related to Joseph Beuys and the early sustainability thinker E.M. Schumacher, are vital to the shaping of a sustainable future. Sacks leads us to the "inner atelier" and gives us colourful insights to the imaginal practice and the development of the Earth Forum methodology as social-aesthetic approaches fostering sustainable development.

After the topics and approaches of the different authors have been presented, in the last chapter of the book we, the editors, provide a brief conclusion regarding the scientific enterprise under the search term of "personal sustainability" and the subjects it might address. Further we indicate some promising highlights that became visible throughout the discussion. Additionally, we want to share some serious concerns involved in the endeavour of personal sustainability research. The book will be closed by a view on the perspectives that show up regarding personal sustainability, above all emphasizing the idea that personal sustainability generally leads to relationship, collective sustainability and culture(s) of sustainability – pointing the way to a next volume.

Notes

1   In contrast, the concept of "sustainability" is more open, carrying very different meanings depending on its use in different contexts. The working definition of "sustainability" used in this book refers to the ability of people and systems to withstand collapse and continue in a viable manner into the future. Often "sustainability" and "sustainable development" are used synonymously, which is also the case with many chapters in this book.
2   In 2014 the *School of Sustainability* was extended and institutionalised at KIT as *Karlsruhe School of Sustainability* (www.mensch-und-technik.kit.edu). The range of teaching content has been enlarged but personal sustainability still plays a major role.
3   Not as an instrument of fitness and relaxation as yoga is often taught and practiced in the modern societies of nowadays.
4   There is no adequate term in English. "Bildung" (German) includes education, but is much more a way of self-cultivation. It is a central term in the enlightenment, based on the classic Greek idea of *paideia* and means the reflexive and self-reflexive acquisition of culture.

References

Banse, G.; Nelson, G.L.; Parodi, O. (Eds) (2011): *Sustainable Development – The Cultural Perspective. Concepts – Aspects – Examples*. Berlin: Edition Sigma.

Berkowitz, B. (1996): Personal and Community Sustainability. In *American Journal of Community Psychology*, August 1996, Volume 24, Issue 4, pp. 441–459.

Bilharz, M. (2009): *Key Points nachhaltigen Konsums. Ein strukturpolitisch fundierter Strategieansatz für die Nachhaltigkeitskommunikation im Kontext aktivierender Verbraucherpolitik.* Marburg: Metropolis-Verlag.

Collins, R. (2015): Keeping It in the Family? Re-focusing Household Sustainability. In *Geoforum*, Volume 60, March 2015, pp. 22–32.

Dawson, J.; Jackson, R.; Norberg-Hodge, H. (Eds) (2010): *Economic Key: Gaian Economics. Living Well within Planetary Limits.* East Meon: Permanent Publications (The Four Keys Series, 2).

Degenhardt, L. (2007): *Pioniere nachhaltiger Lebensstile.* Dissertation. Kassel: University Press.

Dhiman, S.; Marques, J. (2016): *Spirituality and Sustainability: New Horizons and Exemplary Approaches.* Switzerland: Springer International.

Filinkov, A.; Richmond, M.; Nicholson, R.; Alshansky, M.; Stewien, J. (2011): Modelling Personnel Sustainability. In *Journal of the Operational Research Society*, Volume 62, Number 8, pp. 1485–1497.

Fischer, D.; Stanszus, L.; Geiger, S.; Grossman, P.; Schrader, U. (2017): Mindfulness and Sustainable Consumption: A Systematic Literature Review of Research Approaches and Findings. In *Journal of Cleaner Production*, Number 162, pp. 544–558.

Harland, M.; Keepin, W. (Eds) (2012): *Worldview Key: The Song of the Earth. A Synthesis of the Scientific and Spiritual Worldviews.* East Meon: Permanent Publications (The Four Keys Series, 4).

Holz, V.; Stoltenberg, U. (2011): Mit dem kulturellen Blick auf den Weg zu einer nachhaltigen Entwicklung. In G. Sorgo (Ed.) *Die unsichtbare Dimension. Bildung für nachhaltige Entwicklung im kulturellen Prozess.* Wien: Forum Exkurse.

IST (2017): International Sustainability Transition Conference. Program. Retrieved 9 September 2017, from http://ist2017.org/program/.

Jakubowitz, D. (2002): *Genuss und Nachhaltigkeit: Handbuch zur Veränderung des persönlichen Lebensstils.* Wien: Promedia.

Joubert, K.A.; Alfred, R. (Ed.) (2007): *Social Key: Beyond you and me. Inspirations and Wisdom for Building Community. Gaia Education.* East Meon: Permanent Publications (The Four Keys Series, 1).

Kopfmüller, J.; Brandl, V.; Jörissen, J.; Paetau, M.; Banse, G.; Coenen, R.; Grunwald, A. (2001): *Nachhaltige Entwicklung integrativ betrachtet. Konstitutive Elemente, Regeln, Indikatoren.* Berlin: Sigma Verlag.

Krainer, L.; Trattnigg, R. (Eds) (2007): *Kulturelle Nachhaltigkeit. Konzepte, Perspektiven, Positionen.* Munich: Oekom Verlag.

KSN (2017): 'Karlsruhe School of Sustainability'. Retrieved 7 September 2017, from www.mensch-und-technik.kit.edu/english/487.php.

Kuhn, T.S. (1962): *The Structure of Scientific Revolutions.* Chicago, IL: University of Chicago Press.

Kunze, I (2009): Soziale Innovationen für zukunftsfähige Lebensweisen. *Gemeinschaften und Ökodörfer als experimentierende Lernfelder für sozial-ökologische Nachhaltigkeit.* Dissertation. Münster: Ecotransfer-Verlag.

Kurt, H. (2010): *Wachsen! Über das Geistige in der Nachhaltigkeit.* Stuttgart: Mayer Verlag.

Kurt, H. (2017): *Die neue Muse. Versuch über die Zukunftsfähigkeit.* Klein Jasedow: thinkOya.

Leibson-Hawkins, R. (2005): From Self-Sufficiency to Personal and Family Sustainability: A New Paradigm for Social Policy. In *Journal of Sociology and Social Welfare*, Volume 32, Number 4, p. 77.

Mare, E.C.; Lindegger, M. (Eds) (2011): *Ecological Key: Designing Ecological Habitats. Creating a Sense of Place.* East Meon: Permanent Publications (The Four Keys Series, 3).

Marshall, J.; Coleman, G.; Reason, P. (2011): *Leadership for Sustainability: An Action Research Approach.* Sheffield: Greenleaf Publishing.

Meadows, D.H.; Meadows D.L.; Randers J.; Behrens III, W.W. (1972): *The Limits to Growth.* New York: Universe Books.

Naess, A.; Glasser, H. (Ed.) (2005): *The Selected Works of Arne Naess, Volumes 1–10.* New York: Springer.

Parodi, O. (2011): 'Personal Sustainability' – Including Body and Soul. The Karlsruhe School of Sustainability. In: G. Banse, G.L. Nelson, O. Parodi (Eds) *Sustainable Development – The Cultural Perspective. Concepts – Aspects – Examples*, pp. 223–238. Berlin: Edition Sigma.

Parodi, O. (2015): The Missing Aspect of Culture in Sustainability Concepts. In J.C. Enders, M. Remig (Eds) *Theories of Sustainable Development*, pp. 169–187. London: Routledge.

Parodi, O.; Ayestaran, I.; Banse, G. (Eds) (2011): *Sustainable Development – Relationships to Culture, Knowledge and Ethics.* Karlsruhe: KIT Scientific Publishing.

Rauschmayer, F.; Omann, I.; Frühmann, J. (2012): *Sustainable Development: Capabilities, Needs, and Well-being.* London: Routledge.

Roszak, T.; Gomes, M.E.; Kanner, A.D. (Eds) (1995): *Ecopsychology, Restoring the Earth Healing the Mind.* San Francisco, CA: Sierra Club Books.

Routledge (2017): *Routledge Studies in Culture and Sustainable Development.* London: Routledge. Retrieved 7 September 2017, from www.routledge.com/Routledge-Studies-in-Culture-and-Sustainable-Development/book-series/RSCSD.

Schultz, J.; Brand, F.; Kopfmüller, J.; Ott, K. (2008): Building a 'Theory of Sustainable Development': Two Salient Conceptions within the German Discourse. In *International Journal of Environment and Sustainable Development*, Volume 7, Number 4, pp. 465–482.

Turner, G.; Alexander, C. (2014): Limits to Growth was Right: New Research Shows We're Nearing Collapse. *The Guardian.* Retrieved 7 September 2017 from www.theguardian.com/commentisfree/2014/sep/02/limits-to-growth-was-right-new-research-shows-were-nearing-collapse.

Wamsler, C.; Brossmann, J.; Hendersson, H.; Kristjansdottir, R.; McDonald, C.; Scarampi, P. (2017): Mindfulness in Sustainability Science, Practice and Teaching. In: *Sustainability Science*, pp. 1–20. DOI 10.1007/s11625–017–0428–2.

Woiwode, C. (2016): Off the Beaten Tracks: The Neglected Significance of Interiority for Sustainable Urban Development. *Futures* 84, pp. 82–97, DOI: 10.1016/j.futures.2016.10.002.

World Commission on Environment and Development (WCED) (1987): *Our Common Future.* Oxford, UK: Oxford University Press.

2 Sustainability, culture and personal virtues

Reiner Manstetten

To Christian Becker

Introduction

At the beginning of 2015, the Decade of Education for Sustainable Development, which started in 2005 as an initiative of the United Nations, came to an end. Nowadays, when climate change is denied by the present leader of the most powerful nation in the world, even optimists cannot fail to see that the top agenda of global politics in 2017 is dominated by subjects like war, immigration, terrorism, failed states, religious phobias, financial and economic crises, whereas the concerns about the deteriorating environment and future generations have far less importance in public discourse. Part of the problem seems to be a rather abstract and theoretical understanding of sustainable development, which barely puts down roots in human mind, far too weak to give stimulus for fundamental institutional and personal changes. To overcome shortcomings in the sustainable development discourse up to now, in this chapter I argue for a concept of sustainable development that emphasises cultural dimensions and personal virtues. Sustainable development, as I see it, should be understood in the context of a pluralistic culture based on what may be called a *constitution of liberty* (cf. Faber *et al.* 1997: 461–463).[1] Struggling for sustainability, thus, implies to be personally committed to the natural foundations of human life as well as to the social foundations of human interaction and free development of personality.

Although many attempts have been made to clarify the term "sustainable development", current definitions still have common traits with the so-called Brundtland Report "Our Common Future", published by the United Nations in 1987. It defines sustainable development as "a development that meets the needs of the present without compromising the ability of future generations to meet their own needs" (WCED 1987: 41). I would like to emphasise three aspects of this very common definition:

(i)   There are few criteria *which* entities deserve to be sustained and *which* not. If, e.g. the needs of future generations could be met without the existence of tropical rain forests, should it be allowed to cut them down completely?

(ii) Sustainable development is linked exclusively to the needs and interests of the human species. Animals and plants are not mentioned.

(iii) Sustainable development is mainly defined in a negative way: it is a general principle for what should *not* be done. As a result, politics of sustainable development will consist mainly of restrictions on production and consumption that have to be enforced by law and administration. So if there are claims for sustainability on the personal level, they primarily focus on abstinence and abnegation.

Speaking of sustainable development in the lines of the Brundtland definition makes clear that we have to deal with justice and injustice. In times of climate change, polluted oceans, water shortages and desertification in many parts of the world, the global economy is developing in an unsustainable way. It is unjust that future generations are deprived of basic opportunities of life as a consequence of the present way of life (cf. Becker *et al.* 2015). To do justice to future generations, hence, would imply to limit global consumption and production to a measure compatible with the needs of future humans.

Emphasising abstinence as the core of sustainable development, however, may bring forth rather frustrating results. Ethical and political consequences of sustainability understood in this way tend to overburden ordinary people. For most of us, human life is difficult enough without the restrictive demands of sustainable development. Our lives seem to become even more difficult if the challenges of everyday life are extended by such regarding future generations. Eventually, this could lead to rigorous moral postulates, or, even worse, to resignation. What achieving sustainable development demands, seems to be much more than humans, given their possibilities in the conditions of global politics and economies, can afford. This may be one of the reasons why achieving sustainable development often remains a term merely for pious platitudes.

It should not be neglected that, since the 1970s, the public discourse on sustainability has led to considerable changes *ad bonum* in several important fields of environmental protection and politics. Nevertheless it could be promising to elaborate a much more positive meaning of "sustainable development". Supposing that sustainability concerned not only humans but all kinds of life on earth, we could say: sustainable development means that the earth becomes a place where all plants, animals and humans are able to enfold their lives each in its own manner, in the long run. Adopting such an understanding of sustainable development could be an incentive for discovering and developing ways of life more appropriate to humanity than current Western capitalist and consumerist lifestyles and cultures.

In this chapter, I want to introduce some aspects of a more positive and broader understanding of sustainable development as I mentioned it above. Part I deals with some traits of – as I call them – *sustainable cultures*. Encounters with nature as well as a particular understanding of a good life among humans, in harmony with nature, will be discussed. In the light of the question how humans nowadays should lead their lives in order to participate and contribute to sustainable cultures, Part II will discuss pictures of humankind. In this context the unsustainable types of *homo oeconomicus* and *homo mobilis* are confronted with *homo sustinens*. In this discussion, *homo sustinens* is characterised by certain virtues, among which virtues of receptivity play a decisive part. The result of these considerations is that the common concept of sustainability as a matter of public discourse, collective political decisions, and technical and administrative solutions, should be complemented by an idea of sustainable development grounded in personal capabilities that, if shared in communities, could lead to sustainable cultures.

Part I: Sustainable cultures

Nature and culture

The idea of sustainable development cannot be understood without a concept of nature and, as well, a concept of appropriate relationships between nature and humanity. Viewed from the perspective of humankind, nature can be understood as the embodiment of all aspects and circumstances that allow the constitution of human life, insofar as they are not produced by humans themselves. Evidently, nature is the necessary foundation for human life, even if this is sometimes in the sense of restrictions and threats, like big floods or earthquakes. Although in many cases transformed by labour in order to meet human needs and interests, in their original state they have to be accepted as they are. The air we breathe, the water we drink, the sunlight we enjoy, the grounds on which we move, the plants and animals that nourish us are not made by humans. However, we couldn't live without them. The same holds for our bodies: we may develop and improve their appearances and functioning, but as a starting point we initially have to accept and rely on them as they are, along with their occasional weaknesses, pains and diseases.

Too often, nature's useful gifts are taken for granted and it is cared too little about them, their origin and their conservation. The prevalent modern attitude towards nature could be characterised as follows: "Whatever humans do, nature offers her gifts and will offer them for all future times. We may take what we need, without asking about consequences. For us, the gifts of nature are gratuitous" (Benjamin 2006: XI). But this position is misleading. The gifts of nature need to be treated carefully and with respect to ensure their continuity. Otherwise, many of them will deteriorate in the course of time, and such deteriorations can become serious threats for human life. That means, although originally outside the realm of human behaviour and action, nature has to play an important role in the organisation of production and consumption.

Former civilisations often experienced nature as a spiritual source of good and evil powers. They treated nature with attention and gratitude, and developed symbolic forms of exchange, e.g. ceremonies and sacrifices. Doing so, they experienced nature not as an anonymous mass for arbitrary human purposes, but as a self-sufficient and autonomous entity. In consequence, any transformation had to respect certain limits. Such limits cannot be derived from objective parameters; they have to be understood rather as a result of the dialogue between humans and nature. Every generation discovers nature in a new sense, more or less modified by the efforts and impact of past generations. This means that this particular situation of nature generally challenges human creativity demanding answers. The dialogue between humanity and nature is not a theoretical concept, but takes place as a kind of praxis. If the praxis of this dialogue is successful, humanity, as well as nature, play their parts: nature appears as a 'You' for humanity – strange and intimate at the same time –, whereas humanity takes responsibility such that its modifications do not destroy nature's possibilities for its own development (Becker, Manstetten 2004). There is an ancient dictum: *ars perficit naturam*, loosely translated: human art aims at perfecting nature, i.e. manifesting the inherent potentials of nature. Art takes its own paths, but the artist is aware of her dependence on nature. Craftsmen and great artists devoted their works to what Goethe (2008) called "imitation of nature". This phrase did not imply the reproduction of nature's appearance but was related to openness to the infinite creativity of life in all its forms. By intuition and creativity, human art was meant to compete with nature's productivity. The vineyards and olive groves all about the Mediterranean area might serve as examples. They appear both at the same time natural and artificial – founded, shaped, cultivated and conserved by human art, technique, and skill, but developing according to the natural course of seasons.

There is a name for this praxis of dialogue between humans and nature, which is *culture*. To give sustainability a positive meaning implies an understanding of *cultura*.

(i)   In its original Greco-Roman sense, "cultura" is primarily related to "natura". It means the cultivation of nature, the clearing of forests and the tillage of gardens and fields (as evidenced by the term "agricultura", i.e. "agriculture").

(ii) In a derived sense, culture is related to the cultivation of the human nature, of body, soul, and spirit as the basis for personal development and the acquisition of social capabilities. Sports, education and spiritual orientation, thus, are integral parts of culture, as well as the tradition of theoretical and practical knowledge.

(iii) In the broadest sense, culture encompasses all capabilities and institutions that make humans apt for living in society. This holds for values, laws and rules that organise the interactions between the members of society, as well as for all kinds of collective events, e.g. ceremonies, feasts, public assemblies, theatre, music, dance etc. Culture in this sense enables and maintains social cohesion.

(iv) Last but not least, culture, at least in premodern civilisations, is hardly imaginable without common religious services establishing a cult of the gods and the powers that are believed to provide foundation and nourishment for all forms of life.

Additionally, the dimension of time is deeply rooted in the core of culture as it belongs to its very essence that it is transferred from generation to generation. Most civilisations of the past saw the transmission of knowledge, attitudes and orientations as a central matter for their respective societies. Even the treatment of nature in general and land utilisation in particular was a central matter for (ancient) civilisations. In many civilisations, private and public property is conceived as *patrimonium*, i.e. a property whose use is restricted, as it has to be handed over as a heritage to the next generation intact – although its fruits may be consumed by the present owner. An example for such a culture is the ancient Egyptian civilisation. Since about 3,000 years B.C. until the decline of the Roman Empire, the Egyptian culture was materially and spiritually centred around the Nile River. The annual inundations guaranteed the fertility of the soil. Apart from that, the Egyptians developed rather sophisticated irrigation techniques, which could be sustained for thousands of years. But their relationship to the Nile was far more than a matter of technical skills and applications: the fertility of fields and gardens was seen as an expression of the divine power of the Nile, so that religion and spirituality were deeply rooted in gratitude for nature, manifested by the 'You' of the great river which was recipient of prayers and sacrifices. "Egypt is a donation of the Nile" wrote the historian Herodot in the fifth century B.C., and the celebration of this donation was essential for the Egyptian identity.

The good life

Culture, in former times, was nearly always understood – or at least practiced unconsciously – as something to be sustained. But to (purely) sustain was never conceived as the essence of ancient civilisations. The essence was and is rather what Aristotle calls the *good life* (Aristotle, Politics, Book 1). For him, a good life leads to true happiness for individuals and genuine harmony for society (*ibid.*). It is a life in which humans as parts of communities conjointly may unfold their spiritual, political and technical potentials. Essential prerequisites for a good life are particular capabilities of the persons who share an interest in the development of their cultures. Such capabilities are called "*virtues*" by Aristotle (Aristotle 2009, via MacIntyre 1984: 19). Whatever enables humans to develop a good conduct of life bears the name of virtue: in particular self-control, courage, a sense of justice and reasonable judgement. There is an interplay between culture as a collective phenomenon and the virtues, i.e. attitudes, orientations and values, whose origin lies in the souls of the individuals. From an Aristotelian point of view, a culture can be sustained in the long run only if this interplay works without significant turbulences.

As such, sustainability alone can never be a sufficient condition for a good life. The good life does not consist in mere sustaining of given forms of life, but rather in creating and sustaining forms that are valuable to be sustained in the long run. Thus, the question to be answered for sustainable development is the following: which productive capacities, which techniques, which traditions, which political and juridical procedures and institutions, which religious orientations and which attitudes towards nature and fellow humans deserve to be conserved and developed in the long run? On the other hand, although we find different ideas of a good life in different cultures, they have in common an intention towards sustainability, at least as a necessary prerequisite for their continued existence.

Instead of sustainability the sages of the respective civilisations, however, would rather have spoken of durability and transmissibility of their cultures. Sustainability here is understood as the time aspect of an integral whole which concerns all aspects of a society. The aim, thus, is not sustainability itself, but a good life. Such a good life primarily fulfils certain ethical, aesthetical and spiritual criteria. In addition, it is intended to last over time. Hence, to speak about sustainability in terms of culture means to speak of time in the horizon of the essence and identity of a whole civilisation.

Culture and the constitution of liberty

For the presence, this understanding of culture und sustainability may appear somewhat old-fashioned and even misleading. Nowadays, a relationship between culture and nature as it existed in ancient Egypt, has seemingly lost its roots. As Heidegger stated, nature in our days is nothing but an object of demands imposed by human interests (Heidegger 2002: 15). Humans demand from nature what they want, and technology offers effective means to enforce their demands. Like a slave, nature seems to be obliged to obey human wishes. For example the Aswan dam, completed in 1970 and filled with water up to 1976, expresses an attitude unknown in premodern civilisations. The water of the Nile that fills the dam reservoir has lost its spiritual qualities. The Nile itself is conceived as nothing but a store of water for energy and irrigation services that have to be delivered at certain times, according to the needs and interests of humans. In a disenchanted world, where there is no place left for the gods, human economies put a permanent pressure on nature whose autonomy and self-sufficiency is neglected. There is an analogy between the relationship of modern humans to nature and the relationship that they have developed to their own bodies: the body, too, has become a thing that has to fulfil certain desires and functions imposed by the person inhabiting it, or by society. Hence, humans often become unable to listen to the signals of their bodies as the human society has ceased to listen to the signals of nature.

At the same time, liberal societies have given up the idea of a strong common culture. Instead, based on individual freedom, they allow for what we call cultural pluralism or multiculturalism. In the framework of a constitution of liberty, institutions and procedures have to enable free persons to live together in peace, so that an individual pursuit of happiness for everyone under a common law is possible. Concepts of collective obligations as lived in ancient cultures nowadays are suspicious to be hostile to individual liberty. As a consequence, commonly shared and culturally embedded values and habits contributing to sustainability are no longer an essential part of our modern, liberal and individually-focused culture.

There is no way back to culture in the sense of premodern times. The civilisations of the past necessarily were limited according to their stage of development and certain regional circumstances. Sustainable development in current times, in contrast, is a global task solvable only by a global civilisation. Within such a civilisation, an obligatory concept of a good life that is the same for all people appears oppressive or even totalitarian. It is not surprising that such concepts presently tend to arise in societies in which there is little respect for constitutional institutions, human rights or opinions that are opposed to the government's positions. Instead of the renewal of a lost common cultural identity, the reactionary backlashes to allegedly primary cultures often remain nothing but artificial constructs. In the worst case, they result in wars and civil wars originating from that "Clash of Civilisations" (Huntington 1996), which would be destructive for the sustainable development on earth.

But does that mean that there is no longer room for concepts of human culture that are linked to the idea of sustainability in the sense of continuation of certain virtues and respect for the natural limits? In the following passages, I try to outline an approach that is apt to combine sustainability with culture for our times. To this end, I offer the concept of a *culture of freedom*, which, although open to individual diversity, nevertheless implies bindingness to a higher degree than in nowadays-modern culture. However, its binding character primarily does not consist of collective obligations or moral postulates, but rather of certain individual attitudes, values and orientations that may be attributed to *homo sustinens*. In the presence, a sustainable culture has to be based on individual freedom within a constitution of liberty as it is offered, more or less, in modern Western democracies. Individual freedom, however, should not be confused with arbitrariness and irresponsibility against fellow humans and nature. Such confusion is, perhaps, one of the most serious reasons for unsustainable attitudes towards nature and society. Before dealing with *homo sustinens*, for a better understanding it seems expedient to speak of *homo non-sustinens* and his attitudes in the context of present-day culture.

Part II: Sustainability and pictures of humankind

Homo non-sustinens

Lack of interest in sustainability is a peculiar trait of the concept of *homo oeconomicus* as presupposed in mainstream economics. Therefore, it may be argued that the attitudes of *homo oeconomicus* are a main obstacle to sustainable development. This argument is not wrong, but has certain shortcomings. *Homo oeconomicus* is conceived as "rational selfish utility maximizer" (Mueller 1989: 2). His normal needs are characterised by insatiableness, interest in the well-being of others is not assumed. Insofar as his behaviour is based on fixed preferences, it is predictable and calculable. It is true that sustainability is not part of the normal interests of *homo oeconomicus*, for the economic person's horizon normally is limited by her expected lifetime. If future generations play a role for her behaviour, it is completely arbitrarily.

Rather than a picture of reality, however, *homo oeconomicus* can be seen as an artificial construct of mathematical economic theories from the end of the nineteenth and the beginning of the twentieth century. To a certain degree, it surely represents the selfish, individualistic and consumerist attitudes that can be found in Western societies. However, concerning real persons, determining an alleged stability of preference orders presupposes a constancy of tastes, interests and intentions, which is far from current reality. In the rapidly changing circumstances of the modern societies, people are often subject to their volatile tempers, moods and emotions. As a consequence, they lack steady values, orientations and attitudes, also as a basis for action. Because they lack foundation and firmness, they are submissive to the influences of the media, for example Facebook or Twitter and their convictions and judgments are open to manipulation. The only stable factors in their lives seem to stem from ideologies and prejudices – and, perhaps, from a certain constancy in looking for one's own advantage. I call this type *homo mobilis* (or *homo volaticus*), i.e. an unstable human being, moving from one opinion, concept and wish to the other, without finding a safe place for spirit, mind and will. By chance, *homo mobilis* may be enthusiastic even about sustainable development, but the next moment she may change her mind and become concerned with something else like the care for national identity, the fear of immigrants, the breakdown of the financial system or the introduction of a strange religious law. In contrast, any commitment to sustainable development requires the ability to follow certain reasonable insights and convictions in the long run.

Homo sustinens and the constitution of liberty

Modern Western cultures, based on the constitution of liberty, have not and should not have the means to preclude the appearance of *homo oeconomicus* and *homo mobilis*. For it is part of the guaranteed individual liberty that individuals are allowed to behave in a selfish and inconsistent manner, as long as they keep themselves within the laws of their society. However, if all members of a society behaved in that way, their society could not endure in the long run. In reality, many humans, although at times more or less seducible to the attitudes of *homo oeconomicus* or *homo mobilis*, show traits of a quite different nature. They can be touched by ethical arguments, they feel empathy for fellow humans and fellow animals and they search for purpose and meaning in their lives. Additionally, at least sometimes, they realise that the constitution of liberty is not gratuitous, but requires a certain commitment against all forces that are prepared to abolish or destroy it. Furthermore, many of them are moved by the desire to live in harmony with nature.

These aspects could deliver a basis for the striving for sustainability. It is, perhaps, one of the great problems of contemporary cultures, that their foundations are not fostered enough by individual efforts or by the institutions of society. However, the constitution of liberty as well as an open society cannot endure without personal commitment and, if necessary, political interventions and institutional innovations against all forces willing to destroy them. In particular, the hope that sustainable development will come along by the global self-organising market-economy, has turned out to be wrong: economic growth, even if labelled as "green growth", will not solve problems as climate change, water shortage, deforestation or extinction of the species (cf. Becker *et al.* 2015: 66). In fact, the present threats against the natural basis of human life require a decisive commitment for nature's sake as well as for the good life of future generations.

Saying so, I seem to end up in the moral overburdening, which I mentioned at the beginning of this chapter. However, in my eyes the capabilities needed to meet the challenges already exist as real potential in our global civilisation – what matters is if the potential is noticed and sustained through education and public discourse within firm institutional arrangements.

In the last years, there has been some dispute about *homo sustinens* in the circles of ecological economics (Becker 2012; Faber *et al.* 2002; Siebenhüner 2002). My point of view here concerns the capabilities of *homo sustinens* and its cultural embedding – in other words, I deal with the virtues of *homo sustinens* and the corresponding idea of good life. For me, *homo sustinens* is a blueprint for the personal qualities that deliver the basis for cultures which may be sustainable.[2] Thus, for the sake of sustainable development, I argue that it is neither possible nor necessary to outline a certain unifying concept of culture obliging for all members of a society. Instead, focusing on common traits and common virtues underlying all kinds of sustainable cultures seems to be a more promising endeavour.

What are the virtues of *homo sustinens*? Aristotle distinguished between virtues of insight and virtues of will. I'd like to add a third category: the virtues of receptivity.

The virtues of insight of homo sustinens

The virtues of insight concern the concepts of a good life and the possibilities of putting them into practice under the circumstances of our times. For *homo sustinens*, the concept of a good life, as I see it, has three traits:

(i)   The primary interest of *homo sustinens* is to practically answer the question which entities, institutions and values should be preserved, built up and sustained for a good life as seen from the viewpoint of an open society? Among these, the constitution of liberty has to be counted, the principles that guarantee the openness of society as well as the natural foundations of life. Nature in its autonomy and self-sufficiency, and the development of non-human species beyond utilitarian considerations will also be included.

(ii) The second interest of *homo sustinens* is empirical and critical at the same time. It is a kind of stock-taking of the state of present economies, societies and politics. The impartial interest in identifying the status quo has to be guided by the questions in what way the existing entities impede a good life, and in what way they foster it or remain neutral? Are they, in principle, sustainable or not? Answering these questions, it becomes for example obvious that the dominance of *homo oeconomicus* and *homo mobilis* may be destructive: a capitalist culture of selfishness, insatiableness and the augmentation of money and property often leads far away from any kind of good life. The same applies to flightiness, libertinism and consumerism on the one hand and for all varieties of bigotry, narrow-mindedness, nationalism, religious and secular fundamentalism and fanaticism on the other.

(iii) A peculiar interest of *homo sustinens* concerns all kinds of knowledge as well as its transferability to coming generations. Besides scientific knowledge, any culture needs practical knowledge – the know-how of politicians, judges, doctors, teachers, as well as the know-how of practitioners, e.g. foresters and conservationists. In addition, modern societies need, in order to exist and to develop, self-reflection, i.e. all persons who have an influence on the future path of their societies as well as all persons who participate in public discourses should reflect on the economic, political, institutional and cultural developments of their civilisations.

(iv) Not only the production and proliferation of all kinds of knowledge is to be regarded, but also the possibility that important knowledge may be neglected, forgotten or destroyed in the course of time. For example, the indigenous knowledge embodied in different forms of agriculture all over the world is often precious for a sustainable development but forgotten about when modern agribusiness was introduced. Therefore, questions of tradition and its transmission play a crucial role for *homo sustinens*: a society without knowledge of its past and without interest in its manifest and hidden potential for the presence is not likely to have a good future. Rightly, Jan Asmann has pointed out the relevance of the "cultural memory" for the continued existence of any culture.

(v) Fnsight has to be applied to reality otherwise it remains abstract and empty. For this purpose, principles of action have to be flexibly adapted to given circumstances. Analysing circumstances adequately is a necessary prerequisite, otherwise, practical actions become meaningless or misleading. The top-down transition from insight to praxis and bottom-up from given situations to rational analysis is achieved by a human faculty which, following Kant, may be termed as judgement (cf. Klauer *et al.* 2016: 98–118). Thus a good doctor, according to Kant, is primarily characterised not by abstract medical knowledge, but by the ability to find out what is best for the person under treatment (Kant 1991: 61). Distinguishing fake news from true facts, irrelevant information from crucial knowledge, estimating possibilities of actions in complex environments are the tasks of judgement applied by *homo sustinens*.

The virtues of the will of homo sustinens

For (personal) sustainability, the virtues of insight have to be complemented by the following virtues of will:

(i) First of all, the classical virtues, as conceptualised by Plato and Aristotle, have to be developed. Persons without self-control, with no interest in justice, or lacking courage, will hardly be able to make contributions to a good life in practice. The virtue of self-control is the basis for responsibility, the virtue of justice is like the fertile ground on which social interactions may flourish, and the virtue of courage means the readiness to bear sacrifices for one's insight, in particular to defend the constitution of liberty, even at the risk of one's own life.

(ii)   In order to cultivate these virtues, constancy is needed. Constancy should not be confused with intransigence. In contrast, constancy shall include to be open to new insights, but allow sticking to those once acquired, even if advantage or pleasure suggests leaving the chosen path. I argue that the virtue of constancy is most important for any sustainable culture. As a sustainable culture contains certain ideas to be realised over long periods of time, it would seem absurd if the persons who strive for sustainable culture delivered their minds and convictions to the ephemeral moods of Zeitgeist. Constancy implies faith and belief that in spite of errors and mistakes the striving for a good life is worth the effort.

(iii) In our times, a concept of a good life that is not open for a variety of manifestations of culture appears illiberal and insubstantial. The classical virtue of impartiality, therefore, has to be cultivated and expanded to an attitude which in ancient cultures was not appreciated or even unknown: respect for and interest in diverging positions. In the words of Rosa Luxemburg: "Freedom is always the freedom of dissenters" (Luxemburg 1922: 109). This implies an active interest even in positions fundamentally dissenting from one's own – as long as they are compatible with the constitution of liberty.

(iv)   The change from unsustainable to sustainable behaviour requires a particular virtue concerning time, in particular, past time: forgiveness. Without forgiveness, the will of individuals and collectives is too often contaminated by mutual charges whose origin are mistakes, failures or guilt. Readiness to ask for forgiveness and to forgive others releases from burdens of the past that impede present action.

What was said about the virtues of *homo sustinens* up to now seems to have little to do with sustainable development in the usual understanding. This objection is true, but, nonetheless, speaking about sustainable development without mentioning those virtues implies a problematic reduction of the concept. A strong and politically collective will and a society moving effectively towards a more sustainable development cannot be imagined, if those (personal) virtues are not cultivated intensively. This implies great challenges for public discourse as well as for all educational institutions. In particular, for delivering a solid basis for such virtues, ethical and political education has to be fostered.

The virtues of receptivity

On the other hand, it is also true that the questions of sustainable development add decisive new aspects to the traditional catalogue of virtues. Classical ethics is directed towards action, not towards the suspension of action in mere receptiveness. As a result, however, no place is left in classical ethics for an ear open to the voice of nature and for sensibility for nature's presence in all its varieties. This lack of sense for nature has, in our times, led to serious consequences: it is not considered necessary to restrain human action for nature's sake. Nowadays, however, it has become obvious that cultures excluding the dimension of nature from human life could hardly be sustainable. A dialogue with nature, which has been crucial for at least some of the premodern cultures, has to be restored and innovated. What are the virtues that enable humans to get into immediate contact and dialogue with nature?

The virtues addressed in the following are quite different in character and expression from those mentioned above. Although they may imply practical consequences and, sometimes, lead to practical actions, their origin is rather an omission of action, or a kind of response to what first has been received without activity. Nature in its essence can be experienced only if human intentions and purposes are put aside in order to achieve real openness. What the classical Chinese tradition calls "Wu wei" ("non-doing") is a prerequisite for encompassing awareness. The main virtues of a learned receptiveness are the following:

(i) Self-awareness in its full sense. Putting aside all intentions, all interest in gaining pleasure or avoiding pain, all calculations of utility, humans can become purposelessly aware of their bodies as well as of the streams of emotions and thoughts passing through their minds. By getting into contact with the origin of their emotions, moods and tempers, they are freed from the dominance of a particular emotion, mood and temper and open up for their original encompassing and creative nature.

(ii) The same attitude of awareness is appropriate regarding nature in its appearance. Discovering nature's self-sufficiency and creativity as well as the deep connectedness between nature and humanity is possible, as soon as all pressure and demands on nature cease. Experiences similar to those formulated by the German poet Novalis in 1799 may occur:

> Is it not true that all nature, as well as face and gesture, expresses the emotion of each one of the wonderful higher beings we call humans? Does the cliff not become a unique You, whenever I speak to it? And what am I but the stream, when I look sadly into its waters and lose my thoughts in its flow?
>
> (Novalis 1949: 25)

Such experiences may stimulate human creativity and show ways that are more appropriate to nature as the economy of today.

(iii) Learned receptiveness towards nature, be it inner or outer, leads to gratitude. Thanks to nature humans breathe air, drink water and take their livelihood from plants and animals. Thanks to nature, their interior organs, lungs, liver, kidneys, heart do their job day and night without conscious effort. Thanks to nature, humans find themselves in possession of eyes, ears, nose, tongue and skin, which give room for sensory perception, of a brain that enables them to produce thoughts, of arms and legs, hands and feet that allow action. Taking all this for granted, however, is misleading. Experiencing human existence within nature as a true miracle stimulates gratitude that is the basis for respect and careful treatment of nature.

Aesthetical education and spiritual practice

In the Western educational systems, there is a fundamental lack concerning the virtues of receptiveness. Nevertheless, there are sources that could foster them: aesthetical education on the one hand and religious and spiritual practices on the other hand.

The word *aesthetics* is derived from the Greek word *aesthesis* meaning perception, and in its origin at Plato's and Aristotle's, aesthetics is the theory of sensual perception. In the eighteenth century, beginning with the philosophy of Kant and Schiller, the theory of aesthetics focused more and more on learned perception, in particular, on the training of the perception of the beautiful. The beautiful was conceived primarily as the beautiful in nature, secondary as the beautiful in human art. The latter, too, was understood, e.g. by Kant, as a result of nature, namely nature understood as an entity working by means of the unconscious genius in the interior of humankind. Schiller (1954) in his treatise "On the Aesthetic Education of Man" conceptualised an ideal society where humans by means of education in music, poetry and fine arts as well as by encounters with natural and artificial landscapes should be trained in encompassing openness for their fellow human beings as well as for nature in all its manifestation. By means of aesthetics, humans should come into contact with the divine origin of life, and realise that humankind has lost its original path by treating the creation of God as a storehouse for its wishes and interests. In this spirit, Novalis (1949) recognised the true vocation of humankind in becoming the "Messiah of nature" meaning that in its perfection, human receptivity and creativity will bring nature's hidden potentialities to perfection. Aesthetical education was intended to be complementary to the virtues of ethics, which, although necessary for human life, were not considered sufficient for bringing about harmony between humans and between humanity and nature.

Gratitude for the gifts of nature is a root of all true religion. Humans realise that all their labour and work cannot provide for sufficient livelihood and a good life unless their effort is blessed by the creator. Religious ceremonies and worship, in their origin, are meant to express gratitude for the dimensions that lie outside of human disposal. In many traditions, including the Christian and Buddhist monasteries, Indian ashrams or centres of Sufi or Kabbalist Yeshivas, practices fostering self-awareness and awareness of nature have been developed. Although not seldom amalgamated with shortcomings and ideologies of the respective religious doctrines, those mystical practices give room for the development of the human spirit. Primarily intended to bring a person in contact with the inner self by prayer, meditation, and silent contemplation (cf. St. Paul, 2nd letter to the Corinthian, Chap. 4, 16), those practices have effects on the treatment of the external nature. This can be seen for example in the surroundings of Cistercian monasteries or Zen Gardens in China, Korea and Japan.

The core of aesthetic education and mystical meditation is grounded, among others, in its non-intentionality. However, expecting that sustainable cultures could be built solely on aesthetics and mystics would be misleading. Without intention, will, action and institution-building – as well as rationality, sciences and technological efforts – guided by the virtues of insight and will as described above, a sustainable development would never come into being. On the other hand, it is intentionality that dominates the capitalist civilisation of our days. The stress and pressure coming from an excessive intentionality make humans unable to become aware of their inner self and the self of nature. As this unawareness contributes a great deal to the unsustainable traits of the present economy and societies, fostering the virtues of receptivity could be a significant part of a great transformation.

Concluding remarks

Sustainable development should not be confused with infinite duration. The span of human life on earth and even for earthly life in general is limited. Its end may come as the final "Kalpa fire" in Buddhism, or as "Doomsday" in Western religions, or, more prosaically, not later than a billion years by the heating up of the sun, as scientific predictions suggest. But for the time being, be it short or long, sustainable development is a central issue for humanity. I agree with the statement formulated by Becker *et al*.: "We need the courage to prioritize the long-term protection of the natural basis of life, and we need the persistence to continuously adhere to this new prioritization" (2015: 67). It may, however, be misleading to believe that such prioritisation will be fostered by gazing constantly at the deteriorating environment and the seemingly vanishing possibilities of sustainability politics. It is true that the impressions we get from the news are not encouraging. But nevertheless, there is sound reason for hope that, if humanity does its utmost for a sustainable good life, such effort will not be in vain.

Notes

1 The notion *constitution of liberty* is derived from the treatise of Hayek (Hayek 1960). He outlines liberty as prerequisite for wealth and growth and a fundamental basis of civilisation. The constitution is often understood as a basis for neo-liberal politics, the term may as well be applied to the more leftist concepts of Rawls (1971) and Sen (2009).
2 By the way, as sustainability is no value in itself, in my eyes it would be misleading to speak of a "culture of sustainability". I would prefer to speak of diverging concepts of culture, which have in common that they are sustainable.

References

Aristotle (2009): *Nicomachean Ethics*, translated by W.D. Ross. Oxford: Oxford University Press.

Becker, C. (2012): *Sustainability Ethics and Sustainability Research*. New York: Springer.

Becker, C.; Ewringmann, D; Faber, M.; Petersen, Th.; Zahrnt, A. (2015): Endangering the Natural Basis of Life Is Unjust: On the Status and Future of the Sustainability Discourse, *Ethics, Policy & Environment*, Vol. 18, 1, pp. 60–67.

Becker, C; Manstetten, R. (2004): Nature as a You: Novalis' Philosophical Thought and the Modern Ecological Crisis. *Environmental Values*, Vol. 13, 1, pp. 101–118.

Benjamin, W. (2006): On the Concept of History, translated by H. Zohn. In *Harvard's Selected Writings*, Vol. 4 (1938–1940). Harvard: Harvard University Press, pp. 389–400.

Faber, M.; Manstetten, R.; Petersen, Th. (1997): Homo Oeconomicus and Homo Politicus. Political Economy, Constitutional Interest and Ecological Interest. *Kyklos*, Vol. 50, 4, pp. 457–483.

Faber, M.; Petersen, Th.; Schiller, J. (2002): Homo Oeconomicus and Homo Politicus in Ecological Economics. *Ecological Economics*, Vol. 40, 3, pp. 323–333.

Goethe, J.W. v. (2008): Einfache Nachahmung der Natur, Manier, Stil. In *Goethes Werke, Hamburger Ausgabe*, Bd. XII, München: C.H. Beck, pp. 30–34.

Hayek, F.A. (1960): *The Constitution of Liberty*. Chicago, IL: The University of Chicago Press.

Heidegger, M. (2002): *Die Technik und die Kehre*. Stuttgart: Klett-Cotta.

Huntington, S.Ph. (1996): *The Clash of Civilizations and the Remaking of World Order*. New York: Simon & Schuster.

Kant, I. (1991): On the Common Saying: 'This May Be True in Theory, But it Does Not Apply in Practice'. In *Political Writings*. Ed. by Hans R. Seiss. Cambridge, UK: Cambridge University Press, pp. 61–92.

Kant, I. (2000): *Critique of the Power of Judgment*, edited by P. Guyer, translated by P. Guyer and E. Mathews. Cambridge and New York: Cambridge University Press.

Klauer, B.; Manstetten, R.; Petersen, Th.; Schiller, J. (2016): *Sustainability and the Art of Long-Term Thinking* (Routledge Studies in Sustainability). London: Routledge.

Luxemburg, R. (1922): *Die russische Revolution. Eine kritische Würdigung*. Berlin: Verlag Gesellschaft und Erziehung.

MacIntyre, A. (1984): *After Virtue: A Study in Moral Theory*. South Bend: University of Notre Dame Press.

Mueller, D. (1989): *Public Choice II. A Revised Edition of Public Choice*. Cambridge, UK: Cambridge University Press.

Novalis (1949): *The Novices of Sais. Sixty Drawings of Paul Klee*. Preface by S. Spender, translated by R. Mannheim. New York: Curt Valentin.

Rawls, J. (1971): *A Theory of Justice*. Cambridge, MA: Harvard University Press.

Schiller, F. (1954): *On the Aesthetic Education of Man*, translated by R. Snell. New Haven, CT: Yale University Press.

Sen, A. (2009): *The Idea of Justice*. Cambridge, MA: Harvard University Press.

Siebenhüner, B. (2001): *Homo Sustinens. Auf dem Weg zu einem Menschenbild der Nachhaltigkeit*. Marburg: Metropolis.

WCED – World Commission on Environment and Development (1987): *Our Common Future*. Oxford, UK: Oxford University Press.

3 Psychology of sustainability

Psychological resources for sustainable lifestyles

Marcel Hunecke

Introduction

A continual growth in material wealth is not compatible with the principle of sustainable development. Likewise, research has shown that it will not be possible to raise subjective well-being in the early industrialized countries through increases in material wealth without ecological and social costs that would be entirely out of proportion (Randers 2012). The transition to sustainable lifestyles requires a cultural transformation. For this purpose, short-term adaptations achieved by means of technological innovations and organizational efficiency gains will not be sufficient. In addition, there is a need for change towards sustainable lifestyles.

The approach by Hunecke (2013) identifies those psychological preconditions for sustainable lifestyles that are largely independent of moralistic appeals as well as of materialistic incentives. Rather it focuses on individual change processes geared towards sustainable lifestyles that are motivated by increasing subjective well-being. The term *lifestyles* denotes relatively stable patterns in the organization of daily life, regarding behavioural as well as psychological characteristics such as values, attitudes and beliefs. Lifestyles are sustainably oriented if they are informed by the guiding principles of sustainable development. Importantly, these principles should not only be implemented in specific but, as far as possible, in all domains of the organization of daily life, such as energy and food consumption, or mobility behaviour. This approach includes three further characteristics: first, a sufficient number of practicable measures exist that can be used to systematically activate and promote the needed psychological preconditions. Second, the targeted changes in attitude and behaviour have to be achieved on a conscious and voluntary basis and not via strategies of manipulation. Third, measures geared towards promoting psychological preconditions for sustainable lifestyles should be applicable in social systems in order to reach a large number of participants, and should not be limited to exclusively individual, e.g. therapeutic, contexts. In order to cover the psychological preconditions that are needed for such a cultural transformation towards sustainable lifestyles, relevant insights from four fields of knowledge were brought together. These four areas will be introduced in the following: socio-ecological research, environmental psychology, positive psychology and resource-oriented counselling. This chapter presents the relevance of six psychological resources for achieving sustainable lifestyles and points out some ways in which they can be promoted in various practical contexts. The six psychological resources represent important motivational sources for behavioural changes towards sustainability. As such, they can make important contributions for the promotion of personal sustainability.

Four sources of knowledge that can be used in the promotion of sustainable lifestyles

Social-ecological research emphasizes the fact that ecological problems are intimately related to the broader societal context in which they occur. Therefore, these problems cannot be solved by nature- or technology-oriented interventions alone. Instead, they must be analysed from a perspective that acknowledges the interactions between society and nature (Jahn 2000; Becker, Jahn 2006). This requires that societal aspects, such as patterns of production and consumption, social inequality, and the societal conception of a good life be taken into account as well. Furthermore, social-ecological research points to the influence of the individual on ecological problems by shared social mental representations that manifest themselves in collective patterns of behaviour. The social-ecological discourse reveals the importance of the individual by quantifying individual ecological footprints. Using calculators for greenhouse gas emissions, it is by now possible to quantify rather accurately the annual climate-relevant emissions caused by an individual's behaviour (e.g. Hunecke *et al.* 2007). Quantification of this ecological footprint enables each person to relate their individual behaviour to the non-sensually perceivable environmental impact on a global scale. Overall, the field of social-ecological research features considerably more analyses of the interactions between society and nature than on the interactions between society, nature and the individual.

Environmental psychology provides a comprehensive body of knowledge on how environment-related perceptions, evaluations and decision-making processes work on the level of the individual. Since systematic investigation of anthropogenic, ecological problems has started, the last 40 years have witnessed the development of several explanatory- and change models for environment-related behaviour. Examples include the Value-Belief-Norm model by Stern *et al.* (1999), or the Stage Model of Self-regulated Behavioural Change by Bamberg (2013). An in-depth understanding of the motivational bases of environment-related behaviour allows the derivation of specific interventions that target behavioural change. A variety of such techniques have been developed in the field of environmental psychology, and it is possible to systematize the different psychological mechanisms that are involved (Kaufmann-Hayoz *et al.* 2001; Mosler, Tobias 2007). As a general rule, interventions designed for effecting changes in environment-related behaviour aim to modify the relevant cognitive processes, ideally taking into account the situational context in which the desired behaviour usually occurs. However, these interventions do not succeed in initiating the profound motivational changes that are needed in order to effect changes towards sustainability-oriented lifestyles.

Beyond material incentives and legal regulations, the standard repertoire of interventions in the field of environmental psychology operate in the *marketing-mode* characterized by serving the already existing needs and wishes of consumers. Explicitly, this approach can be found in social marketing techniques that are used to promote sustainable behaviour (McKenzie-Mohr, Smith 1999). However, this marketing-mode can only succeed in effecting considerable and lasting behavioural change in those consumers who already have a high degree of sustainability-related motivation. If the latter does not apply, which is not unusual when considering competing aims, such as the individual's wish to reduce behavioural effort, only minor effects can be achieved. The reason for this is that interventions operating in marketing-mode solely affect peripheral aspects of information processing and evaluation. Therefore, these interventions cannot initiate the emotional processes that are crucial for building up lasting motivation for behavioural change.

Positive psychology. At this point, the field of environmental psychology can benefit from the insights of positive psychology. The focus of positive psychology is on furthering those positive emotions that are seen as the prerequisite for the on-going development of a person's personality, as laid out in the Broaden-and-Build theory by Frederickson (2001) or in the concept of *flourishing* by Seligman (2011). In this endeavour, positive psychology does not only concentrate on individual growth processes, but also on the humanistic design of institutions and organizations as the basis on which these growth processes can take place. The field of positive psychology offers most of the available empirical evidence concerning factors that determine subjective well-being and life satisfaction. In addition, positive psychology has produced interventions that can promote subjective well-being outside of therapeutic contexts. Examples include gratitude exercises and the cultivation of forgiveness (Seligman *et al.* 2005; Snyder, Lopez, 2009). So far, however, the insights of positive psychology have not been applied systematically to fostering sustainable behaviour.

Resource-oriented counselling. The fourth domain of knowledge that was integrated by Hunecke (2013) into the conceptual foundations of the psychological preconditions for sustainable lifestyles refers to the resource-oriented approach within the field of counselling. From a broad perspective, everything that a person holds dear and experiences as being helpful in a certain situation can ultimately be regarded as a resource (Nestmann 1996). The resources that are relevant for the approach that is presented here relate to the internal psychological traits and skills that serve to master difficult situations and phases of personal development. If a person is already equipped with certain resources, these can be activated in difficult situations. Furthermore, reflection and learning processes can serve to promote psychological resources and optimize utilization of these resources. Systematic research has revealed a *resource-activating strategy* as one of the most effective modes of action in psychotherapy (Grawe 1998). That said, the promotion of psychological resources is not confined to therapeutic settings, but can also be applied to counselling and educational contexts. The merit of the resource-oriented approach lies in the fact that it gave rise to a variety of methods specifically tailored to build and strengthen psychological resources, long before the label "positive psychology" was established in 2000 (Seligman, Csikszentmihalyi 2000). While resource-oriented counselling has until now been applied almost solely in individual or group counselling contexts, it may also be highly useful in personal sustainability research. This is because the respective methods and techniques, aiming at individual reflection and behavioural change, may inform the development of strategies that target the individual in order to promote a societal transformation towards sustainability.

The presented approach of psychological resources for sustainable lifestyles integrates the four areas of knowledge outlined in the preceding paragraphs. This integration is achieved by looking at ecological problems from the perspective of an individual's behaviour, while at the same time acknowledging that individual behaviour cannot be divorced from its interrelations with societal contexts and nature-related processes. The psychological resources add to the manifold techniques of environmental psychology that aim at effecting environment-related behavioural change. In practice, this is achieved by setting up and encouraging processes of reflection that are in turn needed to build up the motivation for the pursuit of a sustainable lifestyle. The motivation can be created by fostering positive emotions that ensure that a person's current subjective well-being can be maintained or even increased while practicing a sustainable lifestyle. Positive psychology identifies those emotions that are relevant in this process. The resource-oriented approach then lays out measures and techniques to foster systematically the relevant psychological resources.

Three orientations to happiness

The psychological resource approach is aimed at furthering or securing current levels of subjective well-being in the process of a cultural transformation towards sustainable lifestyles. The idea is that if people do not believe that their future lives in a sustainable society will be good or pleasant compared with alternative life models, we cannot expect them to undertake long-term changes in behaviour geared towards a post-material and sustainable way of life. One important insight from research in positive psychology is the distinction of three fundamental strategies that help to increase subjective well-being. In his deliberations on *authentic happiness* Seligman (2002: 262f) distinguishes three orientations to further an authentic and happy life: (a) the pleasant life, (b) the good life, and (c) the meaningful life. Seligman postulates that the *full life* can be seen as the result of the parallel application of all of the three aforementioned strategies (Seligman 2002: 263). This is also the core of the Pleasure-Accomplishment-Meaning theory of subjective well-being that is outlined in the following. According to this theory, each general strategy contributes in a specific manner to a happy life: the experience of pleasure, the accomplishment of certain goals and the construction of meaning. The Pleasure-Accomplishment-Meaning theory that is postulated in Hunecke (2013) differs in several details from Seligman's Theory of Authentic Happiness, which is still strongly linked to the concept of *human signature strengths* (Seligman 2002). Due to their grounding in philosophical and ethical reflections towards the good life, two strategies are well recognized as self-standing ways towards subjective well-being. The distinction between hedonistic and eudaimonic forms of happiness, which can be associated with the *pleasant life* and the *meaningful life*, has been made since the time of antiquity. Seligman has refined his Theory of Authentic Happiness (2011) by distinguishing five areas that contribute to increases in subjective well-being: positive emotions, engagement, relationship, meaning and accomplishment. By also acknowledging the importance of accomplishment, he indirectly defines in a more precise manner his former strategy of the *good life*.

A third strategy, which has been labelled as *living a committed life* (Frank 2010: 104) emphasizes the accomplishment of self-set goals, irrespective of their actual content. Accomplishment of these goals makes the actor proud and establishes satisfaction. Of course these two outcomes can be further increased if the respective goals are regarded as meaningful. However, many goals are pursued for their own sake, and over time it is possible for goals to develop their own dynamics, which are not related to the construction of meaning anymore.

Altogether, the theoretical distinctions that were introduced by Seligman are helpful in identifying the three fundamental strategies of subjective well-being, i.e. pleasure, accomplishment and meaning, although his recent theoretical conception of subjective well-being from the year 2011 has somewhat moved away from these initial considerations. In two empirical studies with English-speaking participants, Seligman was able to verify that subjective well-being correlates positively with precisely these three strategies, namely the pursuit of pleasure, engagement and meaning (Peterson *et al.* 2005; Schueller, Seligman 2010). The findings were replicated by Ruch in a German sample (Ruch *et al.* 2010). In all three studies, it was found that participants who scored high on each of the three strategies simultaneously exhibited the highest subjective well-being. Thus, while the strategies are partly opposed on a reflexive-abstract level, it seems that they are quite compatible in daily practical life. First and foremost, the reason for this can be traced back to the fact that each strategy influences subjective well-being on a different time scale. While the pleasant life is oriented towards the immediate experience of pleasure, the life of engagement requires that goals be pursued over intermediate periods of time if their accomplishment and the associated positive emotions are to be experienced. The most long-ranging orientation is necessitated by the meaningful life, as contents of meaning need to be readapted to individual's life in certain intervals. At the same time, these contents transcend the temporal horizon of an individual life and can never be fully achieved, due to their supra-individual nature.

Subjective well-being and sustainable lifestyles

The Pleasure-Accomplishment-Meaning theory provides a general framework for the manner in which positive emotions that are important for subjective well-being can be fostered. In their role as internal traits and skills, psychological resources assist a person in the realization of strategies of happy living. This is effected in

Table 3.1 Strategies for leading a good life and the associated psychological resources, functions for personal sustainability and positive emotions

Strategy for leading a good life	Psychological resource	Positive emotions	Functions for personal sustainability
Hedonism	Capacity for pleasure	Sensual pleasures	Intensity of experience rather than multiplicity of experience
Achieving aims	Self-acceptance Self-efficacy	Life satisfaction Pride Flow	Greater independence from social comparisons; Strengthening capacity for action
Meaning	Mindfulness Construction of meaning Solidarity	Serenity Security Belonging Trust	Orientation towards goals beyond the individual; Motivation for collective action

such a way that subjective well-being can be maintained or increased by appropriate regulation of emotions. Ultimately, it is possible to identify six psychological resources that can enhance both subjective well-being and sustainable behaviour, as well as systematically modified. Importantly, these resources are also applicable in organizational or institutional settings, where they can furthermore be promoted in large numbers of people at the same time. The six psychological resources are: (1) the capacity for pleasure, (2) self-acceptance, (3) self-efficacy, (4) mindfulness, (5) the construction of meaning and (6) solidarity. Table 3.1 shows the relationship between the six psychological resources, the three strategies for living a good life, and the associated positive emotions. The last column identifies their psychological functions for personal sustainability in the cultural transformation towards more sustainable lifestyles.

The six psychological resources for sustainable lifestyles

The capacity for pleasure describes the ability to experience sensual impressions of different modalities as positive. At this point, only those positive pleasurable experiences that result from bodily-sensual impressions are explicitly addressed. For all human beings, the body exhibits similar potentials and limits of sensual experience. With respect to potentials each person may enhance their sensitivity for the perception of sensory stimuli, e.g. for the modalities of hearing and tasting, by way of training. Concerning limits, each human being requires a certain degree of sleep and relaxation in order to be able to survive in the long run. Strategies for the promotion of sensual pleasures can be especially derived from the potentials of sensual experiences. For example, these include rules for pleasure such as "pleasure needs time", that are taught in the context of behaviour-oriented pleasure trainings (Koppenhöfer 2004) and the strategy of savouring (Bryant, Veroff 2007).

Hedonic experiences derived from aesthetic-intellectual realms are left aside, because they can take such variegated forms, for example in different social milieus (Schulze, 1992), that establishing systematic relationships to sustainable behaviour becomes nearly impossible.

Self-acceptance means that a person is able to embrace all of their positive and negative traits that are represented in their self-concept. Next to self-confidence, social skills and social networks, self-acceptance is an important aspect of self-worth (Potreck-Rose, Jacob 2010). What all of the different strategies to promote self-acceptance have in common is that they enlarge the view on the own person, thereby making it easier to accept all of the various aspects of the personality. Working with a person's own beliefs and norms, and with the core-beliefs (McKay, Fanning 2000) that are derived thereof, constitutes the fundamental and most important strategy in this endeavour. Thus, for the purpose of promoting self-acceptance, a person should first identify the core-belief internal to his or her own biography. Following a period of critical reflection those core-beliefs can – if necessary – be modified or rejected altogether.

Self-efficacy is defined as the belief that one can master challenging situations by virtue of one's own competences. The challenging situations are not tasks that can be accomplished by means of simple routines, but are such that by virtue of their degree of difficulty they require considerable effort and persistence (Schwarzer 2004). Bandura (1997) has identified four basic methods for increasing self-efficacy beliefs: (1) repeated and controlled experience of personal success; (2) modelling; (3) social persuasion; and (4) physiological factors, which can be applied to all areas of skills acquisition and learning, and consequently also to sustainable behaviour. In the theory of planned behaviour by Ajzen (1991), self-efficacy is described as perceived behavioural control. Empirically, it has been shown to be one of the most important predictors for environment-related behaviour (Bamberg, Möser 2007).

Mindfulness means focusing ones' attention fully, intentionally and non-judgmentally, on the present moment. When defined in this way, mindfulness describes both a process "the practice of mindfulness" and an outcome "mindful awareness" (Shapiro, Carlson 2011: 22). A mindful attitude needs to be cultivated over a long period of time, e.g. by practicing meditation or mindful body exercises over years. Mindfulness has proven to be an effective method for stress prevention, enabling a person to identify and de-automatize stress-inducing patterns of thinking and behaviour. By now, several empirical studies have shown direct and indirect relationships between different aspects of mindfulness and environment-related behaviour (Amel *et al.*, 2009; Brown, Kasser 2005; Jacob *et al.*, 2009; Barbaro, Picket 2016).

The construction of meaning as a psychological resource indicates a process by which the individual has to produce their own meaning. The construction of a meaningful experience therefore consists of cognition and an associated feeling (Tausch 2008). Therefore, meaningful experiences by no means always refer to an overarching meaning or life-purpose, but can most certainly also be experienced as single events in daily life. While the beliefs of various cultural and religious traditions may be used in the process of constructing meaning, the selection, adaptation and re-combination of relations of these beliefs always has to take place actively and at the level of the individual. In the approach that is presented here, the aim is explicitly not to impart contents of meaning that are related to sustainability. Instead an open and unbiased search for meaning has to be supported. Nevertheless, the processes associated with the construction of meaning increase the likelihood that people will discover or strengthen either transcendent or socially-directed values that run counter to the individualistic materialism, which forms the often unquestioned values in modern consumer societies.

Solidarity as a psychological resource encompasses two aspects of collective action. The first aspect is the acknowledgement of personal responsibility for the welfare of other people. The second aspect concerns the belief that by engaging in action, one can bring about a real increase in well-being by interacting with others who are working towards the same ends. In a nutshell, solidarity can be understood as a combination of social responsibility and positive self-efficacy beliefs towards collective action. In comparison with the five resources presented so far, it is apparent that a methodological distinction applies to solidarity, namely that it cannot be supported solely on the basis of processes of self-reflection. The development of solidarity and the accompanying turn away from individualistic behaviour do not only have to happen at a cognitive level. They also have to be trained on a behavioural level through repeated practice in concrete interactions with others in groups or in organizations, e.g. by working with children in experiential or theatre education or in the context of the promotion of corporate social responsibility in companies. Research in the field of environmental psychology has yielded a variety of empirical findings that point to relationships between prosocial values and environment-related attitudes and behaviour (Schultz, Zelezny 1998).

The strategy of activating all six resources simultaneously

The six psychological resources do not operate in the same way or with the same intensity in furthering subjective well-being and sustainable behaviour. They behave like nodal points in a dynamic network which can be stimulated from different starting points and can assume different conditions of activation accordingly (see Figure 3.1).

In comparison to its first conception by Hunecke (2013), several specifications have been made in the network of psychological resources depicted in Figure 3.1. First of all, three levels of foundational, transformative and goal-building resources are distinguished. Self-acceptance and self-efficacy are resources on the foundational level that constitute a strong personality, one that – as the humanistic view of human nature holds – is characterized by the pursuit and realization of one's own needs and goals. A personality strengthened in this way, however, is not restricted in terms of the contentual orientation of their life goals. It is thus quite possible for a person with high levels of self-acceptance and self-efficacy to follow a lifestyle that is very materially intensive and therefore not ecologically

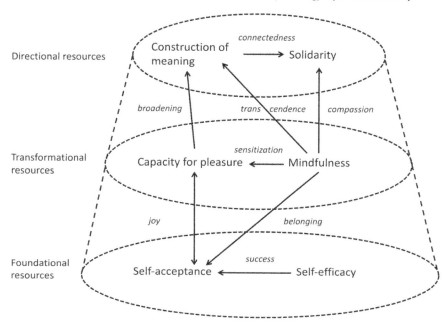

Figure 3.1 Interrelationships between the six psychological resources to foster subjective well-being and sustainable lifestyles

sustainable. This is why the two foundational resources have to be complemented by the transformative and directional resources, namely the capacity for pleasure, mindfulness, meaning-construction and solidarity, if an orientation towards the non-material sources of subjective well-being is to be achieved. The additional level of transformative resources was included into the network in order to underline the specifically transformative function of the capacity for pleasure and mindfulness. These two psychological resources exhibit the greatest potential when it comes to questioning and changing the current lifestyle in a reflexive manner, independently of critical life events and developmental tasks.

Mindfulness already had a particular status in the earlier conception (Hunecke 2013) as a mediator between the foundational and the directional resources. A basic mindful disposition holds the greatest potential for transcending the self-centred focus in one's behaviour, and for opening this focus to a universalist perspective while remaining free from specific convictions about the nature of the world. This function of mindfulness is initially a result of the conscious perception of one's own feelings and needs. In a second step, the perspective is then widened to take in the feelings and needs of other people and other living beings. This in turn is a prerequisite for an orientation towards supra-individual aims and values which go beyond one's own interests and thus abate the striving for material wealth and social status.

When it comes to a person's own lifestyle, the capacity for pleasure has a similarly transformative function, because this resource motivates for changes in lifestyle without determining the specific content of potential goals. Capacity for pleasure aims at promoting subjective well-being via the experience of positive emotions, which are in turn elicited by pleasurable sensory experiences. The Broaden-and-Build Theory (Frederickson 2001) postulates that if enough positive emotions are experienced, the likelihood that persons reflect on their own life and continue to develop their personality is increased. Here, what is meant is a rather continuous reflective process during personal development, and not one that is triggered by critical biographical events or strokes of fate that perforce plunge people into reflections on their lifestyle, and are accompanied by suffering. Overall, an equilibrated balance between the two resources of capacity for pleasure and mindfulness can be seen as the key element for changing materialistically oriented lifestyles. Mindfulness prepares the way for the construction of meaning, while the capacity for pleasures enables short-term positive experiences in everyday life. The transformative force of these two resources is deemed particularly strong in the presence of synergistic effects, e.g. if a mindful disposition carries as a consequence a sensitization for sensual pleasures.

After building up the motivation for changes in lifestyles by transformative resources this motivation must be directed towards sustainability. This orientation can be brought about by construction of meaning and solidarity as directional resources. While neither of the directional resources provides specific value contents, they initiate processes of reflection out of which new values can emerge or already existing values can be strengthened. Regarding these processes of reflection, each directional resource exerts a distinct function. In this context, the construction of meaning can be considered to be largely neutral, as it merely sets the goal of continually updating, in a lifelong process, the search for meaning in one's life. The substantive content of this meaning is entirely indeterminate and needs only to demonstrate a certain level of coherence in order to give the individual a feeling of security.

Ultimately, a transformation of aims and values towards sustainability and post-materialism can be pursued in a multitude of different ways. The approach that is presented here sets out a system directed towards the activation of psychological resources. The crucial characteristic of this system lies in the fact that the selected psychological resources are mutually reinforcing. If, for whatever reason, one of the six resources cannot be activated to a sufficient degree, one or more of the other resources can compensate for it.

As a consequence of their network structure, it is not essential to initiate the activation on one specific level of resources, e.g. by starting with the foundational resources before the transformative or directional resources can be tackled. Rather, it is more important to activate as many of the six psychological resources as possible. In accordance with the Pleasure-Accomplishment-Meaning theory of subjective well-being, different activation pathways for the three strategies for leading a good life, and thus also for the six psychological resources, are available for different people, or groups of people. These differing capacities for activation must be taken into account in the design of measures intended to help specific target groups initiate a cultural transformation towards personal sustainability.

Fostering psychological resources in different domains of application

Measures for strengthening the six psychological resources are directed towards bringing about changes in the individual's processing and evaluation of information to increase the attraction of non-material sources of life satisfaction. These measures can be applied to individuals, for example through counselling or coaching, and to groups of people in different organizational or institutional settings, such as schools or companies. Next to the psychological dynamics of changes in attitudes and behaviour, it is important to consider the aims and the associated inherent logic of the respective organizations when designing interventions tailored for these contexts. Social interventions on a community level aim at changes in larger, socio-spatial units such as cities or municipalities. All these measures have in common is that they must be accompanied by communicative processes and can in no way be replaced by technological means or by pharmaceutical drugs.

In general, the implementation of individual resources is not confined to specific spheres of activity. It is nevertheless possible to name certain resources that can be predominantly applied in certain fields of action.

Health promotion

Three of the psychological resources that were identified to support sustainable development show an explicit connection to the field of health promotion. Most

Table 3.2 Domains of application for the support of the psychological resources for sustainable lifestyles

Domain of application	Mental resource
Health promotion	Mindfulness
	Capacity for pleasure
	Self-acceptance
Coaching	Construction of meaning
	Self-efficacy
	Mindfulness
	Capacity for pleasure
Schools	Self-efficacy
	Solidarity
	Construction of meaning
Companies and non-profit organizations	Solidarity
	Construction of meaning
Community life	Self-efficacy
	Solidarity

obvious in this context is the application of strategies to promote mindfulness. Mindfulness is a central element of stress prevention programs (Kabat-Zinn 1990), therapies for the treatment of depression (Segal *et al*. 2008) and borderline personality disorders (Linehan 1996). Strengthening the capacity for pleasure is also a firmly established element of stress management programs, which ultimately aim at improving self-care (Kaluza 2011). Promoting self-acceptance serves to raise low self-esteem, while reducing the negative secondary symptoms of many mental illnesses that are usually accompanied by a reduction in self-worth. In addition, the construction of meaning strengthens powers of resistance against mental and physical illness through its positive influence on the formation of what Antonovsky (1987) calls a "sense of coherence" with respect to health.

Coaching

Coaching represents a specific form of counselling that is not applied in the treatment of mental disorders, but instead aims at personal development in the broadest sense. Typical topics in coaching courses are the building up of competences, work-life balance, the construction of meaning for one's own life and achieving one's goals and projects (Biswas-Diener 2010: 148).

Regarding the approach towards sustainable development that is sketched out in these pages, construction of meaning, self-efficacy, mindfulness and the capacity for pleasure are the four psychological resources that are most amenable to activation and promotion through coaching. As far as possible, coaching processes should remain open and unbiased in terms of their content, and should not impart specific value-orientations or worldviews. It is to be expected that by promoting psychological resources via coaching, immaterial sources of contentment and happiness that were hitherto not cultivated to larger extents will come increasingly into focus. There are some occasions and opportunities for self-reflection in adult age independent of psychological strain and suffering where individual value-orientations are addressed in order to be changed or strengthened. Coaching provides these opportunities via an interactive form of self-reflection. Another advantage of the coaching approach is its potential to reach people who may initiate a cultural transition by acting as "change agents" (Rogers 2003).

School

Among the six psychological resources, self-efficacy, the construction of meaning and solidarity have a special relevance in school settings. The juvenile phase constitutes a period in a person's life that is central to the development of identity, during which schools are the dominating institutions. From a resource-oriented perspective, processes relating to the construction of meaning should receive special support during this time. There is no other context in which youths have the opportunity to reflect on sources for the construction of meaning from the cultural history of humanity under professional, preferably neutral and open-ended moderation by qualified teaching staff. Furthermore, schools offer an organizational framework that is particularly well suited for practicing interest-led, collaborative and therefore solidary modes of behaviour. This, however, can only succeed if learning processes in schools are not determined by the pressures of competition and success. By now, school teaching programmes that were inspired by the insights of positive psychology have been repeatedly evaluated, with positive outcomes regarding the subjective well-being of students (Seligman *et al.* 2009).

Companies and non-profit organizations

In this context, construction of meaning should not only be applied to the goal of profit maximization for a company, but should be used to locate its work in a broader social or transcendent context. Likewise, solidary behaviour should not only apply to colleagues within the company, but should stretch beyond them to as many groups of people as possible. Usually, the impulse to extend the perspective of the psychological resources beyond the interests of the company does not come from within the company itself, but is introduced from the outside through societal and cultural processes of reflection. An example is the corporate social responsibility approach, which stresses the responsibility of the company to the whole society, including the normative concept of sustainable development (Hahn 2012).

Non-profit organizations (NPOs) are particularly important actors in the cultural transformation towards sustainable development. First, because they are usually the pioneers for the implementation of innovative sustainability ideas and concepts, long before these are taken up by commercial companies and transformed into lucrative business models. Second, a high credibility is ascribed to NPOs concerning the implementation of sustainability objectives, because they are committed to the values and aims of the organization and can operate independently from financial profit requirements.

Construction of meaning is an important motivating factor for members' engagement in NPOs. For this reason, processes related to the construction of meaning should be continually supported through organizational methods, such as regular collegial retreats or workshops. Generally, NPOs also offer good opportunities to support the psychological resource of solidarity. The fact that their goals are aligned with community benefit provides a sufficient value base for communal and goal-oriented action. Moreover, when cooperative activities bring success, collective self-efficacy, respectively political empowerment are raised as well. Therefore only when environmental activists believe that they can make a personal contribution to the achievement of corporate goals, they will enter into long-term commitment for intrinsic reasons to a NPO (Hunecke, Ziesenitz 2011).

Community

The term *community* does not describe a setting that lends itself to a precise definition. Rather, a number of settings can be identified at the community level that in turn can all be characterized by a specific socio-spatial reference, such as a city district or a recreation park. Regardless of the specific setting, two strategies that may contribute to fostering sustainable lifestyles can be identified. The first strategy includes the consideration of subjective indicators in assessments of quality of life at the community level. By now, sufficiently valid measurement scales for the assessment of subjective well-being or subjective life satisfaction in standardized surveys have been developed (OECD 2015). The quality of life in a city, a region, or in an entire country can only be adequately evaluated for purposes of social reporting if the subjective perspective of the people involved can be included. In this context, a successful example can be seen in the state of Bhutan, where a national happiness index was created by summarizing subjective and objective indicators in a methodologically quite well thought-out way (Ura *et al.* 2012).

The second strategy aims at increasing citizens' participation in political-administrative decisions concerning civic or community life at local, regional or national levels. In an elaborate, quasi-experimental field study including 26 cantons in Switzerland, Frey and Stutzer (2000) were able to show that higher potentials of participation in political decisions in communities influenced the life satisfaction of Swiss citizens in a positive manner, when controlling for geographical and socio-demographic factors. Considering that participation in Switzerland has a uniquely high level in global comparison, it can be expected that the influence of citizens' participation possibilities on life satisfaction will be even higher in countries where the degree of democratization is much lower. Thus, those who aspire to initiate a cultural transformation towards sustainability and immaterial sources of contentment and happiness need to provide citizens with sufficient opportunities for participation in the context of civil society.

Final remarks

In short, it is argued that people who have the capacity for pleasure, self-acceptance and self-efficacy; who cultivate mindfulness, pass through processes of creating their own meaning and orient their actions according to the principle of solidarity support the transition towards sustainable lifestyles. By including the perspectives of the individual, the approach that is presented here tries to enlarge the social-ecological perspective that analyses ecological problems primarily as unsustainable interaction between nature and society. Therefore this approach can be seen as a contribution to the field of personal sustainability. However, this should not create the impression that the responsibility for transforming society towards sustainability is solely ascribed to the individual. Such an exclusive responsibility would likely overwhelm most people, who have to manage their daily lives in circumstances and infrastructures that are largely unsustainable. In the programme to initiate a cultural transformation towards sustainable lifestyles, psychological bias must be corrected by ensuring that alongside aspects of individual behaviour and experience, most of all the influence and potential of political and economic relations are taken into account.

With subjective well-being as the motivator, the approach that is outlined here focuses on a dimension for changes towards sustainable lifestyles that is primarily of a self-interested character. However, sustainable lifestyles cannot solely be based on self-interested orientations. Rather, it is essential to have ecological and social norms that ultimately lead to limitations in self-serving behaviour that are self-imposed in a voluntary manner. The psychological resources derived from the Pleasure-Accomplishment-Meaning theory of subjective well-being point out a way that offers the opportunity for ecological and social mind-sets as well as normative orientations to evolve from an originally self-interested perspective.

Another critical point could be that the approach of psychological resources focuses too much on raising the individual's level of happiness. Happiness is always a phenomenon of contrast. Hence it requires, in addition to the cultivation of positive emotions, to a certain degree also the experience of negative emotional states. Supporters of positive psychology, too, acknowledge that it is possible to have too much happiness (Diener, Biswas-Diener 2008: 209ff.). According to this view, change and growth in all areas of life also require feelings of dissatisfaction, scepticism and frustration. As biological creatures, people are not designed to remain permanently fixed in a physiological state of excitement brought on by continual happiness. The Pleasure-Accomplishment-Meaning theory of subjective well-being can act as a guide for people enabling them to identify those areas where they can best cultivate their positive emotions. Ultimately, however, the greatest art of living consists in achieving a balance between positive and negative emotions that meets one's own needs.

While the approach that is presented here is founded on a number of single empirical findings, it has not yet been itself empirically validated as a whole. Due to the sheer variety of the psychological resources postulated in the network (see Figure 3.1), this cannot be accomplished with a single empirical study. However, it is possible to subject individual aspects of the network to empirical validation. Likewise, it is important to investigate potential relationships between the six psychological resources and subjective well-being, as well as other psychological constructs that are considered to be proximate predictors of environmental behaviour, such as behavioural intentions, social and ecological norms, and control beliefs. In the meantime, first empirical results could be generated in this direction. In a study with a sample of 300 participants, with and without practical experience in mindfulness, we found associations between mindfulness, the construction of meaning, and sustainable food consumption (Hunecke, Richter 2017). In another study with a representative sample of 400 participants, we replicated previous results that stand in support of the Pleasure-Accomplishment-Meaning theory of subjective well-being. In this study, we also found relationships between the relevant psychological constructs and ecological norms (Richter *et al.* 2017). The findings from these two studies provide grounds for hope that the identified psychological resources may constitute important conditions for achieving personal sustainability that can be used to initiate a transformation in the direction of sustainable lifestyles beyond the marketing-mode.

References

Amel, E. A., Manning, C. M. & Scott, B. A. (2009): Mindfulness and sustainable behavior: Pondering attention and awareness as means for increasing green behavior. In *Ecopsychology, 1, 1,* pp. 68–75.

Antonovsky, A. (1987): *Unraveling the mystery of health: How people manage stress and stay well.* San Francisco, CA: Jossey-Bass.

Ajzen, I. (1991): The theory of planned behavior. In *Organizational Behavior and Human Decision Processes,* 50, 2, pp. 179–211.

Bamberg, S. (2013): Changing environmentally harmful behaviors: A stage model of self-regulated behavioral change. In *Journal of Environmental Psychology, 34,* pp. 151–159.

Bamberg, S. & Möser, G. (2007): Twenty years after Hines, Hungerford, and Tomera: A new meta-analysis of psycho-social determinants of pro-environmental behavior. In *Journal of Environmental Psychology, 27, 1,* pp. 14–25.

Bandura, A. (1997): *Self-efficacy: The exercise of control.* New York: Freeman.

Barbaro, N. & Pickett, S.M. (2016): Mindfully green: Examining the effect of connectedness to nature on the relationship between mindfulness and engagement in pro-environmental behavior. In *Personality and Individual Differences, 93,* pp. 137–142.

Becker, E. & Jahn, T. (2006): *Soziale Ökologie.* Frankfurt: Campus.

Biswas-Diener, R. (2010): *Practicing Positive Psychology Coaching: Assessment, Diagnosis, and Intervention.* New York: John Wiley & Sons.

Brown, K.W. & Kasser, T. (2005): Are psychological and ecological well-being compatible? The role of values, mindfulness, and lifestyle. In *Social Indicators Research, 74, 2,* pp. 349–368.

Bryant, F. B., & Veroff, J. (2007): *Savoring: A new model of positive experience.* Mahwah, NJ: Lawrence Erlbaum Associates.

Diener, E. & Biswas-Diener, R. (2008): *Happiness: Unlocking the mysteries of psychological wealth.* Malden, MA: Blackwell.

Frank, R. (2010): *Wohlbefinden fördern. Positive Therapie in der Praxis.* Stuttgart: Klett-Cotta.

Fredrickson, B. L. (2001): The role of positive emotions in positive psychology: The broaden-and-build theory of positive emotions. In *American Psychologist, 56, 3,* pp. 218–226.

Frey, B. S. & Stutzer, A. (2000): Happiness, economy and institutions. In *Economic Journal, 110, 446,* pp. 918–938.

Grawe, K. (1998): *Psychologische Therapie.* Göttingen: Hogrefe.

Hahn, R. (2012): ISO 26000 and the standardization of strategic management processes for sustainability and corporate social responsibility. In *Business Strategy and the Environment, 22, 7,* pp. 442–455.

Hunecke, M. (2013). *Psychologie der Nachhaltigkeit. Psychische Ressourcen für Post-wachstumsgesellschaften.* München: oekom (a shortened version in English: www.denkwerkzukunft.de/index.php/englishdocuments/index/MemoPsychEngl).

Hunecke, M., Haustein, S., Grischkat, S. & Böhler, S. (2007): Psychological, socio-demographic, and infrastructural factors as determinants of ecological impact caused by mobility behavior. In *Journal of Environmental Psychology, 27, 4,* pp. 277–292.

Hunecke, M. & Richter, N. (2017): *Mindfulness, the construction of meaning and sustainable food consumption.* Manuscript submitted for publication.

Hunecke, M. & Ziesenitz, A. (2011): ManagerInnen mit grünem Herzen: Zusammenhänge zwischen Werten, personaler Norm, Copingstilen, Geschlechtsrollenorientierungen und dem Engagement in Umweltorganisationen sowie im privaten Umweltverhalten von UmweltaktivistInnen. In *Umweltpsychologie, 15, 2*, pp. 52–76.

Jacob, J., Jovic, E. & Brinkerhoff, M. B. (2009): Personal and planetary well-being: Mindfulness meditation, pro-envrionmental behavior and personal quality of life in a survey from the social justice and ecological sustainability movement. In *Social Indicators Research, 93, 2*, pp. 275–294.

Jahn, T. (2000): *Social-ecological research – conceptual framework for a new funding policy.* Synopsis of the Report for the German Federal Ministry of Education and Research. Frankfurt am Main: ISOE – Institut für sozial-ökologische Forschung. Retrieved 5 May 2017, from www.isoe.de/fileadmin/redaktion/ISOE-Reihen/dp/dp-08-isoe-2000.pdf

Kabat-Zinn, J. (1990): *Full catastrophe living: The program of the Stress Reduction Clinic at the University of Massachusetts Medical Center.* New York: Delta.

Kaluza, G. (2011): *Stressbewältigung: Trainingsmanual zur psychologischen Gesundheits-förderung.* Heidelberg: Springer.

Kaufmann-Hayoz R., Bättig Ch., Bruppacher S., Defila R., Di Giulio A., Ulli-Beer S., Friederich U., Garbely M., Gutscher H., Jäggi Ch., Jegen M., Müller A. & North N. (2001): A typology of tools for building sustainability strategies. In R. Kaufmann-Hayoz & H. Gutscher (Eds), *Changing things – moving people. Strategies for promoting sustainable development at the local level.* pp. 33–107. Basel: Birkhäuser.

Koppenhöfer E. (2004): *Kleine Schule des Genießens. Ein verhaltenstherapeutisch orientierter Behandlungsansatz zum Aufbau positiven Erlebens und Handelns.* Lengerich: Pabst.

Linehan, M. (1996): *Dialektisch-Behaviorale Therapie der Borderline-Persönlichkeits-störung.* München: CIP-Medien.

McKay, M. & Fanning, P. (2000): *Self-esteem: A proven program of cognitive techniques for assessing, improving, and maintaining your self-esteem.* Oakland, CA: New Harbinger Publications.

McKenzie-Mohr, D. & Smith, W. (1999): *Fostering sustainable behavior: An introduction to community-based social marketing* (2nd ed.). Gabriola Island, BC: New Society.

Mosler, H. J. & Tobias, R. (2007): Umweltpsychologische Interventionsformen neu gedacht. In *Umweltpsychologie 11, 1*, pp. 35–54.

Nestmann, F. (1996): Psychosoziale Beratung. Ein ressourcentheoretischer Entwurf. In *Verhaltenstherapie und psychosoziale Praxis, 28, 3*, pp. 359–376.

OECD (2015): *How's life? 2015: Measuring well-being.* Paris: OECD Publishing.

Peterson, C., Park, N. & Seligman, M. E. P. (2005): Orientations to happiness and life satisfaction: The full life versus the empty life. In *Journal of Happiness Studies, 6, 1*, pp. 25–41.

Potreck-Rose, F. & Jacob, G. (2010): *Selbstzuwendung, Selbstakzeptanz, Selbstvertrauen. Psychotherapeutische Interventionen zum Aufbau von Selbstwertgefühl.* Stuttgart: Klett-Cotta.

Randers, J. (2012): *2052: A global forecast for the next forty years.* Hartford, VT: Chelsea Green Publishing.

Richter, N., Strauch, S. & Hunecke, M. (2017): *Orientations to happiness, mindfulness and ecological norm.* Manuscript submitted for publication.

Rogers, E. M. (2003): *Diffusion of innovations.* New York: Free Press.

Ruch, W., Proyer, R. T., Harzer, C., Park, N., Peterson, C. & Seligman, M. E. P. (2010): Values in Action Inventory of Strengths (VIA-IS): Adaptation and validation of the German version and the development of a peer-rating form. In *Journal of Individual Differences, 31, 3*, pp. 138–149.

Schueller, S.M. & Seligman, M. E. P. (2010): Pursuit of pleasure, engagement, and meaning: Relationships to subjective and objective measures of well-being. In *The Journal of Positive Psychology*, *5*, *4*, pp. 253–263.

Schultz, P. W. & Zelezny, L. C. (1998): Values and proenvironmental behavior: A five-country survey. In *Journal of Cross-Cultural Psychology*, *29*, *4*, pp. 540–558.

Schulze, G. (1992): *Erlebnisgesellschaft: Kultursoziologie der Gegenwart*. Frankfurt/New York: Campus.

Schwarzer, R. (2004): *Psychologie des Gesundheitsverhaltens. Eine Einführung in die Gesundheitspsychologie*. Göttingen: Hogrefe.

Segal, Z. V., Williams, J. M. G. & Teasdale, J. D. (2008): *Die achtsamkeitsbasierte kognitive Therapie der Depression*. Tübingen: DGVT-Verlag.

Seligman, M. E. P. (2002): *Authentic happiness: Using the new positive psychology to realize your potential for lasting fulfillment*. New York: Free Press.

Seligman, M. E. P. (2011): *Flourish. A visionary new understanding of happiness and well-being*. New York: Free Press.

Shapiro, S. L. & Carlson, L. E. (2011): *Die Kunst und Wissenschaft der Achtsamkeit*. Freiburg: Arbor.

Seligman, M. E. P. & Csikszentmihalyi, M. (2000): Positive psychology: An introduction. In *American Psychologist*, *55*, *1*, pp. 5–14.

Seligman, M. E. P., Ernst R.M., Gillham, J., Reivich K. & Linkins, M. (2009): Positive education: Positive psychology and classroom interventions. In *Oxford Review of Education*, *35*, *3*, pp. 293–311.

Seligman, M. E. P., Steen, T., Park, N. & Peterson, C. (2005): Positive psychology progress: Empirical validation of interventions. In *American Psychologist*, *60*, *5*, pp. 410–421.

Snyder, C. R. & Lopez, S. J. (2009): *Oxford handbook of positive psychology*. Oxford: Oxford University Press.

Stern, P. C., Dietz, T., Abel, T., Guagnano, G. A. & Kalof, L. (1999): A value-belief-norm theory of support for social movements, the case of environmental concern. In *Human Ecology Review*, *6*, *2*, pp. 81–97.

Tausch, R. (2008): Sinn in unserem Leben. In A. E. Auhagen (Hrsg.), *Positive Psychologie*. pp. 97–113. Weinheim: Beltz.

Ura, K., Alkire, S., Zangmo, T. & Wangdi, K. (2012): *A short guide to Gross National Happiness Index*. Thimphu: The Centre for Bhutan Studies. Retrieved 2 March 2017, from www.grossnationalhappiness.com/wp-content/uploads/2012/04/Short-GNH-Index-edited.pdf.

4 Care of the self and "Bildung" as condition for and result of personal sustainability

Michael Niehaus, Dirk Schmidt and Shirli Homburg

Self-guidance

Man's highest goal, according to Socrates, is to lead a good life (Gorgias 509c, Republic 354a). It is therefore a sign of rationality to consider how one might master one's own life. What constitutes a fulfilled, successful and good life is one of the central questions of Socratic philosophy: not theoretical insight for its own sake, but rather the practice of a good life is its aim. Socrates has become a prototype for the philosophic search for the good life – with all its consequences. His truth-searching dialogic methodology is seen by some as the origin of (self-) education and professional counselling (Stavemann 2002). Socrates assumed that a striving for good is inherent to being human and he intended to serve as a midwife of thoughts for finding the right answers existing within humans. It also became apparent to him that personal happiness, if correctly interpreted, was not in opposition to the societal interests and that happiness in life could only be achieved through an ethically sound life.

"Know thyself" ("Gnothi Seautón") was the short and striking inscription on the antique Temple of Apollo in Delphi. Knowing oneself as a daily exercise was considered the beginning, the foundation for any meaningful thinking about God and the world as a whole, as well as about the lesser issues of day-to-day life. Socrates' activity on the agora in Athens illustrated that philosophizing is ultimately nothing but precisely seeking and searching for this self-knowledge, and that guidance and accompaniment on the path to self-knowledge is the core competence of philosophy (Polednitschek 2013). For Socrates, self-knowledge became a personality-shaping and personality-creating element. Self-knowledge, i.e. insight into one's own desires and actions, was Socrates' top priority. For only when one's own individuality, with its predilections and talents, but also its deficits, becomes transparent does one attain the possibility of purposefully shaping one's own life. Only if one consciously desires the same things that were previously desired unconsciously, Socrates claims, is one able to make the right decisions. From this he concludes that an unexamined life is not worth living (Martens 2004).

In contrast to this, the representatives of the sophistic philosophy offered instruction in rhetoric, grammar, dialectic and other general disciplines – and, also in contrast to Socrates, they offered it for money. The sophists had a great influence on the development of the Greek educational system, but their position remained ambiguous. On the one hand, they helped to weaken the educational privileges of the aristocratic society. On the other hand, the aim of sophistic education was directed to prospective politicians, teaching students oratory for political leadership positions. By contrast, for Socrates the highest goal of *paideia* (German "Bildung")[1] was not to train practical political survival strategies, but education about moral living through pedagogical eros and dialogue. While for Socrates paideia is a self-purpose, for the sophists the purpose of education is to be able to realize your own interests through good rhetoric.

In his "Republic" Plato works this idea of paideia into a philosophical and scientific system of spiritual and moral education to renew the political life in the polis. So Plato can be considered the founder of a systematic training programme that seeks comprehensive education for moral action instead of unilateral individualistic training for political efficiency. Plato's concept of the ideal state is supported by this universal educational philosophy (Moser 2006).

A few centuries later, Kant will again take up this idea, in which he critically questions the conditions of knowledge. Kant asks about the task of philosophy in the search for good life. In the tradition of Socrates and Plato, he concludes that it is primarily the task of philosophy to assist people in their self-enlightenment:

> Enlightenment is man's emergence from his self-imposed nonage. Nonage is the inability to use one's own understanding without another's guidance. This nonage is self-imposed if its cause lies not in lack of understanding but in indecision and lack of courage to use one's own mind without another's guidance. Sapere aude! (Have the courage to use your own understanding!) is therefore the motto of the enlightenment.
>
> (Kant 1963: 3)

In this Kantian way of thinking, philosophy provides the intellectual space in which:

- it is possible to clarify one's own values and concepts;
- one may work on terms and precise definitions of meanings;
- one can cast glances behind the scenes of everyday events;
- different and new perspectives let familiar things appear in an entirely different light;
- radical astonishment and irritation allow us to leave well-travelled paths;
- alternative options for actions and life designs become visible;
- judgement, maturity and autonomy can grow.

Philosophizing, one could say, is a form of empowerment – an instigation to (re-)acquire self-determination over one's own life.

Care of the self – philosophy as an art of life

Care of the self (Latin *cura sui*) is the basis for a philosophical conduct of life. Caring about oneself and for oneself covers all aspects of consciously dealing with oneself, including health and physical as well as mental fitness, managing time, work-life balance, meaning of work, as well as big questions about life's sense and meaning. In other words, self-care is about individual life design and the associated life practices (Hooft 2002). Along with the cultivation of the self its roots go back to Socratic philosophy. Although self-care was actively cultivated in classical antiquity and a wide range of techniques for life aid were available, this tradition (within philosophy) was lost over the centuries. Only at the end of the last century this aspect was rediscovered. Significant influence by the rediscovery of the philosophical art of living was exerted by the work of Michel Foucault (Foucault 1990) and Pierre Hadot (Hadot 1995), as discussed later in the chapter. The reinstatement of the philosophical concept of self-care in the German-speaking world was heavily influenced by Wilhelm Schmid, whose work also represents one of the principal inspirations for this chapter (Schmid 1999, 2004).

The ethical and political character of self-care is Socrates' primary focus. Thus, it can be argued that from the very beginning, self-care was not, as its name might suggest, merely an egoistic concern with oneself. In Socratic tradition, care of the self ultimately occurs through the individual's striving for virtue and excellence, in the framework of which the virtuous and equitable individual soul is always also aware of the good for the society. Therefore, caring for oneself and one's own soul forms the foundation for all social engagement. Self-care is not only a private matter, but in fact always includes a social aspect and occurs in interchange with other people. Socrates himself led a quasi-public life – the agora was his living-room. He did not search for happiness in secrecy and private reclusiveness, but took social responsibility to the point of being willing to die for his conviction. This self-care remains the basis for all leadership activity to this day: without knowledge about oneself, and without taking care of one's self, one is not able to lead others. Or to put it differently: someone who is unable to take responsibility for himself or herself cannot take responsibility for others either (Deslandes 2012).

Socrates' call to take care of oneself, of one's soul, is a recurring topic in the Platonic dialogues. This care for and about oneself requires self-knowledge. One must understand oneself to be able to understand what pertains to others. Such self-care, or should we say education of the self, must begin at a young age and should be an integral part of all parental and academic pedagogy as well as of any professional or vocational training and management seminars (Niehaus, Wisniewski 2016).

While self-care is primarily associated with the soul, it should by no means be equated with ignoring the body. On the contrary, caring for the body and its needs is a part of the Socratic self-care concept. This includes issues of proper nutrition, athletic exercises and the handling of desires. Socrates' contemporaries cared very much about what they ate and drank, which exercises were appropriate for what purpose and what the correct quantities of such measures were. Regarding this, the lines between medical and philosophical discourse were blurred (Rinofner-Kreidl 2005).

The concept of self-care reached a high point in the Stoic movement. This school of thinking clearly differentiated between care in the sense of fearful concern, which was to be avoided, and the prudent care for oneself that the philosophers considered vital. The opposite of self-care was neglecting oneself. In this sense, self-care does not equate to seeking benefits or profit for oneself, but simply prompts the individual not to be indifferent to oneself and to actively work on improving oneself. Thus, self-care primarily means attention to and mindfulness towards oneself, and there doesn't exist any area of life that is out of the focus of intensive and conscientious concern. Again, this concern should not be confused with leading a life full of worries – something which Stoic philosophy was explicitly opposed to – but instead be understood as *the art of living* (ars vivendi) (Gödde, Zirfas 2016).

Many examples for the Stoic care of the self are found in the literarily composed letters of Seneca, who used advice and admonishment to foster improvement in the self of his correspondents, and provided guidance down to the most intimate questions of life conduct. An example:

> Continue to act thus, my dear Lucilius – set yourself free for your own sake; gather and save your time, which till lately has been forced from you, or filched away, or has merely slipped from your hands. Make yourself believe the truth of my words, – that certain moments are torn from us, that some are gently removed, and that others glide beyond our reach. The most disgraceful kind of loss, however, is that due to carelessness. Furthermore, if you will pay close heed to the problem, you will find that the largest portion of our life passes while we are doing ill, a goodly share while we are doing nothing, and the whole while we are doing that which is not to the purpose.
>
> (Seneca 1917: 5)

In Stoic philosophy the care of the self means focusing on oneself so as not to surrender oneself to the mandate of other people or professional commitments. Self-care is associated with strict time management and a number of other behaviours, rules and procedures. The Stoic philosophers provide us with detailed instructions for exercises (Hadot 1998, Ambrosio 2008):

- Self-observation – What do I actually do all day, how do I use the time available to me? What am I doing in this very moment, what am I perceiving, what is the content of my thoughts?
- Analysis of one's thoughts – What are my thought processes focused on? Am I concentrating on what I am trying to do, or am I in fact thinking of other things?
- Meditation – Concentration exercises to focus the thoughts.

- Resolution in the morning and assessment in the evening – Do I have goals for the day? Did I achieve what I planned? If not, why not? Did I set the wrong priorities, did I assess situations poorly?
- Philosophical reading, conversations with friends – Stimuli and advice from familiar people, support for reflection upon one's own life.
- Writing letters, keeping a diary – Expressing one's own thoughts and writing down words and sentences sharpens the mind and fosters self-reflection.
- Preparing for one's own death – Am I living my life in such a way that I could bid it farewell at any time? Am I living my life in consciousness of my own mortality, am I concentrating on the important issues in light of the finiteness of my life?

With the advent of Christianity, essential aspects of the philosophy of self-care were incorporated into religious practice and thus deformed. Self-care and its practices were no longer a goal in itself, but placed under the rules of the Christian religion. This process brought about two noteworthy changes: on the one hand, the focus of self-care shifted more and more from the individual's responsibility for himself towards guidance by others. In a sense, this was a form of professionalization of self-care: the competence and responsibility, but also the authority of interpretation in all issues of self-care was transferred to counselling specialists. On the other hand, the dualism or polarity of body and soul was introduced to the discourse on self-care. The first concern of the soul was now the love of God, not caring for the body; caring for the body was considered a trap for the soul, neglect of the body was supposed to result in enlightenment of the soul.

Pastoral care focuses on cleansing the soul from pollution by sin. Here, self-care is aimed at turning away from the flesh and abdicating all earthly commitments; this requires closely watching oneself and illuminating every corner of the soul. It is no longer only the actions that are important, but in particular also the thoughts which must be meticulously monitored. This new form of care or concern focused on detecting sinful desires. It is this from Christianity modified concept of self-care that has particularly heavily affected western cultural history. Certain techniques of philosophical self-care like the exploration of conscience, the dialogue with the counsellor and the opening of one's soul to a familiar person, found their way into the practices of Christian counselling (Reichenbach 2000). The bodily aspect of self-care is not completely eliminated, but instead reinterpreted within this concept: the church is Christ's body that the church officers must care for, much like in the antique notion of caring for one's body where one required doctors and athletic instructors as advisors, as well as a disciplined way of life, a balanced diet and specific exercises to achieve a good constitution. In this sense, pastoral care represents care for the herd of Christ.

With the establishment of Christianity, the antique form of self-care disappeared from western culture for a long time. It was only in the modern times that the antique self-care tradition was rediscovered. For example, Michel de Montaigne pointed out how little his contemporaries cared for cultivating their souls, instead worrying only about personal riches and their reputation. Self-care was not only pitted against a great number of occupational and social commitments, but also against the bad habits of self-indulgence and regarding oneself unworthy of one's own care. (Moser 2006) Montaigne himself stated that he would willingly abandon himself completely to the care and governance of another – if he only knew whom he could fully entrust himself to. Montaigne believed that nature had outfitted all creatures with a concern for themselves, but that this concern should best be taken off man's shoulders by a competent government (Balmer 2016).

The twentieth century in particular saw the rediscovery of the self-care concept. It became the central topic in French philosopher Michel Foucault's late oeuvre, for instance (Foucault *et al*. 1988). Foucault referred to the antique tradition and developed the concept of self-care further. In his search for self-technologies that help a subject to constitute itself instead of merely being a product of manifold anonymous social forces and unconscious practices, he made self-cultivation and conscious self-governance accessible to the postmodern society. Foucault refreshed the notion of self-care and brought it to the table as a concept for a society whose subjects were already over-governed and had thus become used to transferring their concerns to others. He argued for appropriation of the self with the goal of regaining power over oneself and bringing this power to bear against patronization by an anonymous ruling elite (Balke 2008). Nevertheless, Foucault realized that even in our time, self-care is still seen as something objectionable, as mere narcissism, and therefore a form of egoism, so he emphasized the social aspect of self-care. Michel Foucault has formulated a utopia that focuses on the individual. He is thinking about a community in which subjects feel encouraged to create their own life story, to a permanent creation of their own in their autonomy and not as a product or victim of social discipline and normalization powers. It is about the inner vision, the search for the truth in the soul. The term "self-care" means taking care of oneself and stands for an attitude and the behaviour of a person who undertakes to shape her own life to orient oneself to foreign norms and ideas, but to give it a distinctive own aesthetic form (Gussone, Schiepek 2000).

The reflections of the late Foucault on the art of life are closely related to his theory of power. He does not see power as the quintessence of "evil", which should be combated or avoided. Power comes from "fortune", i.e. something that is able to move or influence. This is the conceptual part contained in terms such as self-empowerment, self-efficacy or empowerment. For Foucault, the subject is not formed against power but in it. Self-care does not mean abstinence from power but the possibility to influence oneself and one's way of life. It means not leaving the government of oneself to others, but to navigate in the complex field of power relations.

Apart from that, in his recourse to antiquity, Foucault discovers an idea of the connection of self-care and public responsibility (Keupp 1996). Just like Socrates understood his philosophizing as being a public act of conversing with the people in the agora, modern Socratic philosophizing seeks a dialogue with the people on the marketplaces of today, in the meeting rooms and boardrooms of corporations and organizations, in politics and the media. Nowadays, the concept of self-care also wins attention in professional contexts. In the area of burnout prevention there are first steps to integrate self-care-practices in the health sector (Gussone, Schiepek 2000).

Exercises in self-care

The next part of this chapter shows what a philosophical art of living means today in the context of personal sustainability. These exercises are the result of many seminars, workshops and consultations that the authors have carried out in recent years with different groups of participants. In the description of the exercises, the oral style of seminars has been deliberately retained. Common to all exercises is the critical self-reflection of the participants, which was initiated by concrete questions about their own lifestyles. In all exercises, it is about changing the view of the world and a transformation of the self (Lahav 2016). When the various aspects of the antique self-care concept are systematized, the following elements become apparent:

- *Self-receptive aspects of self-care* means that one's own self is perceived and taken seriously. The consequence of this self-receptive approach is a great attentiveness to oneself which perceives even the small and seemingly inconspicuous matters of everyday life and places the body and senses in particular at the centre of one's concern. In this context self-care means practicing one's perception, sharpening one's senses and learning sensuousness. Perceiving oneself means recognizing oneself, thereby making self-care a path towards self-awareness – and the other way round. Exercises for cultivating self-receptivity include asking yourself:

  – When did I last truly feel my heart? What does its beating in my chest feel like? When was the last time I felt the boundaries of my physical capabilities? How do my legs feel after a long hike?
  – A healthy mind lives in a healthy body. Which exercises keep my body, mind and soul fit? What is keeping me from doing those exercises more often?
  – How do I train my perception, senses, and my sensuality? Each type of pleasure can be cultivated. What am I doing for myself in this regard?

- *Self-reflective aspects of self-care.* The act of self-reflection is connected to a process of accounting and analysing one's own behaviour. It is the process of taking a step back from oneself, of gaining some distance, which allows to see oneself from the outside. Self-reflection means taking pause from the daily routine, to step out of the flow of events and activities. During self-reflection, one views all things including one's own life from a different perspective. Exercises for cultivating self-reflexivity include asking yourself:

  – When did I last look into a mirror, or when did someone else hold a mirror in front of me? What did I see – whom did I see?
  – What surprised or astonished me?

  − Who or what helps me in taking that step back from myself and viewing myself from outside?

• *Self-productive aspects of self-care.* This means that the self is not simply provided, it is created: I am my own creation, shaped by my own individual constructions of reality. The notion of self-production of the internal and external world has been under constant development since the antique philosophy, leading all the way up to radical constructivism and contemporary systems theory. Insight into this self-production provides enormous freedom, but also imposes great responsibility on us: it is us who are the masters of our fate! We are not victims of the coincidences of life, our genes and social circumstances and compulsions, but rather are challenged to shape our individual selves in a positive fashion. Our attitudes towards different things are what distinguish our lives, and we are capable of changing those attitudes. "Men are disturbed, not by things, but by the principles and notions which they form concerning things", as Epictetus says in his handbook of morals (Epictetus, 1983, 5). Self-care ultimately means changing the self, transforming it on the path to excellence and wisdom. Exercises cultivating self-productive aspects include asking yourself:

  − The fundamental question "Who am I?" This frequently leads us into the very centre of self-production: what is at the core of myself, on what foundation does myself exist?
  − How do I deal with the experiences in my life so far, how do I integrate new experiences into my life?
  − What significance do I attach to various events? What would my life look like if I attached a different significance to these events? For example do I experience myself as being "thrown into the world" or as someone who has chosen and accepted his fate?
  − Am I able to attribute meaning to my life or is it merely a sequence of random events?
  − Do I comprehend myself as something constant and solid, or as something changing and flowing?
  − Nothing is as continuous as change. Am I still the person I was 2 or 3 years ago? What have I changed, how have I been changed?

• *Therapeutic and ascetic aspects of self-care.* The vulnerable self should be cared for and healed, and affects and fervour should be kept at tolerable levels. But it is not enough to regularly examine our attitudes and mindset – frequent exercises are equally important. Asceticism, a term hardly in use anymore today, traditionally means on the one hand training in the sense of physical exercise and gymnastics, while on the other hand it also includes mental schooling and chastity with the ultimate goal of attaining wisdom and virtue. This schooling, aimed at gaining command over one's thoughts and drives, occurs by focusing on fundamental matters. It aims to prevent its exercisers from being distracted by mere sensuousness and lets them dedicate themselves fully to the pursuit of wisdom. In antiquity, self-care was primarily dependent on action. This tradition provides us with a multitude of exercises that can easily be translated into our modern environment. The most important thing is to practice, to act! It is not enough to care for oneself theoretically; one must do so in practice every day. Exercises for cultivating therapeutic and ascetic aspects of self-care include asking yourself:

- The central exercise of self-care is "memento mori", remembrance of one's own death. This means becoming conscious of one's own mortality and accepting the finiteness of all existence. In the face of death, perspectives on one's own actions often change: how much time do we invest into activities and projects that we would abandon immediately if we knew our death was imminent?
- How much time do we waste on mundane things, always carrying the hope that there will still be enough time for the truly important things? *Memento mori* helps us establish the right priorities in our professional as well as our private environment.
- How often do we wish we had invested our time differently in hindsight? When our little children have suddenly become young grown-ups and we ask ourselves where time has gone; when we are plagued by the feeling that we have failed to use our time constructively, that we have not lived our lives the way we wanted to, instead having lived in dreams, plans and visions for the future. *Memento mori* also means: life is here and now, use it. This moment is here to be filled and fulfilled by you, it will never return, there is no second chance. *Carpe diem!*
- When was the last time I thought about my own death? What have I changed as a result of my last insight into the finiteness of all things?
- Change your perspective of time: life is not what may be ahead of you, but what you have already lived and experienced. What does this reversal of perspective change for you?
- As with all other ascetic exercises, the basic rule is: a single attempt is not enough, only regular exercise is valuable.

- *Social aspects of self-care.* Exercising self-care should also be understood as a preparation for caring for others; the ability to govern oneself is a fundamental requirement for leading and guiding others to care for themselves. According to Socrates, self-care always has both social and political dimensions. He viewed himself as an educator of the youth and performed the political duties delegated to him responsibly and without inappropriate zealousness. While other antique teachers and thinkers, like Diogenes, sought happiness in private reclusiveness and shunned their societal responsibilities, Socrates was a paragon of responsible commitment for the common good. Exercises in cultivating the social aspects of self-care include asking yourself:

  - How do I support the people around me? What forms of support do they need and what forms can I give them?

- Who in my circle of friends or colleagues should play a greater role as conversation partner for me in the future? How can I create situations that allow an open and uncompetitive atmosphere for dialogue?
- When was the last time I gave a neighbour or colleague honest feedback?
- How am I working on my self-guidance? How and where do I get support and feedback?
- Would it be good if all the people around me acted like me?

• *Prospective and preventive aspects of self-care.* One's self-care should include considerations of the future. This includes giving thought to what can or will occur, especially fate and death. Self-care aims at being prepared for that which is foreseeable, and many of the things often considered to be strokes of fate are in fact foreseeable: all humans age and suffer from diseases; all humans lose loved ones, and one day have to pass away themselves; all humans, as a part of society, are at the mercy of economic and political constraints, forces and coincidences. Nevertheless prevention, foresightful protection and risk management are possible and constitute another important element of self-care. Exercises for cultivating prospective and preventive skills for self-care include asking yourself:

- What do I expect from my future? What do I expect from tomorrow?
- Am I prepared for unforeseen changes? Do I have multiple alternatives?
- Is my personal way of living sustainable? Do I respect the rights of future generations?
- What am I actually doing to improve or maintain my physical and mental capacities?

"Bildung" as a way of self-cultivation towards personal sustainability

In this chapter we have described the classic concept of self-care as a philosophical art of living and given examples of exercises of self-cultivation. In the German tradition there is another central idea of self-cultivation called "Bildung" (Lessing, Steenblock 2013). It is based on the classic Greek idea of *paideia* and refers to the tradition of self-cultivation (Jaeger 1947). This German term "Bildung" cannot be translated directly into English so it will be used below to explain certain ideas. The meanings connected to the concept of "Bildung" include education and forming, as well as creating, imaging and shaping. "Bildung" refers to the image and thus back to the Genesis Passage (Genesis 1: 26f), according to which God created man in his own image. The concept was introduced into the German language by the medieval theologian and philosopher Master Eckhart. For him man is transformed by himself and is simultaneously transformed by the ground of being. In this respect all human "making" has a limit. In the Christian tradition, Bildung is therefore something intangible, a part of personal salvation. So it can be argued that the concept of Bildung connects the spirit of Athens and the heritage of Jerusalem (Polednitschek 2010).

In the following we discuss the concept of Bildung in relationship to the concept of self-care. In doing so, we focus in particular on the ideas of the German philosopher Peter Bieri (Bieri 2011). In summary, one can say that Bildung is the further context and self-care is a specific technique[2] of Bildung. In our opinion, Bildung and personal sustainability are in a reciprocal relationship. On the one hand, there is some factual knowledge in the sense of Bildung for sustainable development, on the other hand the process of Bildung is a sustainable development. We want to examine this interplay more closely employing Bieris definitions of Bildung.

- Bildung is something you make *with* and *for* yourself. You can be trained *by* someone else, but you form yourself *on your own*. This is not just a word game. We go through a training with a particular objective. Bildung means that we are working to be something – we strive to be in a certain way in the world.
- Bildung begins with curiosity. Curiosity opens the chance to form yourself. It is the insatiable desire to know what the world is all about. It begins in the earliest childhood and it is a challenge to keep it awake for a lifetime. Curiosity covers all areas of human knowledge from the stars to the smallest atoms, from the variety of natural species and into the fantastic complexity of the human organism, the history of the earth and human culture, and the questions about the origin and future of our species. It is always about two things: to know *what* is the case, and to understand *why* it is the case.
- The "Gebildete" (a person who has Bildung and has been formed through a lifelong learning process) is thus a person who is able to orient herself in the world. What is this orientation worth? "Knowledge is power" says Francis Bacon. According to the idea of Bildung this cannot mean to rule with this knowledge over others. The power of knowledge lies somewhere else: it prevents one from being a victim. Anyone who knows about the world can be less easily cast off and is able to fight back when others want to make him an instrument of their interests in politics or advertising.
- Orientation in the world is not the only orientation that matters. To be "gebildet" is also to know what knowledge and understanding exist and what their limits are. This includes questions like this: what proofs do I have for my convictions? Are they reliable? And do they really prove what they seem to prove? What are good arguments, and what is deceptive sophistry? What is a law as opposed to a random correlation? What distinguishes a genuine explanation from a pseudo-clarification? We need to know that if we want to assess a risk and make a judgement about all the predictions we are bombarded with. Someone who is awake will maintain sceptical distance to daily politics or the promises of science and business. The "Gebildete" in this sense knows how to distinguish between merely rhetorical facades and grounded thoughts. He can do this because two questions have become his second nature: "What exactly does that mean?" And "How do we know it is so?" To ask them again and again makes resistant to rhetorical drills, brainwashing and

sect affiliation, and it sharpens the perception of blind habits of thinking and talking, as opposed to fashionable trends. This is a high good, and its name is: mental incorruptibility.

- The enlightened awareness of the educated is not just critical consciousness. It is also characterized by historical curiosity: how did we come to think, feel, talk and live? The Gebildete knows: everything could have come differently, there is no masterplan in our culture. The enlightened consciousness is therefore an awareness of the historical contingency. It expresses itself in the ability to look at one's own culture from a certain distance and to adopt an ironic and playful attitude to it. This does not mean not confessing to one's own way of life. It is merely a matter of moving away from the naive and arrogant thought that one's own form of life is more appropriate than any other.

- The awareness of historical contingency includes also the relationship to the body, forms of courtesy and dignity, ways of celebrating and getting dressed, the relationship to drugs, forms of expressing tenderness, how to flirt and approach each other as man and woman. Here, too, we must be educated, which is expressed in knowledge of diversity, respect for the stranger, and withdrawal of the initial arrogance. To understand a culture is to know its conceptions of moral integrity. The process of Bildung consists of taking note of the fact that in other parts of the world, in other societies and forms of life, one thinks and feels differently about good and evil, that our moral identity is depending on historical coincidences.

- The Gebildete is one who knows about himself and knows about the difficulties and limits of this knowledge. Modern contingency presents a dilemma: I know about the historical conditionality of my views and therefore of their relativity, and yet I cannot help setting them absolutely, because otherwise the seriousness of my beliefs would be lost. In this way, Bildung helps us being autonomous without losing ourselves in postmodern arbitrariness.

- Bildung is understood as a process and a result at the same time, it includes the flexible adaptation to new external conditions and at the same time forms a resistant centre with institutionalized, stabilizing structures. Bildung is based on the fruitful exchange with other people and cultures. It is a form of a conscious and active way of life, it requires a lifelong effort, not to persist in deadlocked tracks but to be open to new ideas and change.

Self-care and Bildung as condition for and result of personal sustainability

Going back to the ancient Greece, we found that the Socratic emphasis on self-care, and the German concept of "Bildung" deliver an essential aspect of personal sustainability. Personal sustainability on the one hand forms part of sustainable development. It is a necessary and so far under-researched part of sustainable development that helps to complement the current discourse. On the other hand, personal sustainability can also be seen as a condition and – as a third aspect – as a goal for sustainable development. Considering these three perspectives the points of contact to the discourse of self-care and "Bildung" are clearly obvious. In this sense, personal sustainability is also nothing new, but has always been part of the German concept of Bildung or of the ancient approach of self-care.

Bieri has suggested that Bildung is the critical assimilation and appropriation of culture. Bildung is always process and result at the same time. Acculturate means to chew and digest (Bieri 2011). It's like the intake of food, which affects the body. So any culture is changing our self, shaping us. The transformation towards personal sustainability thus means an interaction, a process whereby a man transforms himself and is simultaneously transformed. Critically it must be noted that there is a great overlap in terms of personal sustainability, Bildung and self-care, but the different discourses have not yet been combined. On the other hand, the rather natural science discourse of sustainability and the discourse on Bildung and self-care which is located rather in humanities have only few places to come into contact with one another.

In this respect, our contribution is a first attempt to bring the different disciplines into a dialogue and to illustrate the interrelationship between sustainability and education. Further work by Res et Verba – The Sustainability Network! are in preparation.

Notes

1 See sub-chapter " 'Bildung' as a way of self-cultivation towards personal sustainability" below.
2 Self-care is not intended to be instrumental, but a value in itself.

References

Ambrosio, J. (2008): Writing the self: Ethical self-formation and the undefined work of freedom. *Educational Theory* 58 (3), pp. 251–267.

Balke, F. (2008): Begriffe und Konzepte: Selbstsorge/Selbsttechnologie. In: Clemens Kammler C. & Reinhardt-Becker E. (Eds): *Foucault-Handbuch. Leben, Werk, Wirkung.* Stuttgart: Metzler, 286–291.

Balmer, H.P. (2016): *Neuzeitliche Sokratik. Michel de Montaignes essayistisches Philosophieren.* Münster: Monsenstein und Vannerdat.

Bieri, P. (2011): *Wie wollen wir leben?* St. Pölten: Residenz.

Deslandes, G. (2012): The care-of-self ethic with continual reference to Socrates: Towards ethical self-management. *Business Ethics: A European Review* 21 (4), pp. 325–338.

Epictetus: The Enchiridion http://classics.mit.edu/Epictetus/epicench.html (accessed 15 September 2017).

Foucault, M. (1990): *The history of sexuality Vol. 3: Care of the self.* London: Penguin.

Foucault, M., Martin, L.H., Gutman, H., & Hutten, P.H. (1988): *Technologies of the self.* Amherst: University of Massachusetts Press.

Gödde, G. & Zirfas, J. (2016): *Therapeutik und Lebenskunst. Eine psychologisch-philosophische Grundlegung.* Gießen: Psychosozial-Verlag.

Gussone, B. & Schiepek, G. (2000): *Die "Sorge um sich": Burnout-Prävention und Lebenskunst in helfenden Berufen*. Tübingen: dgvt-Verlag.

Hadot, P. (1995): *Philosophy as a way of life: Spiritual exercises from Socrates to Foucault*. Malden, MA: Blackwell.

Hadot, P. (1998): *The inner citadel: The meditations of Marcus Aurelius*. Cambridge, MA: Harvard University Press.

Hooft, S. (2002): Philosophy and the care of the self: A literature survey. *SOPHIA* 41 (1), S. 89–134.

Jaeger, W. (1947): *Paideia. The ideals of Greek culture*. Oxford, UK: Oxford University Press.

Kant, I. (1963): *On history: What is enlightenment? (1784)*. Translated by Lewis White Beck. Indianapolis, IN: Bobbs-Merrill.

Keupp, H. (1996): Gemeinsinn und Selbstsorge. In: Wendt, W.R. (Ed.): *Zivilgesellschaft und soziales Handeln. Bürgerschaftliches Engagement in eigenen und gemeinschaftlichen Belangen*. Freiburg im Breisgau: Lambertus, S. 78–95

Lahav, R. (2016): *Stepping out of Plato's cave. Philosophical Counseling, Philosophical Practice, and Self-Transformation*. Chieti: Edizioni Solfanelli.

Lessing, H.U. & Steenblock, V. (Eds) (2013): *"Was den Menschen eigentlich zum Menschen macht . . ."* Klassische Texte einer Philosophie der Bildung. Freiburg: Alber.

Martens, E. (2004): *Sokrates. Eine Einführung*. Stuttgart: Reclam.

Meyer, K. (2011): *Bildung*. Berlin/Boston: de Gruyter.

Moser, C. (2006): *Buchgestützte Subjektivität. Literarische Formen der Selbstsorge und der Selbsthermeneutik von Platon bis Montaigne*. Tübingen: Niemeyer.

Niehaus, M. & Wisniewski, R. (2016): *Management by Sokrates. Was die Philosophie der Wirtschaft zu bieten hat*. Norderstedt: BoD.

Plato (1903): *Platonis Opera*, ed. John Burnet. Oxford University Press.

Polednitschek, T. (2010): *Meister Eckhart: Philosophisch leben. Zum 750. Geburtstag des großen Mystikers*. Freiburg: Herder.

Polednitschek, T. (2013): *Der politische Sokrates. Was will philosophische Praxis?* Münster: LIT.

Reichenbach, R. (2000). Die Tiefe der Oberfläche: Michel Foucault zur Selbstsorge und über die Ethik der Transformation. *Vierteljahresschrift für wissenschaftliche Pädagogik*, 76 (2), 177–189.

Res et Verba – The Sustainability Network! www.resetverba.eu/, accessed 15 September 2017.

Rinofner-Kreidl, S. (2005): Anleitung zur Selbstsorge. Über den ursprünglich ethischen Charakter von Medizin und Philosophie. *Psychologische Medizin* 16 (4), S. 17–24.

Schmid, W. (1999): *Philosophie der Lebenskunst. Eine Grundlegung*. Frankfurt am Main: Suhrkamp.

Schmid, W. (2004): *Mit sich selbst befreundet sein. Von der Lebenskunst im Umgang mit sich selbst*. Frankfurt am Main: Suhrkamp.

Seneca (1917): *Moral letters to Lucilius*. Translated by Richard Mott Gummere. London: Heinemann.

Stavemann H. (2002): *Sokratische Gesprächsführung in Therapie und Beratung: Eine Anleitung für Psychotherapeuten, Berater und Seelsorger*. Berlin: Beltz.

5   Sustainable development: A matter of truth and love

Oliver Parodi

Introduction – towards a culture of sustainability

At present, we are living in a non-sustainable world. The non-sustainable way in which we deal with the fellow mankind, our environment and our descendants has become broadly and deeply rooted in our global way of living and doing business. It is manifested in the destruction of the environment, poverty, injustice, wars, overused resources, climate change, a decreasing biodiversity, infertile land, etc. We are living in a global and globalised culture of non-sustainability.

At the same time, we also possess enormous technological (and thus economic) means, an immense knowledge and good ideas, concepts, guiding principles and political programmes for a sustainable development (cf. e.g. Schultz *et al.* 2008, UN 2017). But their implementation is held up, the "great transition" (WBGU 2011) largely fails to set in. Many destructive trends continue, although they have been known for decades and countless efforts have been made to stop them, e.g. symptomatically: Earth Overshoot Day (2017).

So there is not a lack of knowledge, neither about the alarming state of the world nor about solution approaches and concepts of sustainability. What is necessary and lacking is their realisation, the transformation and, finally, the actual practice: a lived sustainability that is implemented and taken for granted in every aspect of human life. To live in a really sustainable world, we do not only need technical innovation, a change of our energy supply and infrastructure, but also a change of thinking, a different education, new forms of economic behaviour and sharing, new social orders, readjusted standards, and even new collective and individual patterns of perception – an ultimate and profound cultural change which affects all spheres of life. We need – in the not too distant future – the establishment of a culture of sustainability.

"Culture" means the interplay between individual and collective (Hansen 2011). Thus, heading for a transformation to a culture of sustainability the individual, the person has to be addressed as well as the collective side of culture (institutions, laws, technical, political or economic systems).

To describe the possible, outstanding and necessary cultural change is very thrilling, but not the subject of this chapter. Here, I only want to discuss a few interesting and far-reaching aspects of sustainability. And therefore I address "sustainability" not as an idea or concept but as (a future) practice, an individual and collective way of life and lived culture. Aiming at the realisation of sustainability as lived culture and not only discussing a concept means to move sustainable development a bit from theory to practice, from thinking to living. That brings sustainable development closer to the people, to life, and makes it more human in a way.

Thus I want to address – in the context of sustainable development – some very common and basic human issues first: truth, fear and love (Part I). Then I would like to take two steps back and have a look at human history, introduce a pattern of human relations to the world and the accompanying evolution of the consciousness (Part II) to finally put both parts into relation and dare to take a look at a dawning culture of sustainability, where truth and love are essential and complementary dimensions in the context of an upcoming new relation of human being to the world.

Part I: sustainability, truth, fear and love

In the following, to make the endeavour of sustainable development more human, to bring it closer to people and life, I would like to point out some of the references of the concept of sustainable development to some very basic human aspects: truth, fear and love.

Sustainability as a matter of truth

The pursuit of sustainability has been inextricably linked with the pursuit of truth since its very beginnings, with "truth" also being used *pars pro toto* for knowledge, science and rationality. The fact that sustainable development would be unthinkable without the aspect of truth will quickly become clear.

To begin with, I should point out that when talking of "sustainable development", I refer first of all to the general scientific-ethical-political sustainability discourse (cf. Kopfmüller *et al.* 2001) triggered by the Brundtland Report (WCED 1987), at the core of which is the pursuit of intra- and intergenerational justice: a development "that meets the needs of the present without compromising the ability of future generations to meet their own needs" (*ibid.*). If, in the following, specific concepts, ideas or understandings of sustainable development are meant, this is specified in the text.[1]

The pursuit of sustainable development originally emerged from a new truth spreading in the last century, from the recognition of the *Limits to Growth* (Meadows *et al.* 1972), from the realisation that the resources of our planet are limited and that our lifestyles and economy, aimed at growth and resulting in exploitation (of nature) and pollution, will lead to multiple catastrophes. Ultimately, ongoing growth even threatens the continued existence of humanity, at least as we know it (cf. Jonas 1984). This world-shattering knowledge, this fundamental, scientifically derived truth is essential to the pursuit of future sustainable development.[2]

In addition to this fundamental knowledge, sustainable development needs science in countless forms and activities. The core, the essence and the currency of scientific labour is truth. Theses, statements and assumptions are investigated theoretically and/or empirically to determine whether they are true or false. In achieving sustainable development, science is first and fundamentally needed to generate systematic knowledge in order to understand how, for example, ecological processes take place: what happens to the aquatic ecosystems with increasing CO_2 concentrations? To then identify connections between human (economic, technological) activity and their effects on ecosystems or the essential environmental media air, water, soil and climate. The same applies to economic and social concerns. Here, too, we need science to identify relationships – between education and prosperity, poverty and population growth, ecological crises, political wars and flight, etc. In addition, science is needed to generate knowledge for action: how can sustainable development be achieved? What technologies can contribute, which economic, political and legal framework conditions must be changed, etc.? Science also plays a key role in the development of environmentally sound technologies and processes. And almost any technological development is nowadays based on science or at least uses scientific knowledge.

At this point, it is worth noting that science alone is not enough to stimulate sustainable development, since scientific knowledge and technologies can both support and hinder sustainable development. What is still needed is orientation knowledge: What are the goals of sustainable development, what should a future sustainable world look like? The generation of orientation knowledge goes beyond classical science, is above all a matter of philosophy and ethics (or possibly other value systems far away from science). However, achieving sustainable development without science is unimaginable. Science is therefore a necessary but not sufficient condition for sustainable development.

Taking truth as a basis of sustainable development, it should also be noted that the pursuit of sustainable development is primarily a modern, secular undertaking, and thus does not originate from a religious conviction, a faith (in the sense of one of the faith systems of world religions), but first from an enlightened and areligious understanding of the world. Furthermore, sustainable development is also a rational and therefore justified concept: one sees poverty and misery in the world, environmental pollution and destruction, resource scarcity and, ultimately, humanity's continued existence threatened, and justifies the alternative model of sustainable development on this ground. Here, again, it should be noted that a modern, rational vision is probably necessary but not sufficient for sustainable development.

Finally, it should be mentioned that sustainable development also needs truth in an ordinary, everyday understanding, and this in a double sense: on the one hand, "to tell the truth", that is, not to lie or deny, and prior to this, to first "acknowledge the truth", not to suppress it. While years or decades ago our environmentally and self-destructive lifestyle and economy could largely be suppressed and not acknowledged, the truth of a global unsustainable development is now so obvious, so ubiquitously visible to us that it is hardly possible to further suppress it. It has now seeped into scientific, political and social convictions too broadly and too deeply. The only thing the reactionary forces can do is simple: to deny. And, unfortunately, the populists in the current post-factual and neo-national wave sometimes find open ears.

Sustainability is undeniably a matter of truth. But not only. For sustainable development to take place, it must not only be true, in other words scientifically recognised, rationally grounded and socially acknowledged, but ultimately also lived. But this takes more than pure knowledge. It takes a motor, a motive, for sustainable development to come true, and to bring this truth to life. It takes: love. A sustainable world, a culture of sustainability needs more, above all – like every other cultural practice or daily life – it needs love and will, after all, not be available without fear.

(Un-)sustainability as a matter of fear

Before love we have to address fear. If there was a social driving force for sustainable development during the last 40 years, it might have been fear, or probably concern. The studies of the Club of Rome, from *Limits to Growth* (Meadows *et al.* 1972) to "Beyond the limits" (1992) and analyses far beyond which suggest "from a rational risk-based perspective, that we have squandered the past decades, and that preparing for a collapsing global system could be even more important than trying to avoid collapse" (Turner, Rickards 2014: 16), taught us the meaning of fear: as it is, it cannot go on for long and for good. We as the human race are rushing headlong into our own disaster. A lot of scary news followed, about climate change, rising sea levels, nuclear and other man-made disasters, etc. and joined the ranks of the uneasiness of the modern world. Hans Jonas developed his "Ethics for the Technological Age" (Jonas 1984) around the concept of concern (German "Sorge") – and teaches us the meaning of fear with his written words.

Fear is appropriate and helpful when it comes to avoiding dangerous or even life-threatening situations. Fear supports self-preservation. Given the diagnosis that we are living unsustainably far beyond our limits and the prognoses of multiple catastrophic consequences of our global excesses, the fear of a (near) dark future is absolutely appropriate. Fear is a strong motive, a strong driver, to stay alive.

Despite the appropriateness of today's fear of the catastrophes of a non-sustainable development, fear is a bad advisor when it comes to shaping and establishing something in the long term, to formulate or even more to realise a vision of a just and sustainable world. Fear helps us to leave the established path, hit the bushes, but not to be positive and constructive in finding new ways and solutions that are permanently sustainable. Fear might help us to leave the non-sustainable paths, but is not appropriate as a foundation for a future lived and living culture of sustainability.

Unfortunately one often gets the impression (from politicians, philosophers or even scientists) that sustainability is a matter of fear and a sustainable future can only occur under a repressive 'regime of fear', e.g. an eco-dictatorship.

So, we have to be careful to distinguish between the fear of the consequences of an ongoing non-sustainable development and a future culture of sustainability. The latter may not be entirely free from fear but removes the cause of our contemporary fear of a self-inflicted destruction of humanity indeed.

Fear is working very well as a (personal) situational short-term activating driver. But enduring fear ends up in anxiety, which is a disorder. And anxiety leads to violence or is paralysing, demoralising and leads to deadlock. All this is not useful and rather counterproductive for a sustainable development. So, we have to take care not to institutionalise fear in our societal, political and cultural corpus. This would be, or is already, pathological.

"Sorge" in German (English: "concern") – a central term in Jonas sustainability ethics (Jonas 1984) – does not only include "fear", but also "fostering" and "care".[3] And the political efforts at the national and international level make this concern concrete, for example in the Millennium Development Goals of the UN (2000) and again in the Sustainable Development Goals (established in 2015). The care and will to help the poorer people, societies, and nations, to foster their prosperity (but less their well-being) become apparent here.[4]

Sustainability as a matter of love

Sustainability is a matter of truth. Non-sustainability and the change towards sustainability is also a matter of fear. Both aspects are important, but there are enough of both of them in the sustainability discourse. To realise sustainable development, to bring sustainability to life, a third aspect is required, a motor, a goal and motive that lies beyond fear and truth. It requires love. In my opinion, neither the turn to sustainable development, a future sustainable life, nor a culture of sustainability are possible nor desirable without love.

But love in which sense? "Love" is a very widespread and common term, which has completely different meanings depending on the various contexts – both in everyday language and specialist disciplines. There is a difference if a theologian, a sociologist, a sexual therapist or an artist speaks of love. I would like to address the subject of sustainable development at first from a rather everyday-language understanding of "love".

To begin with, "love" in general shall express a deep affection for, affinity and appreciation of a counterpart here. According to a more narrow and widespread understanding, love is a strong feeling of affection, combined with dear and deep bonds and relation with a person, group, or thing that exceeds the mere purpose or benefit of such a relation. Love is usually characterised by an amiable active attention and dedication for the other. Love is inextricably linked with a feeling of relatedness or the actual connectedness. Those who live their love accordingly are connected with this counterpart. In the context of this chapter, the central element of love is a deep relation and connectedness to someone or something.

Towards which counterpart the love is directed, a human being, a neighbour, a creature, a group, a thing, or something supreme or transcendental, does not matter at first. In terms of sustainable development, we will especially address the love for people, creatures, something supreme and the world as a whole. Love happens in the trustful devotion to the world from an attitude, experience and awareness of deep connectedness.

In addition, love is not only considered as an emotion here, as a purely mental and inner individual experience, but as a principle to guide actions, as a basic attitude towards the world and finally as a mode of human being. Love is (expressed) in actions and behaviour, does not remain a concept without consequences or only a feeling, but is realised in the act, becomes real in actions. So, love should also be understood as a mode of action and behaviour, as a general *modus operandi* of dealing with the world.[5]

But why is love necessary for sustainable development, a future of lived and lively culture of sustainability?

1   Love is, first of all, basically needed in the form of affection for and *appreciation* of a counterpart. A lived sustainable development – and not only one of concept – is hard to imagine or practice without addressing the people, creatures and things around us with love, without the appreciation of and affection for our fellow human beings, without neighbourly or brotherly love (which includes the love for oneself). Just like sustainable development seems in general impossible, or at least pointless, without the appreciation of and caring affection for our children, grandchildren and great-grandchildren. In the same way a lived ecological sustainability would seem absurd, or at least monstrous, without the appreciation of other living creatures, of natural things, of ecosystems, of nature as a whole, a creation or something transcendental. Of course love can take very different forms here, from the concrete appreciation of individual natural things like animals or trees to a lived "deep ecology" (Naess 1973) and abstract forms of appreciation of a transcendental nature. *Which* forms of love are necessary, adequate and fruitful for a sustainable development may be argued, but hardly about the fact *that* it is required.

2   Love is based on *deep bonds* and *actual connectedness*. Even appreciation is based on bonds, precedes them. Connectedness is the starting point and necessary precondition for (real) appreciation. Without a (affectionate, open, top quality) relation to people or things one cannot perceive them as such and thus not appreciate them. Without such connectedness one remains unaffected, impassive and things seem worthless.

   Ecological sustainability might be rationally justifiable, but at least its realisation is likely to fail if there is not a certain degree of relatedness of the human beings to their ecological fellow creatures. Sustainable development aims at a global and intergenerational justice, a sound ecosphere, and, finally, at a human race, a community of all humans embedded into a living "eco nature" (Parodi 2008: 139–144). This can hardly be achieved if the human beings do not feel related and connected to their fellow humans and fellow creatures, do not realise and acknowledge their similarities and differences – and do not recognise that they are basic parts of a larger context.[6]

Especially this involvement in larger contexts – as a specific form of connectedness – plays an important role in sustainable development. The concept of sustainable development puts the human being explicitly into larger contexts and entireties, e.g. into an ecosystem which is superior to or underlies the human existence. Moreover, sustainable development explicitly puts the individual as a link into a chain of generations, into a stream of human ancestors and descendants. Those who do not experience, take in, or feel this relation (re)constructed in the theory of sustainability first-hand, those who do not experience themselves as connected to the ecosystem (or nature), as a human being among other human beings, as life in the midst of life that wants to live (Albert Schweitzer), sheltered in the chain of ancestors and descendants of the human race, have little reason and motivation to dedicate themselves to sustainable development. Worldwide solidarity, intergenerational justice and environmental protection are basically a matter of this connectedness.

3   Love covers and encompasses the *human being in its entirety*. It goes way beyond thinking. It bridges the gap between the theory of sustainability as theoretical conception and the world (with appreciation and bonds), without being only based on thinking and reasoning. Love addresses human beings as a whole, captures them in their "Leiblichkeit"[7] and carries them into the unknown sustainable future.

In the end, a certain appreciation of and connectedness to the world are actually necessary preconditions for its (deeper) understanding. If we reject the world, we cannot enter into a dialogue with it, thus it remains silent and does not reveal itself. So an open sympathetic inner attitude towards the outer (and inner) world and an actual connectedness are also the basis for our intellectual edifices and theories. In the end, the kind and extent of our connectedness to the world determines the degree, type and appropriateness of our findings and understanding of the world. This means that our current valid truths are products of our respective (kind of) connectedness to the world. Love – or the absence of love – eventually forms our truths.

If love captures the human being as a whole in its cognitive, mental, emotional, and physical dimension, the related appreciation and relations go way beyond what is thought and discussed in ethics (e.g. in the context of "value judgements") – maybe not regarding its contents, but the manner in which these contents are justified and how they address the dimensions of human being. Love goes beyond the rationale, captures the whole human being. On this basis a "leibliche Vernunft", a subjective body rationality can evolve, a rationality built on life and experience. What ethics think, love can live.

Here I would like to make a small digression. What is especially important about love regarding sustainable development is the *modus operandi*, love as act and form of existence, as a basic attitude towards the world. This implies that the counterpart, the specific 'object' of love, is less important in the first instance. If it is not about an all-embracing love, sustainable development calls for an extension of the horizon of love, to appreciate more things, be more and more actively connected. The target horizon would be a lived global anthropocentrism ("all humans will become brothers and sisters") through to the point of an eco-centric holism, where all living creatures and systems are precious. Attitudes and actions which attach value and love only to a certain group (family, nation, race) and deny it to others at the same time disrespect, disregard or exploit them, are not welcome in the discourse and pursuit of sustainable development.

4   Love as the *motor and vector of change*: fear enables us to escape, to leave the paths which lead into disaster, to flee from the danger of the looming catastrophes of an unsustainable development. But this fear is not suited to provide orientation, e.g. in which direction we should realign us and our lives. The truth, however, can contribute considerably to this orientation, even more so the more seriously we take it. Nevertheless, experience shows that truth is a weak momentum to set out and change our life. This is not only true for individual ways of life but also for societies as a whole.[8] But love provides us with orientation and sufficient motivation. It drags us into a direction, towards a goal, and, together with the truth, at best into a sustainable future. And love as a basic attitude also makes us stronger, enables us to withstand the adversities, setbacks and uncertainties of change which would inevitably be associated with the transformation of a sustainable development.

Conclusion I: sustainable development is a matter of truth and love – (until now) not as a concept but in its realisation. Recognising that love is part of a sustainability transition means to broaden our understanding of it and acting towards a sustainable future. It means also that the human being as human being and being (of) humanity has to be taken much more into account in our search for sustainable development. The endeavours of sustainable development are above all scientifically based (relying on the idea of "truth") but in this they overemphasise the scientific, mental, rational and technological access to the world – and remain blind for a lot of human dimensions and humanity. Within the concept of *personal sustainability* such human aspects of the journey to sustainability could be discussed, elaborated and even exercised.

Furthermore, the common concepts of sustainable development are still too much bound to the dominant worldview of modern times and thereby emphasise the separation of human beings (from the world) – that's the common way (scientific) truths are generated nowadays – and not their connectedness – the way love takes place.

Part II: I, You, It – a typology of human relationships to the world

Next, I want to step back and take a look at the attitudes and relations of human being to the world throughout the history of humankind. Which attitudes and positions towards the world has he taken? What kind of relations has she lived, is she still living? I want to retrace this human-world-relation exemplarily on the basis of the human-nature-relation and understanding.[9] Doing so, I'm not looking for the respective concepts of nature but for the relations the human being had and has to the world (surrounding him). In the context of this chapter, the different kinds of relation are interesting. And, not explicitly but implicitly, the issues discussed in the first part are shining through every now and then.

I want to base my reflections upon a typology of human-nature-relations Ernst Oldemeyer (1983) worked out. It had been developed in the course of the reappraisal of the anthropological development of the human-nature relationship and the respective evolution of human consciousness.[10] Within this typology, the basic human attitudes towards nature are classified into four different types of relation, according to the linguistic framework of personal pronouns "I", "You", "He/She/It" and "We". Oldemeyer points out that it is no coincidence that the fundamental forms of the human relation to nature "succeed one another in a certain order" (*ibid.*: 17).[11] It is important that these types do not supersede each other by wiping out and replacing the old one with a new, but rather in a "process of overlapping, overlaying and reshaping" (*ibid.*).

So, even if the predominant type changes over time and characterises the common attitude towards and the handling of the world, all of the former types are still present, existing and are alive in a way. You find traces or layers of them today in personal attitudes or different cultures, worldviews – and different understandings and undertakings of sustainable development.

Having a closer look at this typology and the different human-world-relations below enables a deeper understanding of the endeavour of sustainable development and puts it in a framework of human history and evolution.

I-I relationship – magical-mythical relation to 'nature' (type 1)

In prehistoric times in terms of cultural history, every distinction made at the beginning of the human reference to nature is preceded by unity. I-(human) is at one with I-(nature). For lack of distance, there is yet no concept or understanding of nature, no science or philosophy. Human being at first *is* 'nature'. There is no distinction at the beginning of human history. By and by, human beings experienced themselves as self and different from other natural beings. But still life is full of overwhelming direct experiences, the world is full of "alluring and threatening" (*ibid.*: 21) forces. The human being acts "as a participant in the whole of nature" without any reflective awareness of this and occurrences of nature are seen as proof for and expression of the participating creatures. They are perceived not only in an anthropomorphic, but also in a phytomorphic and zoomorphic way. Later the behaviour of humans towards other entities of nature (humans as well as deities) is borne out of the participants' ethos of mutuality.

I-You relationship – holistic nature (type 2)

The establishment of the second type goes hand in hand with the emergence of the first philosophies of advanced civilisations, which freed themselves from the view and relation of the myth. This is also the time when the pre-Socratics started to philosophise about the characteristics of nature. The human being perceives itself as different from nature. Although it sees itself as a separate being, it is significantly nevertheless in a very close relationship with it. This relationship can be egalitarian-fraternal, but also strictly hierarchical. The hierarchy can thereby run both ways: the human being considers a natural-divine being as 'super-you', but it can also treat an animal, a plant or another surrogate 'subhuman' as 'sub-you'. Nature (physis), here still used as a totalising concept, denotes the structure of the universe as a whole and is "not yet narrowed down to a partial concept of a specific realm of being" (ibid.: 23). The questioning focus of early philosophy is on the existence and becoming of things. With reference to the becoming and decay of creatures, nature as a whole is often considered biomorphically and organismically as a creature of its own. Physis is what unites the opposites (life/death, beginning/end, male/female) in harmony (Heraclitus), it is what 'wafts' through the cosmos and puts it in its circular motion (Philolaus).[12]

On the transition to a type 3 relationship, nature – as a whole – is no longer considered anthropomorphic. "It is neither a first person to identify with, nor a second person to communicate with" (ibid.). It is slowly becoming a third person. The former participant ethos changes into the "cosmos ethos" which does not set any specific norms in dealing with things of nature any more, but sees the only virtue in recognising cosmic rationality and blending in: "Wisdom is [. . .] acting in accordance with nature by listening to it" (Heraklit 2007, fr. 112 and 106, own translation). "The cosmos is alright if all the beings, also human beings, follow its intrinsic law" (Oldemeyer 1983: 24).[13]

I-It relationship – nature as object and counter-world (type 3)

The human being is now perceived as outside to the natural union of beings. It is no longer a participant, but discovers nature as something exterior, something it is facing. Nature is reduced to an object of one-way observation, treatment, use, etc. The human is thought of "in the position of a principle opposed to nature. So in the end, this subject is constituted as an extra-natural instance and is thus removed from the 'nature union' of beings with regard to its crucial aspect, i.e. as a subject" (Oldemeyer 1983: 25). Human relationship to the object "nature" can turn out very differently, ranging from exploitation and elimination to shelter and care.

Nature is no longer referring to the cosmos as a whole, but represents only one region of being. In the completed dissociation from nature, the human being experiences what will later be criticised or complained about as "alienation". The degree of alienation and its assessment differ here, depending on whether the human being sees itself confronted with an it-nature as a construct of (divine) works, as mechanical process, as random product or even as self-organisation.

Regarding the normative-practical attitude of the human being towards nature in Greek philosophy, the so far valid cosmos ethos becomes obsolete with the disappearance of the numinous from the it-nature. A significant difference to the second (and first) type is expressed in the ethical neutrality of the reference to nature. In Aristotle's view, physis creates plants for the sake of animals, animals for the sake of human beings "which implies that the higher-ranking being is entitled to use the low-ranking one, a right that is not balanced by an explicit commitment in the opposite direction" (*ibid*.: 28).

The platonic and Jewish-Christian concept of a Creator God and nature as object that is produced (natura naturata) for example does not represent a mere I-It relationship but rather an "I-(super-him)-It relationship" mediated by a third, divine person. However, since the Creator God itself is perceived in a distance to his work, nature is stripped off its own dynamics and divinity and thus devaluated. According to the Old Testament's view, the human being itself is (like nature) also the work of the Creator God, but has an outstanding position as being created "in the image of God", as the "reflected glory of the super-nature in nature" (*ibid*.). Normatively, two divine mandates have to be considered together, i.e. *the mandate to rule* to "fill the earth and subdue it, and have dominion" (Gen 1,28) and the *mandate to work and keep*: God put man "in the Garden of Eden to work it and keep it" (Gen 2,15). With the repulse of God in the wake of modernity's enlightenment, the mediated I-It relationship becomes a completely unmediated one: the human being fills God's gap and the normative boundaries of nature conservation are subject to the arbitrariness of human's shaping of nature.

Leucippus's and Democritus's ideas paved the way for a third subtype of a mechanistic-materialistic I-It relationship which can still be found in today's atomistic, mechanical and materialistic ideas in science and everyday life. Here an obvious order is inherent in nature that follows firm principles. Nature, in the beginning above all a subject of thinking, of opinions, more and more becomes the object of processing and use. Descartes separates the thinking substance from the material nature, the subjective mind becomes the counter-term of nature. Without divine impulses for creation, ideal patterns and teleological work, the path becomes clear for the total availability of nature. This is expressed in Galilei's maxim of (natural) sciences: "Measure what is measurable, and make measurable what is not so" (Galilei, cited by Oldemeyer 1983: 32) as well as in the imperative of the dominance over nature by Descartes and Bacon. In this third subtype, nature is countable, measurable, calculable and predictable.

Based on Descartes' emphasis on the concept of the self-aware human, a fourth subtype of a transcendental-idealistic notion of nature was developed where nature is reduced to a product, to a manifesting correlate of a subjective human mind and consciousness. Nature as a phenomenon becomes both materially and formally dependent from the independent activity of human self-awareness. Laws of nature are not given, but are, in the end, created by the subject (based on its experience). "The understanding creates its laws (a priori) not from nature, but prescribes them to nature" (Kant 2001, § 36, A 113, own translation). The question concerning nature as a thing in itself – if this is still asked at all – has to remain unanswered since this thing is in principle beyond the realm of the human cognitive faculty. Here, within the cognitive, the subjectivistic turnaround becomes clearly recognisable: Nature remains *natura naturata*, but is as a phenomenon no longer seen as the product of a Creator God but as a *product of human consciousness*.

In light of the consequences of a possessing relationship to nature and a culture in crisis, the fifth subtype – an aesthetic-sentimental relationship to nature – emerged where the value of nature and culture are reversed. Culture with all its accomplishments appears as barbarian 'un-nature', as perverseness of an originally free and happy natural state: "God makes all things good; man meddles with them and they become evil" (Rousseau 1998: 107). Nature is what we once were and what we should become again. The barbarian phase of culture is often seen as an intermezzo of alienation that has to be overcome. This includes a sentimental backward look at an original, lost state that has to be regained (*"back* to nature"). Even though this view of nature prepares the fourth type of an I-We relation, it does not overcome the type of an I-It relation at first. After all, the human being is clearly outside this in its sentimental-romantic view towards nature. Nature should be pursued, not overcome; however, in its separation from the human being, nature remains a *sub-region* of the world that is initially not accessible to the human being. In today's *nature conservation*, this excluding view is passed on and not only expressed in an attitude of mind but also geographically precisely manifested in the landscape: as fenced-in preserves for nature ("nature *reserve*") from which the human being and its actions are excluded.

I-We relationship – 'nature' as an overall system (type 4)

Since the beginning of the nineteenth century, a fourth type of relationship to nature emerges, which turns out to be structurally different from the aforementioned types. In worldviews and scientific theories like Goethe's approach to nature, Schelling's philosophy of nature, the theory of evolution, the dialectical materialism, or relativistic and quantum-theoretical physics, tendencies "to get beyond a differentiation in opposite terms, a mechanistic objectivism, and a transcendental not-me attitude of nature" (Oldemeyer 1983: 35f) can be perceived to overcome an I-It attitude of the human being towards nature. Ecology and systems theory contribute to the "overcoming of the opposite term and to constituting a holistic understanding of nature" (*ibid.*: 36). A categorical shift towards the plural takes place in the understanding of the human-nature relation. Nature is no longer something identical-indistinguishable, also not an (communicative) opponent, or a remote third party (as God or object), but the encompassing, impersonal whole.

The human being sees itself as *observer and participant* in an all-embracing whole. The human being knows that its becoming and actions are embedded in this whole; it also knows that, as an element *within* this 'nature', it will never be able to capture 'nature' as a whole, but only ever catch sight of 'nature' from its respective position *perspectively*, for example as an open system of systems, as a network of hierarchic systems. The normative consequence in such a relation to nature would be that natural system contexts have to be considered in their own self and viewpoints of ethics of nature and humans have to be balanced. Those things that were, according to the age-old form of reference to nature, "carried out inconsiderately and uncritically in projection and retrojection, would be, in line with this new type of understanding, practiced critically and in full awareness" (*ibid*.: 37). In such an understanding, the conceptual definition of 'nature' does no longer need the opposite concepts of human, culture, mind, or technology. "Nature" as a counter concept dissolves.

In this manner, the dissolution of these opposed concepts of nature and culture cannot only be observed from a science-oriented perspective in the form of ecology or ecosystems, but also at the opposite side in contemporary cultural theory and science. Regarding nature and culture, Hansen says: "Where we can recognize a *dialectic co-operation* today [. . .], older theories assumed a super- or subordination" (Hansen 2000: 267, own translation). The third type of nature, the basis of older cultural theories, is being overcome. "The relation between nature and culture is just *not either-or*, but an *as-well-as*; it is not an addition, but an interaction" (*ibid*.: 29, own translation).

Sustainable development in the context of the human-world-relations

As extension of the 'ecological turn', the emerging and establishment of the ecology movement since the 1970s, the striving for sustainability for me is clearly part of a motion, a shift from an I-It relation to an I-We relation of human being to the world. It is not completed yet, but still ongoing.

In the context of sustainable development the human being sees itself as participant in a global ecosystem and an all-embracing "web of life". Life, an all-embracing oneness or at least planet earth is seen as the (impersonal) bigger whole in which human existence is integrated.[14] The world (of sustainability) is seen and sometimes experienced as a We-world. The human being experiences this world as an observer and participant from an inside perspective. In the concepts and worldview of sustainability "ecology" and "ecosystem" supersede the term and idea "nature". 'Nature' is no more a counter concept of human and culture.

What is crucial for me for the further debates and actions for sustainable development is that the later relation types don't obliterate but *include* all previous types in a process of addition, integration and overlaying.[15] For a vivid I-We relation and a future culture of sustainability we need to have subsumed the I-I, I-You and I-It relations – the identity, the close relatedness with and the distinction from and reflection on the world. So, all of the previous types play their role in an upcoming culture of sustainability.

In debates about sustainable development none of these types can be wiped away completely, arguing that it is overcome today. As paradigms and *dominant relations* they are overcome – even the I-It relation. But as included, subsumed and integrated aspects of an I-We relation they are still vital and vivid. The overlaid coexistence of these relation types is important for being whole as a human being and for a holistic and integral relation to the world around (and in) us. Quite on the contrary, in my opinion negating and suppressing one of the aspects will lead to some sort of dysfunctional relation to the world. That happened, e.g. by the exploitation of the planet and fellow humans, in the course of the paradigm of an I-It relation while denying an I-You (and I-I) relation during the last two centuries.

Bringing sustainable development to life would mean bringing an I-We relation collectively to life and vice versa. A culture of sustainability would mean a lived and collectively shared I-We relationship. This would mean a new era, actually a new step in the history of mankind related to a new form of human being, relatedness and consciousness. Conversely, trying to realise sustainable development within a (still dominant) I-It relation must fail.

This step to a culturally embedded and collectively lived I-We relation to the world, the transformation from our global culture of non-sustainability to global cultures of sustainability, would probably be as revolutionary as the industrial revolution or perhaps the neolithic turn from hunter-gatherers to agriculture – and similarly unpredictable. The transformation to sustainability means a big adventure. Nobody can know where this journey is leading us. The only thing we can and have to do is head for sustainability, trust in mankind, follow the truth with love, live in truthfulness and let things go.

Conclusion – sustainability as a matter of truth and love in the horizon of an I-We relation

Sustainable development is a matter of truth and love (Part I). As a way of transition sustainable development goes with an I-We relation that is increasingly coming to life (Part II). Both thematic fields discussed before are important for bringing sustainability to life.

But one question is still open: what have truth and love got to do with the typology and evolution of human relations to the world? A lot. First of all you can locate "truth" and "love" roughly within the typology. Love is first of all a matter of an I-You relation. Love grows or happens in the connectedness to a close (and similar) counterpart, respectively in the willingness to connect. Whereas the home base of truth is clearly the I-It relationship.[16] All endeavours based on or closely linked to truth like science, rationality, the paradigm of the modern age, and nowadays the knowledge-society are expressions of an I-It relation of humans to their surrounding world.

So, as argued above, love comes first. Love is probably older than truth in human history. And like the I-It relation is based on an I-You (and I-I) relation, truth in a way builds on love, as pointed out in Part I. It is crucial that just like the relation types do not supersede each other by replacing the old one with a new, truth can never replace love. Even if our modern times, in which the 'truth-complex' is super elevated, science is the one (and only) authority of world interpretation, rationality the only sanity, the brain the most important part of the human body, etc., suggests so. Humanity and a human life are never possible without the foundation of love (and identity as expression of an I-I relation).

Becoming sustainable, taking the step from an I-It-dominated world to an I-We means not following truth and skipping love – or vice versa: skipping truth, following love (only). That is a crucial point, because there are trends and views that are striving for a sustainable future only by love and heart, denying truth and science as valuable and sensual agents for sustainable development. That is dangerous and reactionary. There will be no sustainable development without truth. We have reached the level of an I-It relation, the respective consciousness, we are on the edge and way to a culturally implemented I-We relation, and we should not turn back, glorifying and heading for the golden ages and return to any kind of pre-modern state of being.[17] Considering the inhumanity and barbarity of an excessive I-It relation that took place during the last 200 years – e.g. in the destruction of our environment, social alienation or the massive technological killing in two world wars – the wish to reinstall former times and respective human-world relations (I-I and I-You) is understandable, but such an escape to the past is neither realistic nor desirable to come really true. Further, in the context of the evolution of human consciousness that would mean to give up a part of our human abilities and of our humanity.

As dangerous as this possible romantic roll-back or even more dangerous would be a deadlock, caused by the insistence on and persistence of a still-dominating I-It relation that is deeply inscribed in our political, economic and technical systems. There are strong and culturally dominant forces keeping the I-It paradigm alive that impede sustainability transformation or try to cut the idea of sustainable development down to an I-It relationship and reduce sustainability only to a matter of resources and purpose. Cutting sustainable development to a question of resources remains in the old paradigm of an I-It relation, looking at earth only as a place and resource made and available for us as humans.

By the dawning of a culture of sustainability, by the transformation to a collectively lived I-We relation, love and truth both are in a process of overlaying and reshaping. Both are embedded in a broader context, a deeper understanding of the world and a new form of being connected to the world, respectively in the sense of an I-We relation even being (part of) the world. With a sustainable development based on an I-We relation the horizon of both, truth and love, widens. In fact, the global "We" is the horizon of sustainable development. And even the depth of truth and love increases. Living in a We-world as 'interbeings' changes our way of understanding and living truth and love. A culture of sustainability means a new quality of life and being human.

At long last, this brings us back to the topic of the book: personal sustainability. Everything I wrote about truth, fear, love and the different human relations to the world can be seen and understood in the light of sustainability as a collective undertaking – but even as personal issues. For me the transformation to sustainability is a question of culture and requires a deep cultural change. "Culture" means the interplay and interrelation between the collective and the individual (Hansen 2011). So, for a cultural change or transformation both are needed: the collective *and* the individual side.

If you look at the topics discussed above, you can address them to our society, our modern culture, to our economic system and to our politicians – but you can ask yourself also: what do truth and love mean for me? What is inside, what beyond my horizon of love or truth? Am I aware of or do I already live an I-We relation? What quality do my I-It relations to the world have? Am I connected? Can I meet my 'environment' in an I-You manner? Do I see myself embedded in a web of life or a transcendent oneness? Do I only see or even live that? Am I personally part of the change to sustainability, transforming myself (a bit) or still stuck? Dealing with sustainability is about collective and institutionalised truths but also about very personal ones. Sustainability is even a matter of personal truthfulness.

And ultimately, love and especially connectedness are always personal. They take place via perception, the senses and the body (respectively the subjective body – German "Leib"). Human connectedness to the world can finally only be made by individuals. The perception of and even the dealing with the world are ultimately such of human individuals. That still remains a fact even if our contact to the world nowadays is technically mediated and modified to a high degree, and thereby standardised and brought in line collectively. But even in our modern mass society the access to, the dealing with and the way of connectedness with the world is a matter of each person, of us at the end of the day.

Notes

1 In this chapter I use the terms "sustainable development" and "sustainability" almost synonymously. There's no political or conceptual difference addressed behind, however, "sustainability" points more at a status, whereby "sustainable *development*" emphasises a development or being in process of change.

2 Conversely, there is reason to believe that certain advanced cultures and civilisations perished because the knowledge of the limits to their growth and the consequences of their actions remained hidden to them.

3 The concept of "care" includes both fear and love.

4 However, what makes wealthy countries provide development assistance? What is the UN's motivation to pursue sustainable development goals? Of course it is concern. But how much of this is unselfish attention and how much is political strategy, the will to maintain the existing global balance of powers, fear of social unrest? Even the efforts of wealthy nations regarding the sustainable development of less-developed countries might not be driven by real altruism and care, but rather by their concern about their own interests, increasing global tensions, terror and war, which also affect the prosperous world, through refugee movements which resemble a mass migration. And maybe the Western world and its colonialism are also to blame for significantly contributing to the world's injustice over decades and centuries.

5 Here, in the context of sustainable development the focus on "love" is not on desiring "Eros" as a specific manifestation or (physical) dimension of love. The polar erotic attraction, e.g. as sexuality surely is a vital and powerful (biological) motor in and for life. But Eros in many ways is just as well volatile and shortsighted. So, in this context and chapter first and foremost the smoother, broader and more 'cultivated' forms of love "philia" – love towards friends – and "agape" – love from and towards something transcendent – are addressed.

6 The humanistic Ode to Joy by Friedrich Schiller ("An die Freude" published in 1808), much later chosen as the European Anthem, enunciates this bond of all people very directly, since "all people become brothers".

7 To translate this German term into English is difficult, the most adequate expression would be "corporeality", the German term is derived from the German term "Leib" which can be translated as "subjective body".

8 For example, we know for decades that we consume and exploit the global biosphere much more than it is possible in the long run. But we still keep on going, the Earth Overshoot Day (2017) is still moving closer.

9 Most of the time in human history the relation to "nature" was the most important (or only) relation the human being had.
10 Oldemeyer developed the categories of his typology following Martin Buber (in particular Buber 1973). In its content he refers to a lot of philosophic and anthropological studies e.g. A. Gehlen, W. Dilthey, J. Gebser, M. Eliade, K. Jaspers and E. Topitsch.
11 This and all following quotations of Oldemeyer are own translations.
12 This understanding of nature (physis) as polar and complementary whole can be found throughout all holistic concepts of nature of the occident (from Bruno, Spinoza, Leibniz, Herder, Goethe, etc.), or nowadays in ecological movements, alternative scientific approaches (to self-reinforcing tendencies and self-organising principles of nature) or in philosophies of the Far East.
13 "This attitude had led to an ethos of minimal intrusion, which is more pronounced and distributed within the cultural area of the Chinese Taoism than in the Western World" (Oldemeyer 1983: 24).
14 The first reports and photos taken during the upcoming space travel from outer space showing the earth as a whole in the 1960s had a deep impact on the sustainable development movement and are still often used as symbol thereof.
15 Similar to the evolution of the cerebral cortex the brain stem was not extinguished but 'overlayed' and the function of the whole brain was reshaped – but the brain stem is still active and vital.
16 "Truth" here understood in the meaning(s) mentioned above in the first part. There is even "truth" in an I-You relation, but that "truth" differs, is much more personal, intensely and 'subjective'. If we speak nowadays about "truth" we use it normally in an ('objective') I-It manner.
17 This may happen anyway by disaster if we are not able to manage the sustainability transition by design.

References

Buber, M. (1973): *Das dialogische Prinzip*. Gütersloh: Gütersloher Verlagshaus.
Earth Overshoot Day (2017): Homepage. www.overshootday.org, accessed 18 August 2017).
German Advisory Council on Global Change [WBGU] (2011): *World in Transition. A Social Contract for Sustainability*. Berlin: WBGU.
Hansen, K. P. (2000): *Kultur und Kulturwissenschaft: eine Einführung*. Tübingen: UTB.
Heraklit (2007): *Fragmente*. B. Snell (ed.). Düsseldorf: Artemis & Winkler.
Jonas, H. (1984): *The Imperative of Responsibility: In Search of an Ethics for the Technological Age*. Chicago, IL: University of Chicago Press.
Kant, I. (2001): *Prolegomena zu einer jeden künftigen Metaphysik, die als Wissenschaft wird auftreten können*. Pollok, K. (ed.). Hamburg: Meiner.
Kopfmüller, J., Brandl, V., Jörissen, J., Paetau, M., Banse, G., Coenen, R. & Grunwald, A. (2001): *Nachhaltige Entwicklung integrativ betrachtet. Konstitutive Elemente, Regeln, Indikatoren*. Berlin: sigma.
Meadows, D. H., Meadows, D. L., Randers, J. & Behrens III, W. W. (1972): *The Limits to Growth*. New York: Universe Books.
Næss, Arne (1973): The Shallow and the Deep. Long-Range Ecology Movement. *Inquiry*, 16, 1–4, pp. 95–100.
Oldemeyer, E. (1983): Entwurf einer Typologie des menschlichen Verhältnisses zur Natur. In: Großklaus, G. & Oldemeyer, E. (eds) *Natur als Gegenwelt. Beiträge zur Kulturgeschichte der Natur*. Karlsruhe: von Loeper. pp. 15–42.
Parodi, O. (2008): *Technik am Fluss*. München: Oekom.

Rousseau, J.-J. (1998): *Emile oder Über die Erziehung.* Rang, M. (ed.). Stuttgart: UTB.

Schultz, J., Brand, F., Kopfmüller, J. & Ott, K. (2008): Building a 'Theory of Sustainable Development': Two Salient Conceptions within the German Discourse. *International Journal of Environment and Sustainable Development,* 7, 4, pp. 465–482.

Turner, G. & Rickards, L. (eds) (2014): *Is Global Collapse Imminent? An Updated Comparison of The Limits to Growth with Historical Data.* MSSI Research Papers. Melbourne, Australia.

United Nations [UN] (2017): *Sustainable Development Goals.* www.un.org/sustainable development (18.08.2017).

World Commission on Environment and Development [WCED] (1987): *Our Common Future.* Oxford, UK: Oxford University Press.

6 Sustainability in crisis

A perspective of subjective body as a 'healing' force

Sabin Wendhack

Introduction

While sustainability is an idea that is very present in Western culture and life, the transition towards sustainability and to a sustainable way of life has turned out to be rather problematic – if not disastrous. The problem doesn't seem to be that situations that are destructive in an ecological or social way and human behaviour promoting them are not recognised, on the contrary: in Germany for example, at least since the 1970s, many of the problems are widely known, nowadays the radio stations and television channels repeat them in their news many times a day and the newspapers are full of according information. Talking about missing sustainability has become a habit in society and the knowledge about it is to some extent common knowledge. Nevertheless, the adequate reaction of people and societies to this knowledge seems to be somehow missing, at least in many cases the reaction doesn't seem appropriate: even if there is a lot of initiative towards a more sustainable way of living together, this still resembles more a drop in the ocean than a mainstream way of living. Action and behaviour promoting the disastrous conditions are still predominant.[1] So even if the knowledge is more or less available, it is not followed by adequate consequences and somehow seems detached from a sensible reaction to it.

Having in mind the enlightened human being meant to be thinking and acting in a reasonable and autonomous way, this is not easy to understand. The reasons provided whenever a conversation gets to this point, such as "humans don't change" or "that's how humans are", are rather simple, but at a closer look these explanations don't really explain anything. They tend to tag this detachedness as 'normal', that way eliminating the discrepancy and consolidating the prevalent attitude and the status quo. What's happening here and what could be a reason for the reluctance of human beings and societies to realise change that is urgently needed?

Sustainability in crisis

The social and ecological situation in the world can be perceived as a state of crisis. Familiar patterns of conduct have reached their limits, there are ideas about the causes of the situation and potential solutions, but new attitudes and ways of life have not yet been identified and adopted by a broader basis of people. However, the desperate situation provokes a lot of thinking and ideas on how to solve the problems. At the same time, the at least partial awareness of the disastrous situation of the world on the one hand and of the insufficient answers to it on the other lead to desperation, resignation and repression (Böhm 2015: 34–36). Society ends up in a kind of stuck state and, in the end, all the knowledge present in society has not led to the necessary changes.

In this chapter I want to suggest that interpreting the situation as a crisis in this way makes it resemble a mental crisis of an individual person: in case of such a mental crisis the known concepts of self and the world, as well as habitual behaviour, don't work out for one's own life any longer (Kast 2013). There are also many ideas and often a lot of thinking about problems and potential ways to improve the situation, which often take little effect. In the end there may be resignation or desperation, leading to the person getting stuck in the situation.

In case of mental crisis, what people need is not some kind of advice or a better understanding of the situation (in terms of facts). They don't need solutions and someone who tells them what to do. They might go and see a therapist whose job would be to support them with the integration of the conflicting parts of themselves. Such integration usually enlarges the scope of action and so opens up new possibilities to address their life and the world. That means that by integrating the inner situation of a person, the relationship between the person and the outer world improves (see for example Perls *et al.* 1994). In consequence it extends the capacity of the person to relate to the world. That means, what is needed is rather not solutions or knowledge, but more likely some sort of 'healing' that results from integration. What exactly is addressed by "integration" here?

"Integration" shall be understood as a process of integrating yet external experience into the own being. Actually, a process like that has been described in many contexts. For example, it is how education (German "Bildung")[2] is achieved: outer contents are incorporated into the mind and change the whole human being. Second, such a process is the basis of any therapeutic context: Sigmund Freud noticed the healing force of integrating repressed experience into the conscious mind, which was the beginning of psychotherapy (Freud 1969: 278–279, 574). Apart from that, and perhaps more generally, a similar process can be found regarding human growth or development with a more or less spiritual focus. For example, Martin Buber described such a course of integration: by encounter, a part of the world that is external to oneself is recognised and incorporated into the own experience (Buber 2002: 90–91). Thereby, the person is spiritually developing and growing and his or her relationship to the world is extended and intensified.

What is to be overcome by integration is a sort of 'disruption' between a person and the world: in the best case it is not-knowing or ignorance that constitutes the gap, as it might be addressed by education. In the worst case it is repression that is used to avoid contact and relationship with parts of the inner and outer world; this is the case addressed by psychotherapy. While the earlier gap can be overcome easily by gathering knowledge, the latter gap is more persistent: a person interrupts the relation to the world on purpose.[3] This has at least two consequences: first, it needs effort to keep up the disruption or detachedness, as it is the human's natural state to be in touch (Buber 2002: 22). Apart from that, as the connection is effectively lost, it is not fully perceived and understood what happens on the other side. It might be that the individual can even see and know it with their mind, but as it is not perceived with the person's whole being or better, as it is not felt in its totality, the person is not able to react in an appropriate way. It is this type of detachedness that I want to propose as a reason for people 'knowing of' or 'could be knowing of', but not reacting in a fruitful way, for example in regard to an unsustainable way of life.

In case of an individual mental crisis, "healing" would refer to the integration of such disruptions and to reconnecting to the detached inner and outer contents. How would integration be approached? In psychotherapy, integration would mean perceiving the situation, feeling it, dedicating oneself to it without separating and excluding pieces of it and the inherent emotions as not wanted (see for example Perls *et al.* 1994). As mentioned before, integration isn't a process taking effect only in pathological contexts: all human learning, development and growth grounds in such a process. The task – or at least the opportunity – of a human being in the world is to live his or her life, which includes perceiving his or her situation, not only rationally but experiencing it with all his or her being. The permanent request to integrate experience that is external to the person so far, experience that is at least unknown and often unwanted, constitutes on the one hand a most common, on the other hand, a very essential quality of human life. In this picture, the human situation is not separated from its surroundings and ex- and intensive relations between them are crucial for a rich human life.

What is the motivation to draw a picture like this and compare the situation of sustainable development to a situation of mental crisis of an individual? First, I want to draw attention to the similarities that I find remarkable. Things don't develop in a fruitful direction, but a problem is not easily admitted. The problem doesn't seem to be one of knowledge, but one of missing relationship. Somehow re-establishing the relation to the detached parts is not wanted, as this would mean to perceive what is really going on and feeling the respective emotions. At the same time, occupation with the issues, analysis of the situation and working on solutions is ever increasing, somehow missing the point. Which means that the perspective, from which the issues are commonly approached, might not be adequate.

Furthermore, the similarity of the crisis taking place in sustainability transition to the mental crisis of an individual shall be used to suggest that by learning from psychotherapy the sustainability crisis could be (and might need to be) "healed" rather than solved. This approach seems promising, as concerning the mental crisis of individuals a lot of theoretical knowledge, practices and tools are already available (see for example Revenstorf 1994). There is knowledge about attitudes and approaches that have proved to be more helpful than others (see for example Roth, Fonagy 2005). The transfer of the advanced understanding of mental crisis to the crisis of sustainability transition could be taken advantage of in two different ways:

First, even if sustainability transition is an issue of society, it is the individual forming part of that society who doesn't take into account knowledge about or doesn't adapt his or her behaviour to their knowledge about the situation of the world. So in the end, looking at sustainability transition, it is the individual who is detached from his or her own situation.[4] And many detached individuals form a detached society. In consequence, the first useful aspect of the idea of transferring knowledge from psychotherapy to sustainability crisis is the expectation that the individual in a healing process contributes to sustainability transition as he or she enlarges their possibilities to relate to the world and therefore will be able to feel his or her situation and that of the world to a greater extent. This, so the hypothesis states, will provoke him or her to act and live differently than in a detached state.

Second, society as a whole could be considered to need to be healed more likely than to be solved or told what to do. Also society as a whole is required to integrate issues and developments that are exterior to it so far, it can react in a positive way and dedicate itself to the task or refuse commitment.[5] However, this interpretation shall be mentioned as a possibility, without being discussed in this chapter.

Here, an interpretation of individual mental healing shall be given in order to suggest that such healing might have effects on sustainability transition. As mentioned above, the perspective that is generally taken when addressing sustainability issues (as well as that often taken reacting to a personal mental crisis) might not be adequate. So a shift in perspective might be needed. In this book, supplementing sustainability discourse by the idea of "personal sustainability", we want to draw attention from the collective to the individual part of the problem and from an exterior to an inner, personal one. In this chapter, I want to argue on top of that for the importance of a shift of perspective within what we call "personal sustainability": even when addressing the individual instead of the collective part of the problem, even when taking inner aspects into account in order to get a better view on the whole situation of sustainability, the outcome is strongly determined by the perspective that is applied. In the following, I would like to draw attention to a perspective, different to and less common than the one we normally take, as I expect it to be more helpful addressing the situation.

When addressing individual mental crisis, an approach, for example one from behaviour therapy (Revenstorf 1994), can propose solutions and elaborate strategies to be able to cope with the problems in a better way. Or, on the contrary end of the scale of forms of psychotherapy (Perls *et al.* 1994, Revenstorf 1994, Neidhöfer 2014), there are approaches (for example, depth psychology or body therapy) that might allow a deeper access to the problems. Of course, for the treated individual, they also mean more work, more time, more emotions, overcoming more reluctance, more deep investigation of the situation, all dedicating the whole person and not only the mind. In individual psychotherapy, with problems that are deeply entangled with the psychic structure of a person, that means when they root in early age, and/or when they turn out to be persistent, an approach of the second type is recommended as it accesses the causes and not only the symptoms (compare Revenstorf 1994). I would like to transfer this diagnosis to sustainability transition: the problems have been persistent and are deeply rooted in our culture for a long time. Therefore, in order to allow 'healing' of the situation, I would recommend to also adopt an approach of the second type of deeper access.

How does such an approach in psychotherapy address problems and change individual situations? It seems not to be by increasing knowledge, at least not on the level of the mind, nor by proposing solutions, nor by relying on methods or strategies and not by access via the mind. Earlier, I spoke about a process of integration and about building relationship by engaging in it. What is the subject that is addressed and changed by this process? Where does integration take place?

The missing perspective: subjective body

When Freud talks about such a process, his language is quite mechanistic; sometimes he suggests entities entering into a kind of hydraulic relation.[6] That means, while the problems he addresses are from a 'mental space', he nevertheless uses expressions from a materialistic scope to describe them. Buber's process of integration is located within what he calls the "subjectivity" (Buber 2002: 66). He understands this as the essence of a person, where personal growth is realised. Apart from that it is the space where a person meets their surroundings and so the contact between the person and the world takes place. It is the situation from which a person can orient his- or herself towards encounter, towards the other (or reject it). When talking about the process of integration that is allowed by encounter and relationship, Buber claims that these issues cannot really be talked about as they are not part of a perspective on the world that orders and uses it, but of encounter. In consequence, what he offers more likely has the character of hinting at something than that of a description.

Nevertheless, Buber sometimes employs the German term "Leib" (Buber 2002: 24) in these contexts. For the meaning of "Leib" there is no simple expression in the English language. Therefore it is hard to translate. It means something that takes about the same location as, but has a very different quality compared to, the human body. While the body ("Körper" in German) is an expression used in a physical or materialistic context, "Leib" inherits a very different spirit: it can be perceived by sensation and therefore is a term referring to a phenomenological access to the world.

Like Buber, Freud deals with the point where the individual meets what is exterior to him or her. This is the space where contact can be admitted or rejected and experience can be integrated into one's own being, allowing relationship. That way, in a therapeutic sense, healing of disruption is possible, in the ordinary sense of living one's life, learning is possible, or in a sense of spiritual development, human growth and maturing of the person is possible. In this chapter, I want to suggest that both authors seem to miss a kind of medium in which the process takes place. Freud helps himself with presenting what he recognises as mental movement in materialistic images. Buber talks of the things that cannot be put in words and points in particular directions to introduce a kind of inspiration in the reader.

However, it is Buber himself who starts employing the term of "Leib". In Germany, since the 1960s, there has evolved a new field of phenomenological philosophy. It is called "new phenomenology" or German "Leibphänomenologie" and was constituted and promoted mainly by Hermann Schmitz (Schmitz 1980). Schmitz has developed a perspective on the world that is grounded in the term "Leib" and describes the phenomena in a way that is still very different to common ways of seeing things.[7] In consequence, the approach offers ways to describe thinking and action which wouldn't be possible without it. Within this philosophical discipline "Leib" is often translated as "subjective body".

What can "subjective body" mean? It addresses a space that is located where we are used to find the (physical) human body. We access this space and it is at the same time the space where we are affected by the world. So, in this perspective, the person and the world are not separated in the way they are in common views. There is no limit between the person and the world (as would be the skin referring to a physical context, or the mind, addressing a mental context). The person and the world inhabit the same space and are affected by each other within this. Schmitz, for example, no longer understands emotions as entities (of whatever kind) located within the person. He describes them as atmospheres that are in the first place independent from particular persons but invade space (and the persons who are in it). He differentiates between the basic character of emotions as atmospheres and the additional property of personal concern (Schmitz 2005: 91ff). The latter is a quality that an emotion can have besides its characteristic feeling for a particular person. In consequence, an emotion can be felt, for example, when entering a room full of people who are in a certain mood: it feels different when I enter a room where people meet after a funeral has taken place than a room where people got together because of an anniversary. Given that people physically behave in exactly the same way (e.g. sitting around a table eating, engaged in conversations), I nevertheless perceive a difference. This is the case even if I don't know the people and therefore am not personally involved in the situation.[8] From this example it can be understood why Schmitz considers emotions to be atmospheres: I can perceive these emotions like, for example, the weather, without necessarily being personally involved. By describing situations like that, Schmitz releases our mental situation from being located within us, as personal inner states or contents that are exclusively accessible by ourselves. He creates a terminology that allows us to talk about a space in which we, as entities possessing subjective bodies, meet each other and the world.

Among the psychotherapeutic approaches aiming at changes on a deeper level within the psychic structure of a person there are approaches considering the human body as the medium where relationship takes place. Wilhelm Reich is seen as the founder of this type of therapy known as "Körpertherapie" in German. Even if he uses the term "Körper", which can simply be translated as "body" (Reich 1989: 470ff.), he refers only partly to the physical human body. He describes a context exceeding what is understood by body[9] and refers to – as for example Loil Neidhöfer, who affiliated Reich's approach, puts it – some sort of space ("field") that can be accessed by more than one person. This allows contact of materially different persons by overlaying their "fields of life energy" (Neidhöfer 2014: 53). A space of this kind is considered as the medium where contact and relationship can take place and where integration and healing is possible.

The two mentioned approaches, represented by Hermann Schmitz and Wilhelm Reich and his followers, both assume a different perspective than we normally take when we look at problems or crises, be it individual mental or such of sustainability transition. While the first one of new phenomenology is a philosophical one, setting up a terminology to describe the world from such a point of view, the latter takes advantage of it in practice and uses it for healing processes. Both approaches have in common that they consider our rather materialistic common perspective, that overemphasises the mind, to be insufficient in terms of their respective subjects. For Hermann Schmitz it was not able to represent the world in an adequate way, Wilhelm Reich missed something that would enable him to support and heal his patients. Both of them developed their terminology or respectively their practice in a similar direction: the subjective body that allows being in touch with the world not by the mind but sensing and perceiving. Or, as we always are in touch with the world in the respective way, having the adequate perspective or not, more likely: which allows to describe contact and relationship in a different way and to draw more attention to our respective experience, in turn leading to development and refinement in this field.

How are we able to access this perspective of subjective body? As already implied in the explanations above, access to this perspective isn't possible via the mind, especially not via thinking (Reich 1989: 482, Feldenkrais 1978: 79–80). It doesn't work via the senses as we tend to use them either. For example, the normal way of seeing or hearing is not a good way to enter the perspective of subjective body, as these sensations are generally processed using the analytical mind. However, employing the senses in a different way may lead to a respective perspective: in yoga, for example, hearing is not practiced as detecting contents from sound but as a type of listening without classifying anything with the analytical mind. Nevertheless the main access to a perspective of subjective body lies in a sort of sensing with the body, or better with the subjective body. Through the subjective body we can perceive a lot of things by focusing on it, feeling it and expanding it (or oneself) into the world and that way allowing contact. Practice can lead to bodily perceptions drawing 'landscapes of sensation' within the person, landscapes of ourselves in contact with us, other persons and the world.[10]

There is one big disadvantage when telling a story like that: it is not very common to access such a perspective of subjective body. As our way of life nowadays is deeply rooted in thinking and knowing, classifying and evaluating the phenomena we meet, we have neglected this kind of access to the world. Even if part of such a perspective is common and accepted,[11] it is often considered ordinary and of low interest, especially in a scientific context. Another part might be – at least at the moment – not accessible by our awareness. This means, even if our body is connected to its surroundings in that way, and we obtain or send information via that connection, making use of it for our lives, we're not aware of what's going on and possibly wouldn't easily accept such a view. Beyond that, we might have completely lost a part of our capacity to orient ourselves, to move and act within the perception of the subjective body, while focusing on concepts, ideas and other activity of the analytic mind.

Implications of a shift in perspective

In this chapter I tried to show and promote a perspective that is different to our common access to the world. The main motivation to draw attention to such a view on the world is that, within this perspective of subjective body, a different picture of our situation as human beings in the world becomes visible: we're not separated as individuals but deeply entangled with the situation in which we find ourselves. We're part of our surroundings. And, note well, this connection is not a concept or an idea, but a kind of physical condition. As I tried to show, referring to authors from different contexts, it is a very basic condition of our humanness, a way that we are in the world, a 'bodily truth', and we are able to perceive it via our subjective bodies.[12]

Accordingly, this connectedness cannot be accessed via the mind. That means it cannot be argued for and it is not sensible to try to prove it within a theoretical approach. All that can be done is to draw attention to it and hope that the reader will be inspired and discover his or her own experience that they are able to associate with it. However, in our culture and way of living, we're not very familiar with such kinds of experience. It is not appreciated very much and therefore its potential is neglected. In consequence, neither our capacities to perceive ourselves and the world through our subjective body, nor those to move, act and express ourselves within the respective space can be expected to be very elaborate at the moment.

Therefore, even if we don't perceive the perspective of subjective body in a strong way, it needn't mean that it's not there or has little potential for us. On the contrary, it would be most plausible if it were generally hard for us to discover such a perspective. The reason for that would be that we have little experience and practice with consciously employing it. What is more: it could even be the case that the perspective of subjective body is a part of the world we intentionally don't want to integrate into our worldview, just because it would mean being connected to the world in a very different and much more intense way than we're used to. Being connected in a more intense way here would mean having less control and being at the mercy of emotions to a greater extent, including emotions such as helplessness and impotence. Let me repeat that it could even be the case that we're reluctant to reincorporate such a way of perceiving the world back into our awareness and understanding of ourselves and the world.

In this chapter, it is suggested that the detachedness from our surroundings can be spotted rather as an artificial than as a "natural" state. Even if "natural" would not assume any biological condition where any normative implications could be drawn from, more simply and less ambitiously, it could rather mean something like "efficient in a gentle way" in a sense of little loss in friction and reluctance and high potential for vital life – for the individual person, as well as for the community. Thus, even if a connected situation is not considered as the primordial state for our human being, it nevertheless might be more favourable for the individual as well as for the community.

What could this more favourable situation look like? Taking into account and appreciating subjective body could be expected to create and foster a 'field' among humans and between humans and the world. This 'field' shall be understood neither as an abstract idea nor as a metaphysical entity but as a rather profane web of actual relations, a custom of being in touch. The intensity of such a field would be constituted by the particularity of mutual perception on the one hand and by the potential to create a spontaneous answer to that perception as an expression of the own being in this very moment on the other. Even if during a process of reconnecting a person has to deal with many and intense emotions, living through them reduces the fear that goes along with their retention and leads to relief in the long run. That means such a field would be less determined by fears and restraint than our way of living at the moment. Relief and absence of fear, however, create the inner space for an attitude oriented towards the world. In consequence, the common field would be nourished by curiosity and lust for life and allow and support vitality in turn.[13]

Focusing on subjective body means expanding oneself into the world. This does not only mean taking more space for oneself and it does definitely not mean blocking this space for the others, isolating oneself against outer influence. On the contrary, it is supposed to come along with sharing the space with others and the world. It implies perceiving and feeling the other and the world, allowing them to enter the own person on the one hand and influencing and forming the common space in a gentle way by the own particular contribution of being on the other. In consequence, a strong, autonomous human being would not locate his or her autonomy in self-sufficiency but in taking responsibility to reconnect and get back into contact and relationship with him- or herself and the world. Autonomy would not mean to isolate oneself from the other and outer, but to be strong enough a personality and connected intensely enough to oneself, to others and the world, to be able to open oneself for the outer, to be able to stand while perceiving the other. Strength would not mean employing power in order to maintain the own isolation against others, but to be strong enough to experience the world, to share space with others and to feel one's own emotions connected to that. Hence such an approach would imply dedication and surrender to what is not oneself.

Re-establishing the missing touch can be considered an important task in terms of 'healing', development and growth, be it for the individual or the whole society. It is based on a decision that everyone has to take over and over again: to integrate experience that is external to oneself[14] and thereby extend contact with oneself and the world, or to reject the impact of that experience. It's a task to engage in such processes, but it's not only a task. I think, apart from favourable consequences for our common world and its situation, a focus on relationship would also mean a better life for ourselves. Even if it is very difficult to reconnect at points where connection was interrupted on purpose, even if that means to be confronted with emotions and truths that are very hard to be felt and integrated, the rewards of vitality, extended possibilities to live and relate to the world, absence of fear and being in touch with the world are nourishing and valuable. They might even exceed all that we know of at the moment and lead us to a new form of being humans.

What is extremely important is that for our steps in this direction we absolutely need each other. As we're generally not aware of our own detachedness, we have to rely on the relationship with other people to find our way to reconnect. Apart from that, when it comes to opening up and feeling our actual situation, sometimes our inner situation might not be bearable without the support of others. The community with others, incredibly important for our development as humans and as society, is the only way to be able to cope with the huge task we face: that of establishing a sustainable way of life allowing for our future. Mastering this task even rudimentarily will only be possible together. It is a project having a dimension that cannot be realised by individuals or by groups of people. I think it will need every single person to add his or her part. Contributing a particular part that cannot be supplied by any other person will require the person not as a follower but as the actual other. It will need the developed person, not a person only adapted to any outer circumstances. Therefore it is necessary that we support and challenge each other in developing and growing – each to his or her very distinct subjectivity. Allowing a community of individuals like that might transcend all kinds of known togetherness as humans and as world.

Conclusion

The reasons why I think that changing our perspective in a direction of subjective body would promote sustainability transition lie in the potential of establishing a field of dense and direct relations as described above. Thus, in the end it is not the perspective of subjective body itself that is supposed to turn around sustainability transition but its potential as medium for relationship. Getting more familiar with the perspective would mean respecting, appreciating, promoting and creating a different web of relationship among us human beings and also among us and our surroundings, including nature as our ecological environment.

Such a modified field of relationship could mean various changes: there could be more touch with oneself, with the other and with the world, which would mean more support[15] and less loneliness; our domination by fear would decrease and our lives would be free and happy to a greater extent. The first reason why I would expect an influence on sustainability transition is that the accompanying relief would allow us to change and adapt our behaviour to our situation in a more unpretentious way. The second reason is that being in touch with our surroundings in a more ex- and intensive way would enable us to perceive the situation in a more direct and complete way, not only with a distant, analytical mind but with our whole person, i.e. by our subjective body.

Being in touch as described creates the opportunity to act with respect to the whole situation instead of only on behalf of a detached individual. This opportunity is set up by direct affection, which means that we're perceiving the situation in a sufficiently detailed way and including our emotional situation that enables us to act with respect to it. At the same time, because of the bodily connection to the situation, there arises a subjective necessity to act with respect to it: being in touch and aware of that connection it is similarly not imaginable that we hurt our surroundings as it is not imaginable that we hurt ourselves, as that would hurt our subjective body. Human behaviour that is hostile to life, while it can be justified and performed on the basis of concept, cannot be imagined as developing from real bodily (including emotional) connectedness to the situation and the world. That is applicable, for example, to the German Nazi regime as well as to poisoning our water. A consequence of the proposed perception of our connectedness with the world is supposed to be that sustainability issues will also change their character and meaning for us: they will no longer be abstract contents of the mind or subject of moral claims. If we perceive them as part of our direct situation, caring for them will become a subjective necessity.

Notes

1 To mention an example from Germany: the waste produced per capita is increasing (Eurostat 2017).
2 The well-known German term "Bildung" refers to a process of education, including the evolution of the person. According to a humanistic understanding this is not that much a process of the mind as it is considered nowadays. It is rather seen as a process affecting the person as a whole and changing her or him (see for example Heafford 2016).
3 Speaking of "on purpose" here is questionable. For sure it is not the conscious part of a person that decides not to relate to the world concerning certain issues. However, the lack of relation to the world in these issues is more than an accidental fact: within the psychic constitution of the person, including his or her worldview, it has a function (or let's say a purpose) to omit just these issues. Respectively, it is a task to reintegrate such issues.
4 Of course the human's situation has been locally extended and has become much more complex very quickly in the last 200 years. To stay in touch with it is a huge and ambitious task that is not easy to fulfill.
5 These days, this can be illustrated by the difference in reactions to and dealing with refugee flows for instance.
6 Freud talks for example about "repression" or "upwelling" (Freud 1969: 507).
7 Actually, sometimes it is not even that different to common ways of seeing things, but to perspectives that qualify to enter the scientific scope.
8 These examples describe perceptions that are very ordinary for us. However, we don't have the language to describe them accurately. It is remarkable that, especially in scientific language, there are few possibilities to address such experience. If it is expressed, it is normally done in common language, which is, as common language, not appreciated in scientific contexts.
9 Wilhelm Reich, for example, spoke of sensing the expression manifested in the body of another person that would be permitted by our own body automatically provoking an imitation of that expression (Reich 1989: 478).
10 There are authors and schools based on approaches similar to that of the subjective body. A known author would be Moshe Feldenkrais (1978). Also many Eastern traditions, for example yoga, provide a similar concept of space: akasha (Vivekananda 1981).

11 To give an example of commonly applied subjective body: the adequate physical distance to other persons is considered as dependent on situation and relationship. In this case it is obvious that it is evaluated via subjective body and not determined by deliberation.

12 Apart from the Western authors thinking in this direction, many Eastern schools of wisdom, which dispose of very old knowledge that has been passed on for a very long time, quite naturally assume a similar access to oneself and the world via the perception of subjective body. For example the yoga tradition (Vivekananda 1981). However, this knowledge seems to be seen as a different type of knowledge and therefore generally not linked to the scientific knowledge of our Western culture. There are exceptions in recent times, such as Ken Wilber (2006).

13 As this bodily connection is already there, of course such a 'field' is already existent. However, appreciating and drawing more attention to it could intensify and strengthen it enormously.

14 "External to oneself" shall not only refer to what is external to the own person. On the contrary, a big part that is "external to oneself" in this sense are characteristics, emotions and experience the person is deeply involved in, but not aware of, for example the repressed experience Freud talks about.

15 Here, support is not referred to as any particular or conscious act but as a very basic biological condition, known to be effective particularly in our early ages: confidence from feeling in touch with our surrounding.

References

Böhm, I. (2015): Modelle gelebter Nachhaltigkeit zwischen Theorie und Praxis. Ökodörfer als Kulturen der Nachhaltigkeit. KIT (Masterthesis). Retrieved 15 September 2017, from: www.quartierzukunft.de/forschung.

Buber, M. (2002): *Ich und Du*. Gütersloh: Gütersloher Verlagshaus.

Eurostat (2017): Waste per capita in Germany. Retrieved 5 July 2017, from: http://ec.europa.eu/eurostat/tgm/table.do?tab=table&init=1&plugin=1&pcode=sdg_12_50&language=en..

Feldenkrais, M. (1978): *Bewusstheit durch Bewegung*. Frankfurt am Main: Suhrkamp Verlag.

Freud, S. (1969): *Studienausgabe. Band I: Vorlesungen zur Einführung in die Psychoanalyse. Und Neue Folge*. Frankfurt am Main: S. Fischer Verlag (13. Aufl. 1997).

Heafford, M. (2016): *Pestalozzi: His Thought and its Relevance Today*. Florence: Taylor and Francis.

Kast, V. (2013): *The Creative Leap: Psychological Transformation through Crisis*. Asheville, NC: Chiron Publications.

Neidhöfer, L. (2014): *Intuitive Körperarbeit. Schriften zur Körpertherapie 1990–2002*. Hamburg: Endless Sky Publications.

Perls, F., Hefferline, R., Goodman, P. (1994): *Gestalt Therapy: Excitement and Growth in the Human Personality*. Gouldsboro, ME: The Gestalt Journal Press.

Reich, W. (1989): *Charakteranalyse*. Cologne: Kiepenheuer & Witsch.

Revenstorf, D. (1994): *Psychotherapeutische Verfahren*. Stuttgart: W. Kohlhammer GmbH.

Roth, A., Fonagy, P. (2005): *What Works for Whom? A Critical Review of Psychotherapy Research*. New York: The Guilford Press.

Schmitz, H. (1980): *Neue Phänomenologie*. Bonn: Bouvier Verlag.

Schmitz, H. (2005): *System der Philosophie. Band III/2: Der Gefühlsraum*. Bonn: Bouvier Verlag.

Vivekananda (1981): *Raja-Yoga*. Freiburg: Bauer-Verlag.

Wilber, K. (2006): *Integral Spirituality: A Startling New Role for Religion in the Modern and Postmodern World*. Boston, MA: Shambhala Publications.

7 Developing intra-personal skills as a proactive way to personal sustainability

The preventative side of the mental health equation

Helena Lass

Introduction

There is no health without mental health. Mental wellness and health are among the biggest fields of future exploration and development. When it comes to mental health and health of the inner in general, the main focus has been on disorders and the cure. This narrow approach has left people feeling that mental wellness has no relevance in life unless a mental illness occurs. In reality all humans possess an internal realm and experience intra-personal events on a daily basis such as feeling emotions, learning, thinking, planning, focusing and leading our attention, having an ability to investigate, gaining an insight etc. Mental wellness in its rightful context would mean a certain ease in directing those internal processes. This becomes possible if we are able to differentiate between specific intra-personal functions and understand their patterns and combinations. This cannot be reached as long as all inner processes are lumped together simply as "the mind". Besides being too abstract and vague, the current terminology does not highlight another matter of high importance – the distinction of the Self and the intra-personal functions that can be led by the Self.

For the current work, the realization about the relevance of human's intra-personal functions was checked against medical science, clinical practice, evidence of empirical experience and the author's personal experience on the subject. The author suggests that addressing the psycho-behavioural and intra-personal functions may revolutionise the understanding about the fundamental under-pinnings of psychiatric disorders, possibilities for primary prevention and even more, provide a framework for exploring human capacity that is not defined by disorders. This chapter proceeds from the premise that intra-personal functions and events emerge in parallel with brain neurodynamics and coordinate the functioning of each other through instant feedback loops. The chapter debates that the topic of known mental health disorders encompass only a small fraction within the vast territory of all intra-personal functions. The reductionist view of equating mental health with mental ill-health has pulled the approach to intra-personal out of context and caused stigma, a limited view of the human with a narrow focus on the brain. This has resulted in the loss of an open mind towards empirical evidence and is in fact obliterating progress to provide practical value to the society and improve intra- and interpersonal sustainability.

Although considerable progress in understanding the internal functioning of humans has been made in psychology, the author finds the overall effect insufficient, reflected in the sustenance of problems and challenges people experience. The majority of methods in psychology have been developed as forms of intervention for a therapy setting, not as proactive education. Positive psychology has somewhat expanded the scope of psychology into non-therapy applications with examples from gratitude exercises and the cultivation of forgiveness. The direction and hypothesis in positive psychology nevertheless follows an analogous mindset where positive qualities are lacking, need cultivation and therefore require methods to introduce the missing competencies. The main premise is that furthering positive emotions is the prerequisite for an ongoing development of a person's personality. The author rests on a diametrically opposite viewpoint that there is an excess of negative internal reactions and habits, and therefore a need to introduce methods of becoming aware and discontinuation. These fundamental differences will be addressed in detail within this chapter.

Mindfulness, being one of the youngest forms of psychotherapy alongside psychoanalytic and cognitive-behavioural, is the first of its kind, helping people go beyond the mind while observing the mind and providing methods to explore one's internal functioning in an independent and self-sufficient manner. Nevertheless, the author wishes to emphasise that 1) none of the existing interventions in psychology has been designed for proactive education and therefore cater to the needs of therapy, not education; 2) none of the existing models are constructed with placing the actual Self into the centre of human identity and while exploring the intra-personal sub-functions to a limited extent, do not explore how and under what conditions does the Self exercise command over the internal functions; 3) none of the existing modalities in evidence-based psychotherapy has provided an applicable education towards re-establishing the human's most natural state, where we identify with Self rather than ego nor provided methods to systematically discontinue the automatic reactions that people have started to consider normal and become identified with.

Intra-personal functions

The following section describes what the intra-personal functions are, how they relate to the current terminologies and how they can bring us closer to a function-based approach for proactive prevention and mental wellbeing. The term *intra-personal* is used by the author to discern emotional-mental and awareness-related inner functions from the somatic ones. It enables an umbrella concept that is not reserved to any specific sector of psychology, pathology or intervention. A structured approach to intra-personal functions enables the entities that people describe as the mind, Self, awareness, subconscious, spirit, ego etc. to obtain a clearer meaning and a practical reference. The intra-personal functions can be classified into three meta-types: emotional functions, mental-cognitive functions and awareness-related functions. Every individual is not only potentially capable, but indeed requested to direct these functions if we aspire to live harmonious lives and build sustainable societies. The Self, as described later, lies outside of these functions and should be attributed as their chief conductor. The term *mental* will be reserved for the mental apparatus wherever possible, concerned with sustaining and mentally processing data.[1] The term *mental health* is avoided if possible, and if suitable, replaced with a more accurate term of *intra-personal health*. The general term *mind* will also be substituted with a more accurate, specific equivalent of a function, event or an entity. Obviously, affects, mental functions and awareness are massively inter-penetrant; however, an initial separation into three meta-functions and the Self beyond these functions is presented for purposes of clarity.

As the result of personal observation and clinical experience, discussed in further detail in the chapter, the author holds the educational deficit in intra-personal skills as the main factor that pre-disposes and even causes the majority of current social as well as mental health problems. A radically new perspective that transcends our modern understanding about genetics, somatic functioning of the brain and current theories in psychology is needed to introduce a fundamental change in intra-personal topics. This can open up a different avenue for intra-personal wellness and education beyond the concept of therapy or disease. Further, this new perspective that stems from a holistic understanding about the Self, the intra-personal functions and their consequent effect on physiology will help explore human capacity and quality of life in a new light, supporting humanity in the quest for meaning, productivity, creativity and fulfilment.

Current status in mental health

The World Health Organization (WHO) predicts that by the year 2030 depression will be the single major burden of disease. Lifetime prevalence of depression is 15–20 per cent, 10 per cent of the world's population has at least one mental health disease. While the WHO notes that this is the "silent epidemic", many people think that this would never concern them, their family or colleagues. Besides direct healthcare costs and subjective suffering, mental illnesses also have dire consequences on productivity, the ability to work, performing social roles and participation in family-life. It could be that by, or even before the year 2030, we have a population who are physically fit, but mentally inept. A number of studies have shed further light on how this affects society in general. The Pan-European Matrix Study (2013) outlined that workplace-related depression cost the 27 EU nations' economies, businesses, healthcare systems and society nearly €617 billion per year. In the USA, Greenberg and colleagues' paper published in the *Journal of Clinical Psychiatry* (2015) found similar results. They concluded that the total economic burden of depression-related costs to businesses is estimated to be $210.5 billion per year, representing a 21.5 per cent increase from 2005.

The Director-General of the WHO, Dr Margaret Chan, stated at the World Bank and International Monetary Fund Spring Meeting that: "The cultural and historical contexts for taking action in different countries vary considerably, but all face one common barrier: stigma. Mental disorders are something people don't want to know about. This must change, and I see some encouraging signs."

It is not correct to regard mental ill-health in a narrow manner as is still the norm. Instead, intra-personal ill-health makes up just one sub-fraction of the total landscape of intra-personal health and wellbeing. Not all intra-personal topics have by far automatically to do with mental illness and are therefore free from the risk of stigma.

Intra-personal wellbeing should not be considered only as a goal in itself, but also as a sign of fluency in basic life-skills. Learning intra-personal skills refers to an enhanced ability in managing and directing the three types of internal meta-functions, in this regard universal skills, very similar to learning to read. Once a person learns to read, the ability itself turns into a basic skill that enables the development of further skills through reading. Being awareness-based, intra-personal skills are the pre-requisites of a fulfilling life and a more harmonious and sustainable society. We need to know how to deliberately direct awareness in order to learn effectively, differentiate lasting values from fleeting ones to support our choices for a meaningful life, and learn to individually connect cause with consequence to become responsible citizens. One can contribute and reach goals considerably better if there exists know-how about conscious application of awareness to effectively process data, orient in changing environment, and become aware of and regulate one's emotional as well as mental reactions.

Additionally, there are even bigger concerns. First, there is an increasing lack of qualified service providers in mental health and even if people become comfortable with seeking help, the current model will not be able to cater the rising demand. Second, with our current healthcare built upon the disease-centric paradigm, it mostly addresses the consequences. With absent emphasis, know-how and a model for proactive education on intra-personal skills and wellness, the society faces rising healthcare costs, damage to economy through lost productivity, decline in the quality of life and collective frustration with deepening mistrust in medicine and evidence-based psychology all at the same time. There-fore, from a perspective of social and personal sustainability, prevention needs to become increasingly important next to cure.

Mental health disorders – not just a question of genes or accidental infection

In essence, psychiatric disorders are not isolated, sudden illnesses that need attention when there is an outbreak. All psychiatric illnesses develop over time as cumulative subtle changes in the intra-personal functioning, starting long before clinical signs present themselves, which marks a certain crossing of a threshold. Without education to apply awareness to notice the reaching and crossing of the threshold, expressed as repeated and cumulative daily emotional and mental dysfunctional reactions, people do not discover the problematic developments early enough. Also, the education about intra-personal wellbeing and mental health provided in schools and generally in society is theoretical, too illness-centric and statistical in nature, lacking practical know-how about methods to independently regulate one's emotional-mental reactions, mental processing and the application of attention. Without a simple and structured education about these universal intra-personal meta-functions, their forms of further combination and expression into various internal events, and the ability to observe them in real time, people remain unable to identify the determinants of the dysfunctions and correct them effectively. As a result, people are not equipped to prevent suffering caused by dysfunctional reactions, their cumulative development into mental health disorders and remain unequipped to deliberately sustain their state of wellbeing after an illness has been treated. A known pain point of psychiatric diseases is the percentage of relapses after treatment: 80 per cent in schizophrenia, 60 per cent in depression and anxiety disorders. When neural circuits have been corrected with medication, what causes them to become dysfunctional again? A closer look into the current findings from neuropsychopharmacology reveals that despite the ruling monoamine theory of depression and anxiety disorders,[2] the imbalance in monoamines is not the primary aetiological[3] factor, but most likely a secondary one. And while, according to Dr Stephen Stahl, over-activation of circuits, expressed as sustained psychiatric symptoms, may over time lead to the loss of synapses, dendrites and neurons (2008: 230) contributing to brain damage caused by sustained emotional-mental symptoms, we might ask what activates the dysfunctional circuits in the first place? It is common knowledge that relapses of psychological and psychiatric conditions occur in the presence of stress, a triggering agent. In order to further our understanding of what happens as the result of a triggering agent, we need to focus on what gets triggered, not on the triggers themselves. The author has observed that subsequent intra-personal events in the form of automatic emotional-mental reactions are always triggered while differing in their content from person to person. These automatic internal reactions, discussed in detail as emotional-mental complexes in the following paragraphs, are the bridging agents that translate the environmental stimuli into activation of neural circuits and changes in neurochemistry of the brain. The author claims that these automatic emotional-mental complexes are the internal events that constantly create the brain's ever-changing biochemical and electrical environment.

There is no single gene known to cause psychiatric illnesses. The overall genetic predisposition to psychiatric diseases is below 50 per cent, mainly influencing individual sensitivity to life stressors. At the same time, increasing understanding about neuroplasticity raises questions of whether some brain changes may be caused by mental illnesses, rather than pre-existing and causing them. Schizophrenia genetics re-emphasises a critical role for other factors besides genes, particularly the environmental ones. For example, Howes and Kapur (2009) state in their paper that people who reported low maternal care during their childhood react to stress with increased striatal dopamine, which is strongly correlated with the onset of psychosis. They further argue that psychotic symptoms, especially delusions and hallucinations, emerge over time as individual's own explanation to the experience of aberrant salience, being an internal emotional-mental reaction rather than an isolated hallmark of the disease. How else is low maternal care translated into low levels of dopamine than through personal emotional-mental reactions to the situation, where emotions of loneliness, abandonment and sadness remain internally triggered over a period of time, are later mentally constructed into a narrative and thereafter kept in reactivation through memory. Hereby we know that genes and environmental factors do not exist in isolation, but rather in interaction. The author estimates that it is the intra-personal reactions that, through epigenetic processes, are responsible for mediating brain changes through (re-)activating illness-corresponding circuits for the symptoms to emerge as well as for a relapse to occur. Hence, the brain "forgives", but does not forget.

Perhaps one of the most salient findings as witnessed in several recent brain studies is the observation that the adult brain can still change significantly in both structure and function as a result of experience (Maguire *et al.* 2000; Draganski *et al.* 2004; Boyke *et al.* 2008). Not only long-term, but also relatively short-term practice has been associated with neural changes in adults. Pascual-Leone and his team observed (2005) that performing a five-finger piano exercise for 2 hours on 5 consecutive days resulted in an enlargement of primary motor areas representing finger muscles. This study also marked a significant turning point by stating that mere mental practice (visualising the movements) of the same finger exercise results in a similar reorganisation of the motor cortex as was observed in the group of participants who physically practiced the movements. It is now commonly held that the brain undergoes continuous changes in response to each sensor input, motor act, association, reward signal, action plan and awareness itself (*ibid.*). Many other reliable neuroimaging studies have also concluded that motor imagery and motor execution activate similar, although not entirely identical neural networks (Lotze *et al.* 1999; Kosslyn *et al.* 2007; Munzert *et al.* 2009). When rephrasing, there is strong and repeated evidence that intra-personal events have direct effect on the function and structure of the brain and therefore the skills to direct these events can most likely lead to changes in wiring and neurotransmitter activity in the human brain.

The conclusion that the experience of intra-personal events and the activation of corresponding neural circuits in the brain occur in parallel, is of high practical relevance. The evidence from studies allows concluding that the activation between the "mind" and the brain is regulated through constant feedback loops. Simply put, thoughts and emotions, regardless if they are automatic or intentional, activate a circuit, and repetitive activation of circuits turn a state into a trait, an emotional-mental habit. Whereas research often focuses on psychiatric disorders as the outcome of exogenous factors that can't be altered (be it genes, environmental stressors or early childhood adversity), this chapter suggests them to be at least partially caused by an endogenous condition. This means that structured methods and skills to discontinue dysfunctional intra-personal reactions in the midst of everyday activities can provide fast and possibly even more sustainable results than current forms of treatment, as pharmaceutical agents tend to alter the circuits and monoamine levels only temporarily and are therefore needed as a lifelong regimen. Focusing on intra-personal skills allows us to move towards an education that acts as primary and secondary prevention at the same time not being a form of therapy and rather a segment of education on basic life-skills.

Problems of the current paradigm

The majority of problems in personal wellbeing, professional excellence and intra-personal health exist due to the global lack of understanding on intra-personal functions and respective skills. Current solutions are either substitutive in nature (consumerism to activate positive emotions, use of stimulants and addictive substances to alter internal states, use of entertainment and other activities to get "mind off things") or do not provide practical skills that can be implemented independently. Breakthroughs have been modest. Unfortunately, the current understanding of emotional-mental and attentional dysregulation, the core presenting features of psychiatric distress, lack clarity and systematic understanding, as can be witnessed from increasing prevalence of psychiatric disorders. There is urgent need for practical methods, not only scientific discoveries from neuroscience that tend to focus on increasingly narrower aspects of brain function.

So far, the medical science has been excessively one-sided. The author emphasises that this retrograde path where the physical brain itself remains the primary object of investigation, will not provide practical keys for turning the course of mental illness epidemic and the overall reaction-derived problem-points in society. When looking at the current bias in science, focus has been on studying the anatomical, more precisely the brain and the genes, instead of studying intra-personal functions. The golden standard has emphasised investigating the somatic, making weak assumptions about the intra-personal realm based on that. For centuries there has been little disciplinary will to move beyond the safe harbour of regarding humans as bio-robots.[4] The main argument being, that if the physical body is well and all the organs function as they are supposed to, humanity will reach optimum health and therefore the somatic-focused studies should be prioritised. The current trends however provide more and more evidence that there is more to health than the health of our organs and that intra-personal functions play a vital part in both wellness and illness. As the realisation about the interplay between intra-personal events and their correlating brain functions emerges, so does the need to understand the intra-personal from a more empirical aspect with effective methods to alter and direct internal reactions and events.

Syndromal[5] classification of disorders, characteristic of psychiatry, has become a barrier to noticing the dysfunction from the aspect of the three intra-personal meta-functions. Due to progress in neuroscience we understand more about neurons, circuits and responsibilities of distinct brain regions; however, practical applications of these discoveries for the benefit of people remain minimal. It is clear that if problems are not solved, they escalate. Many superficial observations about the internal nature of humans have, due to being widespread, quietly turned into standard assumptions in society and are often accepted without further discriminative evaluation (for example that automatic activation of emotions is normal; it is in human nature to be erroneous; the sum of emotions and mental processes is our identity etc.).

It is known that the aetiology of psychiatric diseases is diverse, but scientific studies are still conducted in an isolated manner: of 12,060 PubMed articles on major depressive disorder published between 1980 and 2014 about 93 per cent, studied only one key variable and only 7 per cent studied two or more. The lack of published works on the intersecting agents that drive depression is striking (Wittenborn *et al.* 2015). Kendler *et al.* (2011) suggested new frameworks in place of the common approach and recommended a shift from seeking an 'essence' that is directly responsible for a mental disorder to delineating the complex causal mechanisms that underlie psychiatric syndromes. Since traditional psychometric approaches often assume a linear and latent variable model and cannot estimate intra-individual effects, network and dynamic methods have been recommended by Borsboom and Cramer (2013). As long as the interests remain exclusively focused on the brain and the triggers, while discarding basic systematisation that considers the three universal intra-personal meta-functions and the Self, we will first ignore the automatic emotional-mental complexes that as explained later, currently determine behaviour. Second, no effective method for self-direction can be developed, if the Self remains unaddressed and is left out of the equation. Third, focus will remain on solutions that are substitutive in nature or demand for an intervention by another person (i.e. a therapist). Fourth, the intra-personal domain will lack a mutually understood framework for systematisation, each theory and method seemingly standing separate from another.

The author encourages all concerned scientists and clinicians to keep an open mind. It is more likely that our unwillingness to change perspective from the brain, the triggers, life events and presenting symptoms towards intra-personal functions is simply impeding progress on topics of ultimate concern. A. K. Wittenborn *et al.* suggest that more empirical studies and models that expose the multiple drivers of depression and how they intersect are needed (2015). When talking about proactive prevention, the subject of interest shifts radically from medication to education, consequence to cause and reaction to proactive initiative. In fact, this is needed for the whole field of psychiatry to move forward, with the current chapter being one of the first attempts in this new direction. Even to consider that intra-personal functions directly affect neural circuits and their underlying genetic controls is enough to introduce a new starting point for understanding intra-personal wellbeing and its sub-category of psychiatric disorders in a more integrated way. The author strongly believes that further progress in providing practical as well as sustainable methods for proactive self-leadership and prevention depends on a structured investigation of the more intangible intra-personal functions, including their combination as various internal events and reactions, in an empirical way.

The known and the unknown – the conscious and the subconscious

The intra-personal, just like the brain, is a multi-layered system that works in hierarchical ways. In regard of self-direction skills, it is necessary to understand the differences between the conscious and the unconscious. In neurology the awake state is equated with being conscious and the states of general anaesthesia and coma with the unconscious. Looking towards psychology, "conscious" can generally be understood as everything that one can have deliberate access to and that is readily available for observing and becoming aware of. Conscious always refers to an informed and voluntary choice. On the other hand, "subconscious", "unconscious" and "non-conscious" are largely used as synonyms and refer to personal data, emotional, mental and physiological, that exists, although access to this data remains out of our deliberate control. Subconscious events are events that lack the presence of consciousness, being run by automation whereas people sense to have little power of direction over them. The border between subconscious and conscious is fluid, not rigid, and runs on the edge of the capacity to become aware. For example, with low capacity to become aware, the subconscious processes remain largely unnoticed by that person, as if being on autopilot, although other people may easily recognise them. While the majority of limitations on freedom seem to be imposed from the outside, from society and external regulations, there is little realisation as to the scope of our limitation from within. Typically a person lives with an illusion of much greater self-control and free will than is actually true. Wherever we have an option of choice, we seem to be free to act according to our free will, for example choosing between ice-cream flavours, a holiday destination or a perfume. However, this choice is seriously limited by advertising, range of possibilities, wish to be liked, desire to be different or blend in, previous choices, habit, cultural preferences, an active emotion and many other factors. Having a real choice implies a high degree of consciousness.

According to Ingvar Villido, a practical researcher of awareness with empirical experience spanning over 30 years:

> There are two options with awareness. The first is that one knows to have awareness, has discovered it. The second is to be oblivious of it, not having discovered it. Not having discovered one's own awareness is one of the saddest tragedies possible for a person. During that time, during that subconscious period, a person is unable to lead their life. Instead, very complicated psychophysical reactions are in charge, combined of emotions, mental data and behaviour. As such, two ways of being and acting can be outlined: reaction-based and awareness-based. Unfortunately most of the humanity currently leads a reaction-based life.
>
> (Villido 2005)

The observations and empirical experience of the author allow to claim that the subconscious material surfaces regularly during our daily tasks as automatic emotional-mental reactions in response to data already present and then sinks again into the depth of the subconscious when the data ceases. For example, one does not feel irritated all of the time and knows what kind of data – people, situations, sounds or images activate this emotional reaction of irritation.

What most people refer to as "being conscious", can in the current chapter be more accurately described as a state of ordinary subconsciousness, an automated way of living and reacting while awake. The role of subconscious processes in generating human behavioural tendencies has been extensively discussed in several recent papers (Bargh, Morsella, 2008 and Bargh, Morsella, 2009). When it comes to behaviour and agendas it could in fact be said that people do not alter between consciousness and subconsciousness, but between different levels of unconsciousness. On ordinary level of subconsciousness people are identified with the ego[6] and follow an subconscious automated routine, unaware of the Self. Sinking into an even deeper reactive subconsciousness occurs when automatic emotional-mental complexes get triggered, manifested as irrational behaviour that is later on difficult to comprehend even by the persons themselves. Taking the frequency of automatic reactions and absence of both knowledge and identification with the Self, the ordinary subconscious state can be deemed to be most people's usual state. A similar conclusion was reached by Bargh and Morsella, stating the "unconscious mind" to be the rule, not an exception (Bargh, Morsella, 2009). As long as the ordinary and deep subconscious state remains the behavioural "norm", the automatic complexes will also remain to rule over intentional conscious will, creating various forms of suffering.

The fundamental root of dysfunction – confusion of identity

The topic of this paragraph is the least studied and explained by modern science. This is because the ego and Self, the main topics in this paragraph, can be discovered, experienced and discerned only empirically by the person who has set out to do so. The following explanations reflect the discoveries of the author, resulting from 15 years of awareness practices, while the aim of the current chapter is to provide only a short introduction to the topic. What most people understand as "I" is in fact a mental concept, a representation of oneself in the descriptive word form, perceived as a vocal "I" in thoughts. This mental "I" is constructed by language and is daily in constant change, depending on the ongoing mental process. The thoughts "I am a nice person" and "I am not good for anything" do not mean that there exists more than one you. These thoughts merely describe situations, attributes and states and should not be mistaken as an identity. The word "I" comes from Latin, meaning ego, the false self. Carl Gustav Jung says: "The 'I' lies at the centre of the field of consciousness and comprises the empirical personality – personality as we are aware of it and experience first-hand" (Murray 1998: 15). This is a misleading starting point. Since it is easily possible to become aware of the vocal "I" (everyone can observe the thoughts that contain the word "I"), this vocal "I" clearly is an observable object. The "I" is not the centre of consciousness, rather a dynamic object onto which our awareness can fall. Therefore a question arises – who is the non-vocal witness, silent behind the scenes? The ego largely consists of two parts: the mental "I" and one's emotions. In the view of the author, ego is not only seen as someone being an egotistic person, but as a tendency to perceive oneself as an emotional-mental identity. Identification with the ego-derived identity substitutes identification with the Self and creates a fundamental confusion. Although a very common aspiration in society, it is impossible to find stability from the ego, as the mental content along with emotions change all the time. Second, trying to make the ego non-vulnerable or somehow protect it is useless, because the ego is not one's real identity to begin with. According to Villido:

> The biggest problem with the ego is that it replaces the real Self. Replaces in a seamless and practical way, in all aspects of life. Usually till death or until the person starts to apply more of awareness. Ego is a substitutive agent that consumes the life of the person, while the human itself remains in the background.
>
> (Villido 2011a)

The child first says "I" at about the age of two. Until then it refers to itself in the third person or by name "Ann is hungry". In psychoanalytic theory the moment when a child is able to say "I" is regarded as a leap towards consciousness. From the perspective of mis-identification with the mental "I", it marks the introduction of a fundamental flaw. Rather, a child must acknowledge and be aware of one's body, thoughts, emotional states and awareness as functional parts of oneself and also be encouraged to retain the real identity, the Self. In his lecture in 1941 Paramhansa Yoganada proclaimed: "My sole desire is to give you the Truth, that you may experience what I experience. The purpose of this life is to find your Self. Know your Self" (2008a: 398). Every person having abandoned the true identity of the Self encounters an unexplained longing for something "deeper" and "truer", commencing the quest to find oneself. This flaw of misplaced identity cannot be corrected by any other means than by practically realising that the ego, the pseudo self, in fact is not the Self. Suffering is not caused by a weak ego in need of restoration. No matter how weak or strong the ego becomes, identification with it is a misunderstanding. Instead, suffering is caused by identifying with the ego in the first place. Villido describes the relations between the ego and Self as follows:

> One of the biggest problems of a human is that he does not in fact know who he really is. And this results *exactly* from a habit of being aware of the objects while forgetting one as an observer. Once you become the observer, you will understand that your awareness, the tool you use for observing, falls on objects and through that process, those objects become accentuated, objective. In that regard there is no difference, either you use the eyes to observe the external or you observe your internal world. (. . .) As such it is irrelevant what you observe, it is important to *be* the observer.
>
> (Villido 2008)

The Self, or true identity, is radically different from the ego. It is silent and one senses it as continuity. It is that same entity able to witness and know about the mental as well as emotional events in the first place. No matter how much objects, internal or external, change, Self is always stable, witnessing the change, while remaining beyond change itself. C. G. Jung also investigated the subject and around 1918 made a discovery that the psyche rests on a fundamental structure that is able to withstand threat to mental stability and emotional balance. He came to call this entity Self, inspired by Indian Upanishads that refer to higher personality as the atman and counted Self as the human's highest authority (Murray 1998: 153). To initially become aware of and thereafter re-identify with the Self would mark the restoration of every human's most natural and sane state. Until that moment, there remains a never-ending famine to find peace and happiness, most often compensated through consumerism and a hunt for more positive emotions. To be able to Self-direct,[7] a fundamental distinction between the intra-personal functions to be led and the Self as the ultimate commander needs to take place. As long as the entity of Self and awareness as its tool remain unaddressed, there will be no such distinction and all attempts for education on self-direction (including effective direction of emotional-mental events and reactions) will remain without profound results. This would also mean obliteration in locating fundamental methods for cure and prevention of emotional-mental problems or seriously tackling psychiatric illnesses that can also be looked upon as amplified consequences of misplaced identity and the resulting compensatory mechanisms. During his lecture in Los Angeles in 1942 Yogananda explained:

> If at this moment you could completely calm your body, your thoughts and your emotions, you would instantly become aware of your true Self, the soul that is a reflection of the omnipresent Spirit of God hidden inside of you. Every person is innately wonderful; he has only to rid himself of the mask of ego. You imprison yourself in various moods and this is the cause of all your sorrows.
>
> (2008b: 220–229)

The emotions

The term emotion is used as an umbrella concept that includes subjective affective feelings, desires and urges that are different from the mental data and somatic sensations. Emotional reactions are typically triggered by perceptions as primary data as well as by secondary data, usually in correspondence to analogy. As proposed by Jaak Panksepp, it could well be that one's ability to perceive the emotional pain of others is possible partly through mirror-neurons (2006), the emotion's neural correlates. As a practicing psychiatrist, the author has noticed that regardless of advances in neuroscience, people are still no closer to effectively directing their own emotions: having freedom to intentionally activate, sustain and discontinue an emotional activity. Rather, observation confirms that emotions tend to auto-activate in the presence of data, often able to override the wisdom of analytical power and obstructing insight, resulting in emotionally biased decisions and actions. The lack of command over these automatic reactions means that even if undesired, the emotion becomes activated regardless. In this regard people are often mis-emotional: they do not respond to situations in their environment with the most adequate emotional activation. It is a widespread false belief that this kind of auto-activation of emotions is an inevitable part of human nature. Relying on the previous paragraphs, the author claims that massive automation of emotional activity is due to the somewhat temporary absence of the regulatory role of the Self. At the same time, while the command remains in the hands of subconscious automation, the conscious Self cannot be realised and a sensation of being a victim to one's own internal reactions is gradually accepted.

Since many psychiatric disorders reflect dysregulation of the emotional system, the topic of emotion regulation becomes especially important. For example individuals with general anxiety disorder show deficits in emotion regulation (Tull *et al.*, 2009), such as a greater negative reactivity to, and poorer understanding of emotions (Mennin *et al.*, 2005). Until people are educated to exercise methods of conscious control over their emotional activation, it is only a matter of time when some of the destructive automatic emotional-mental complexes get triggered and initiate a cascade of problematic events, including irrational or destructive behaviour. The importance of emotional activation cannot be discarded simply because it is difficult to study the topic. As stated in previous paragraphs, all intra-personal events, including emotional activations, have their corresponding neural circuits in the brain. This aligns with the work conducted by Panksepp, stating that at present, the evidence is most consistent with the findings that our core emotional feelings (e.g. fear, anger, joy, various forms of distress) reflect activities of massive subcortical networks (2005). However, it has to be said that most widespread forms of emotion regulation such as suppression, ignoring and acting out are more like poor compensatory mechanisms and not means of regulation. Without the possibility to go deeper into this topic, the author wishes to emphasise that effective regulation must address the frequency of involuntary and automated activation rather than emotions themselves. Emotional independence would be gathered as being free to independently either engage into an automated training pattern or discontinue its development at any point according to conscious will.

The subconscious automatic complexes

Every person has experienced some intra-personal disturbances that do not seem to be linked to environmental causes and are out of proportion to any observable stimuli. Examples would be sudden sadness, anger, feeling of revenge etc. that occur seemingly out of the blue. Carl Jung proposed a theory on complexes back in 1910 and presented it titled as "A Review of the Complex theory" later in 1934 in Germany at the 7th Congress for Psychotherapy (Murray 1998: 41). In his theory Jung refers to a "feeling-toned complex" composed of a dual core "image" (a personal mental representation of the objective reality) and an emotion as the "glue" that knits the various associated elements together and holds them in place

(Murray 1998: 49). From the field of neuropsychopharmacology, Stephen Stahl in his *Essentials of Psychopharmacology* explains:

> A feeling of anxiety can be triggered not only by an external stimulus but also by an individual's memories. Traumatic memories stored in the hippocampus can activate the amygdala, in turn, to activate other brain regions and generate a fear response.
>
> (Stahl 2008: 731)

Since the activation of every emotion and thought activates corresponding neural networks, their automatic activation as complexes most likely causes configuration of neural networks, up- and down-regulating them according to the frequency of emotional-mental events. Panksepp proposes affective states to be the underlying psycho-neural substrate for many behavioural choices (1998), indicating the utmost importance to address the mechanisms of emotion activation and deactivation.

As a result of personal and professional observation, the author agrees that people react constantly to data presented in their daily lives with an activation of an automatic emotional-mental process, closely followed by a physical reaction, resulting in subsequent behaviour. This subconscious and automatic emotional-mental reaction will be called a complex. The dysfunctional automatic complex initiates behaviour over which the person has only limited or no control at all, although one may well remain informed about the dysfunctional nature of the actions. Therefore the author considers the automatic complex equal to a compulsion. Like a training pattern, complex has a command value, but goes into operation without adequate assessment of the situation or intentional will of Self.

The mechanisms of complex formation, auto-activation and discontinuation are alike for all people, but the contents of the complexes for each individual are different. Villido states that:

> The emotional, mental and physical systems work alongside each other. All of these three types of functions occur in parallel, during one and the same time. And all of these three are tied together by the subconscious and form complexes. The ego is an assembly, a unit of complexes. All of these complexes are learned, acquired from others. This is the life that people live (. . .). If you exist as your Self, you use nothing of that triad and it will remain on its own. You discover it in action, that it is your duplicate, speaking on behalf of you. It is an absolutely automated system at work, only without insight and awareness. These complexes are a substitute until Self is realized.
>
> (Villido 2011b)

According to Jung, complexes act as if they were instincts by producing an automatic reaction to situations or persons and function in humans as the equivalent of primitive instincts in other mammals. Complexes are human-constructed instincts (Murray 1998: 52). The emotional-mental reactions activated by complexes are automated and do not respond to reasoning, which explains the limited effect of current therapies that exclude awareness and Self. The automatic emotional-mental complexes are the autopilot, subconscious regime of humans, the opposite of a conscious choice. And although some of the automation can be very helpful in everyday life, they leave little room for free choice due to their compulsive nature. When allowed to dominate, they turn a human being into an automated being, sleepwalking through life.

While Jung saw automatic complexes mainly as possible contributors to psychiatric disorders, the frequency of automation allows proposing a more wide-spread role and scope. In fact complexes, if not consciously discontinued, are permanent and determine fate. At the time Jung concluded that a complex could never be completely eliminated, only thawed out or modified with an attempt to restructure the ego (Murray 1998: 53). To the knowledge of the author, no other scientists have pursued investigation about automatic complexes and methods of their discontinuation thereafter. However, in the light of more recent information, for example experimental clinical work conducted by the author as well as practical explorations of the intra-personal sphere by Villido, the author would like to put this conclusion under re-consideration. Villido suggests that:

> The current problems in humanity are caused by the emotional-mental, complex-driven human. (. . .) The complexes cannot be eliminated by the ego, because ego is part of the complex. Awareness introduces an effective tool to release these units – complexes that are ineffective and cause suffering.
>
> (Villido 2009)

To somewhat control people and their reactions, some triggers have been regulated by laws, rules, agreements, social norms, religion etc. Such emphasis on controlling the triggers is insufficient, since it encourages external solutions while discouraging personal responsibility along with the development and need for methods of Self-regulation. Also, as long as there is no emphasis and education about discontinuing the complexes, the frequency and involuntary eruption of emotions will not be resolved in any fundamentally different way. Progress in prevention and cure of psychiatric diseases will also remain questionable, since the automatic activation of disabling emotions is one of the core elements for most of them[8] alongside with the mental element.[9] Only when automatic complexes are discontinued, can the actual identity be re-established and Self is free to decide upon the internal reactions as well as direct all internal functions in an optimal way. The author has applied specific awareness-based methods for discontinuing her own automatic complexes for over 7 years and has during the past 3 years educated others on how to discontinue theirs. During the course of this period, it has been revolutionary to find that in most cases a large number of complexes can indeed be totally eliminated independently by people themselves. However, there is no space to provide details of these case studies, their methods and process in this short chapter, as it would require an article of comparable length.

On the importance of awareness for the emergence of new education

It can be said that all people are born with and possess awareness. Nevertheless, by observing people's values, most place more emphasis on the objects that they become aware of, instead of awareness itself. Children mimic the values that are expressed by the people surrounding them and gradually continue to use their awareness only to a minimal extent. When the author describes her own practical experience with awareness, then first it is an ability that one uses to become aware of any type of objects – visual, auditory, olfactory, taste-related or tactile, sensation-type. In this chapter feelings and thoughts are also considered as objects that one can become aware of. It is also possible not to observe any specific object at all and just remain aware of the vector of the awareness itself. When one becomes aware of the whereabouts of one's own awareness, a static state is discovered. Hereby the author first distinguishes consciousness in the dynamic form and calls this awareness. Secondly, when describing the static form of the same quality, this can be seen as a state and is then referred to as consciousness. Third, awareness can also be called a tool. Awareness becomes a tool when one discovers their own awareness and learns to apply it deliberately to differentiate between the internal objects and the Self, followed by intentional discontinuation of all emotional-mental identities that are not the Self. As a means of discovery and influence, awareness forms the basis for all intra-personal skills.

In regard to awareness it is crucial to differentiate it from thinking. The mental apparatus is fundamentally different from awareness, being responsible for storing data into memory and reproducing it from there in various forms. Evidence from stroke victims attests that the mental contents (thinking, remembering, naming, recognising) are actually more transient and fragile than awareness itself. It is possible to lose one's memory completely and still be able to notice and be aware (Panksepp 2005). We do not need thoughts to become aware, in fact empirical observation confirms that thoughts arise as descriptions and analogies milliseconds to seconds after becoming aware of the objects. Some simple examples: when a person steps outside and wind blows against the face, then first one becomes aware of the tactile sensation caused by the strong wind that may thereafter be commented by the mental apparatus as "what a strong wind today"; when entering a mall, one can become aware of the noise caused by people speaking and the music which may thereafter be commented as "what a terrible noise" with the possibility of evolving into a mental project, an essay on the topic of noise and calm. These realisations challenge the widespread social belief about thinking being the most important characteristic of a human, with many superficial interpretations of the quote by R. Descartes: "I think, therefore I am."

By 2014 awareness as a topic had been an object of research in more than a thousand various scientific studies, with over 500 of them conducted in 2013 alone (Thompson, Gauntlett-Gilbert, 2008). In the past 10 years this field of study has seen tremendous expansion. Thompson and Gauntlett-Gilbert's study in 2008 (Bögels et al. 2008) pointed out that well-trained awareness produces better control over impulses and decreases emotional reactivity in challenging situations. There are links between intentional awareness and the ability to notice (Bootzin, Stevens 2005) and better quality of sleep (Schonert-Reichl, Lawlor 2010). In a study by Schonert-Reichl and Lawlor (2010) it has been stated that deliberate awareness training can decrease stress and increase self-confidence, it also enhances relationships, attention, self-esteem and helps to create an optimistic attitude (Ritchhart, Perkins 2000). And as opposed to the scattered mind, better awareness supports creativity, psychological flexibility and ability to both memorise information and use it efficiently (Williams, Kuyken 2012). Mindfulness-based cognitive therapy (MBCT) reduces the risk for relapse in depression for patients with a history of at least three episodes by 50 per cent (NICE 2016). MBCT for depressive relapse prevention is more effective than standard care and according to the National Institute for Health and Care Excellence (NICE) clinical guidelines should be offered for people who are currently well but have experienced three or more previous episodes of depression (Black 2014). If just becoming aware of objects, a cornerstone of mindfulness practice, produces these initial results, we can only speculate what the effect of gaining full use of our awareness would be. Even more – what would be the effect of restoring the right identity, the Self, with practical confidence to consciously direct all the intra-personal functions? Since all people possess awareness, there also lies a huge dormant potential to use it intentionally and more often to progress towards the true identity and also find solutions to the most pressing problems in psychiatry, ecology and society in general.

Conclusion and future perspectives

The physical and intra-personal are two relatively independent parallel systems with tangled interaction patterns. Nevertheless, the majority of people's everyday problems stem from the intra-personal sphere and cause disturbances intra- and inter-personally to a greater or smaller degree. It can indeed be estimated that everyone, without a structured education on intra-personal processes, is at risk for developing a psychiatric disorder. As elaborated in *The Essentials of Psychopharmacology* by S. Stahl, the hypothesis is that mental illnesses are not caused by a single gene nor by a single subtle genetic abnormality but by multiple small contributions from several genes, all interacting with environmental stressors (Stahl 2008: 180). Something else has to occur from the environment to make the inheritance of silent risk manifest as illness. That "something else" is often known as "stress" (Stahl 2008: 185). As has been explored in the chapter, the environment does not affect the brain directly; it uses a bridge – the intra-personal events. We should consider the three main intra-personal functions as a connection point, a gateway between the environment and the brain. As long as psychology and psychiatry exclude awareness and Self from the scheme of understanding human functioning and nature, all aspirations to understand the totality of human functioning will remain incomplete. In a society where we move towards a more holistic worldview, prevention-oriented and personalised intervention, Panksepp and

Harro estimate that future mind medicines may be quite specific to more discrete emotional traits, and may work optimally in the context of therapeutic environments that enhance emotional education (Panksepp, Harro 2004).

In order to discover new ways to do things, also a new route and new methods of investigation have to be applied. When looking for answers, we should not be so dependent on outward circumstances or solutions. To give them too great an importance increases their power over us and creates a bias in our focus towards the external. There is no need to fight stigma, instead to comprehend that intra-personal wellness is a vast arena that has to do with the quality of life and is not reserved only to mental illnesses. This chapter has argued that health and sustainability of an individual and the collective depends almost entirely upon personal awareness to provide an ability to perceive the internal as well as physical environment around us in a realistic manner. Also, to change and adjust the environment, so that one can thrive without jeopardising the ability of future generations to do the same. It is suggested that an approach based on a structured understanding of the intra-personal sphere and includes the Self may shed some much-needed light on proactive strategies in achieving and improving total wellbeing. It is evident that people need effective education to direct their emotions; thoughts and other mental functions; attention, ability to investigate, differentiate and awareness itself along with returning the gaze towards the Self – the true identity always there, yet unnoticed. Hereby the author poses a hypothesis that by empirically exploring intra-personal functions and events, improving intra-personal skills for self-direction, a more sustainable way of handling and preventing problems can emerge, increasing personal and communal resilience. Proactive interventions to increase the quality of life as well as prevention in psychiatry can be furthered through education. This new education will emphasise conscious focus on the individual as a starting point for transformation towards sustainable lifestyles and society. To change one's internal functioning is the most positive step one can take to contribute towards increase for personal and world harmony.

Notes

1   Data can be classified as primary and secondary. Primary data is perceived directly through awareness via five perceptual organs: visual, auditory, tactile, taste and smell. Secondary data is derived from memory and includes: emotion, thought-memory-imagination, visual, auditory, tactile, taste and smell.
2   One of the current dominant hypotheses that depression and anxiety are caused due to imbalance of neurotransmitters in the brain, mainly of monoamines such as serotonin, norepinephrine and dopamine.
3   The factor(s) causing an illness.
4   A general assumption prevalent in society and science that if the body is fully intact and its organs function without hindrance, then there is no basis for complaint. As a result the focus in investigation and solutions has been body-centric with minimal interest on the intra-personal. It is well reflected through the development of medical faculties, where there are hundreds of body-focused specialties and just one psychiatry, whereas in some communities psychiatrists are still not considered as "proper" doctors regardless of receiving the same medical training during pre-residency as the somatic doctors do.

5   A syndrome is a set of medical signs or symptoms that correlate and usually appear together. A depressive disorder is a clinical syndrome.

6   Mental-emotional definition of "I" that is expressed in ordinary daily life as a conglomerate that leads our behaviour and decisions via automatic emotional-mental reactions, substituting the leading role of the Self.

7   Self's ability to become aware of the automatic reactions as well as consciously initiated intra-personal events and the consequent capability to direct them.

8   Sadness, apathy, worthlessness and other in the case of depression; anxiety and insecurity for anxiety disorders; strong emotional cravings that alter with intense worthlessness and sadness for addictions; horror, agony and helplessness in post-traumatic stress disorder.

9   Thoughts of not being needed, frequent involuntary memories of sad events etc. for depression; different topics of worry, doubt and loss of control for anxiety. The content varies somewhat for each disorder, however the involuntary aspect remains.

References

Bargh, J. A., Morsella, E. (2008): The unconscious mind. *Perspectives on Psychological Science*, 3(1): 73–79.

Bargh, J. A., Morsella, E. (2009): Unconscious behavioral guidance systems. In C. Agnew, D. Carlston, W. Graziano, & J. Kelly (Eds), *Then a miracle occurs: Focusing on behavior in social psychological theory and research*. New York: Oxford University Press.

Black, D. S. (2014): Mindfulness-based interventions: An antidote to suffering in the context of substance use, misuse, and addiction. *Substance Use & Misuse*, 49(5): 487–491.

Bögels, S., Hoogstad, B., Lieke, D., Schutter, S., Restifo, K. (2008): Mindfulness training for adolescents with externalizing disorders and their parents. *Behavioural and Cognitive Psychotherapy*, 36(2): 193–209.

Bootzin, R.R., Stevens, S.J. (2005): Adolescents, substance abuse, and the treatment of insomnia and daytime sleepiness. *Clinical Psychology Review*, 25(5): 629–644.

Borsboom, D., Cramer, A. (2013): Network analysis: An integrative approach to the structure of psychopathology. *Annual Review of Clinical Psychology*, (9): 91–121.

Boyke, J., Driemeyer, J., Gaser, C., Büchel, C., May, A. (2008): Training-induced brain structure changes in the elderly. *Journal of Neuroscience*, 28(28): 7031–7035.

Draganski, B., Gaser, C., Busch, V., Schuirer, G., Bogdahn, U., May, A. (2004): Neuroplasticity: Changes in grey matter induced by training – newly honed juggling skills show up as a transient feature on a brain-imaging scan, *Nature* 427: 311–312.

Greenberg, P. E., Fournier, A. A., Sisitsky, T., Pike, C. T., Kessler, R. C. (2015): The economic burden of adults with major depressive disorder in the United States (2005 and 2010). *Journal of Clinical Psychiatry*, 76(2): 155–162.

Howes, O. D., Kapur, S. (2009): The dopamine hypothesis of schizophrenia: Version III – The Final Common Pathway. *Schizophrenia Bulletin*,35(3): 549–562.

Kendler, K. S., Zachar, P., Craver, C. (2011): What kinds of things are psychiatric disorders? *Psychological Medicine*, 41(6): 1143–1150.

Kosslyn, S. M., Ganis, G., Thompson, W. L. (2007): Mental imagery and the human brain. *Progress in Psychological Science Around the World*, 1, Neural, Cognitive and Developmental Issues: 195–209.

Lotze, M., Montoya, P., Erb, M., Hülsmann, E., Flor, H., Klose, U., Birbaumer, N., Grodd, W. (1999): Activation of cortical and cerebellar motor areas during executed and imagined hand movements: An fMRI study. *Journal of Cognitive Neuroscience*, 11(5): 491–501.

Maguire, E. A., Gadian, D. G., Johnsrude, I. S., Good, C. D., Ashburner, J., Frackowiak, R. S., Frith, C. D. (2000): Navigation-related structural change in the hippocampi of taxi drivers. *Proceeding of the National Academy of Science U.S.A*, 97(8): 4398–4403.

Matrix Study (2013): Economic analysis of workplace mental health promotion and mental disorder prevention programmes and of their potential contribution to EU health, social and economic policy objectives. (http://ec.europa.eu/health//sites/health/files/mental_health/docs/matrix_economic_analysis_mh_promotion_en.pdf, accessed 15 September 2017).

Mennin D. S., Heimberg, R. G., Turk, C. L., Fresco, D. M. (2005): Preliminary evidence for an emotion dysregulation model of generalized anxiety disorder. *Behaviour Research and Therapy*, 43(10): 1281–1310.

Munzert, J., Lorey, B., Zentgraf, K. (2009): Cognitive motor processes: The role of motor imagery in the study of motor representations. *Brain Research Reviews*, 60(2): 306–326.

Murray, S. (1998): *Jung's Map of the Soul*, Peru, IL: Open Court Publishing.

National Institute for Health and Care Excellence (NICE): Clinical guideline [CG90]. Published date: October 2009, last updated: April 2016. (www.nice.org.uk/guidance/cg90/chapter/key-priorities-for-implementation, accessed 15 September 2017).

Panksepp, J. (1998): *Affective neuroscience, the foundations of human and animal emotions.* London: Oxford University Press.

Panksepp, J. (2005): Affective consciousness: Core emotional feelings in animals and humans, *Consciousness and Cognition*, 14(1): 30–80.

Panksepp, J. (2006): Emotional endophenotypes in evolutionary psychiatry. *Progress in Neuro-Psychopharmacology & Biological Psychiatry*, 30(5): 774–784.

Panksepp, J., Harro, J. (2004): The future of neuropeptides in biological psychiatry and emotional psychopharmacology, Goals and strategies. In J. Panksepp (Ed.), *Textbook of biological psychiatry* (pp. 627–659). Hoboken, NJ: Wiley.

Pascual-Leone, A., Amedi, A., Fregni, F., Merabet, L. B. (2005): The plastic human brain cortex. *Annual Review of Neuroscience*, 28: 377–401.

Ritchhart, R., Perkins, D. N. (2000): Life in the mindful classroom: Nurturing the disposition of mindfulness. *Journal of Social Issues*, 56(1): 27–47.

Schonert-Reichl, K. A., Lawlor, M. S. (2010): The effects of a mindfulness-based education program on pre- and early adolescent's well-being and social and emotional competence. *Mindfulness*, 1(3): 137–151.

Stahl, S. (2008): *Essentials of Psychopharmacology, third ed.* Cambridge: Cambridge University Press.

Thompson, M., Gauntlett-Gilbert, J. (2008): Mindfulness with children and adolescents: Effective clinical application. *Clinical Child Psychology and Psychiatry*, 13(3): 395–407.

Tull M. T., Stipelman, B. A., Salters-Pedneault, K., Gratz, K. L. (2009): An examination of recent non-clinical panic attacks, panic disorder, anxiety sensitivity, and emotion regulation difficulties in the prediction of generalized anxiety disorder in an analogue sample. *Journal of Anxiety Disorders*, 23(2): 275–282.

Villido, I. (2005): Recorded lecture in Estonian, 7 June 2005. Tallinn: Lilleoru MTÜ.

Villido, I. (2008): Recorded lecture in Estonian, 7 December 2008. Tallinn: Lilleoru MTÜ.

Villido, I. (2009): Recorded lecture in Estonian, 15 December 2009. Tallinn: Lilleoru MTÜ.

Villido, I. (2011a): Recorded lecture in Estonian, 25 January 2011. Tallinn: Lilleoru MTÜ.

Villido, I. (2011b): Recorded lecture in Estonian, 25 November 2011. Tallinn: Lilleoru MTÜ.

Williams, J. M. G., Kuyken, W. (2012): Mindfulness-based cognitive therapy: A promising new approach to preventing depressive relapse. *British Journal of Psychiatry* 200(5): 359–360.

Wittenborn, A. K., Rahmandad, H., Rick, J., Hosseinichimeh, N. (2015): Depression as a systemic syndrome: Mapping the feedback loops of major depressive disorder. *Psychological Medicine*, 46(3): 551–562.

Yogananda, P. (2008a [1941]): Recorded lecture in Encinitas, California, 16 February 1941. Lecture reprinted in *Man's Eternal Quest*. Kolkata, India: Yogoda Satsanga Society of India.

Yogananda, P. (2008b [1942]): Recorded lecture in Los Angeles, California, 22 March 1942. Lecture reprinted in *The Divine Romance*. Kolkata, India: Yogoda Satsanga Society of India.

8 Inner conflict resolution and self-empowerment as contribution for personal sustainability on the case of intentional community practices

Stella Veciana and Kariin Ottmar

Introduction

Only quite recently transitions research has started to examine the potential of innovative social practices developed by intentional communities and ecovillages[1] for catalysing sustainability transitions. In particular there is an emerging interest in the research field of personal sustainability aiming to understand personal preconditions and motivations to choose such sustainable lifestyles. This line of research also focuses on possible ways of evaluating the reciprocal influence between individual behaviour and wider socio-cultural transitions.

This chapter aims to address the influence of personal sustainability on transition pathways in conceptual, methodological and empirical terms. It explores how three selected community-design practices foster personal sustainability competences of community members, especially for inner conflict resolution and self-empowerment. Furthermore, the community-led approach to personal sustainability is explored regarding its actual and potential interactions with wide-scale systems transformation. This perspective seeks to broaden the established notion of sustainable development by including "alternative developments/alternatives to development" (Gudynas 2011). In a provisional classification Eduardo Gudynas lists for instance conviviality, deep ecology, economies of care, interculturalism and buen vivir as "alternatives to progress and modernity" (Gudynas 2011: 47).

In our research this view on systems transformation is related to "alternative sustainable development" approaches used by diverse members of the Global Ecovillage Network (GEN).[2] Through sharing best practices, innovative solutions and honouring the deep-rooted traditional knowledge and local cultures, GEN seeks to build bridges between policy-makers, academics, entrepreneurs and sustainable community networks across the globe in order to develop strategies for a global transition to resilient communities and cultures. The network encompasses intentional and traditional communities all over the world, while each community designs and implements its own local pathway towards a sustainable and solidary future (GEN 2015: 2). In this way GEN demonstrates a meaningful conceptual and hands-on shift regarding the historical notion of the so-called developed and undeveloped world perpetuating the global divide of former colonial powers and ex-colonies after World War Two. GENs "lived sustainability" can be related to the "multi-level perspective" (Geels 2002 and 2011, Maassen 2012, Steinhilber *et al.* 2013), approach in the way it revises the self-perpetuating socio-technical regimes and their ideas about a successful life.

Besides nurturing alternative niche-initiatives for a fulfilled life, the ecovillage movement aims to transfer their socio-ecological innovations from the margins to mainstream following a common goal of integrating the social, economic, ecological and cultural dimensions of sustainability transitions. GENs common alternative vision of development embraces North-South Partnerships with regional networks in all continents aiming for mutual learning and taking responsibility for socio-ecological justice on a global scale (Veciana, Neubauer 2016: 41). It is precisely in this inclusive way that GEN embraces personal sustainability along with alternative perspectives to sustainable development.

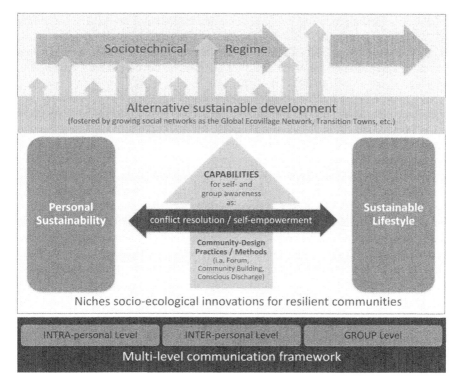

Figure 8.1 Personal sustainability and alternative sustainable development on the case of community-design practices/methods.

Elaborated by Veciana upon Geels Multi-level perspective (2002: 1263)

Within this alternative notion of sustainable development, embedded in the everyday life of communities, personal sustainability is understood as a lifelong learning process (GEESE 2009). In the following section particular barriers and drivers of personal sustainability are examined on three distinctive levels.

Personal sustainability barriers and drivers at the intra-personal, the inter-personal and the group level

Our Common Future from the personal sustainability perspective

The most quoted definition of sustainable development published by the United Nations World Commission on Environment and Development in *Our Common Future* (WCED 1987) also known as "Brundtland Report" emphasizes particularly the needs of the present and future generations. The needs of the present should not compromise the ability of future generations to meet their own needs, particularly the basic needs of the poor for food, clothing, shelter, jobs and their legitimate aspirations for an improved quality of life (WCED 1987: 37). In this chapter we part from Gudynas' alternative view on this established notion of sustainable development by going beyond material needs and the understanding of quality of life based on a raw material-, energy- and pollution-intensive industrial production. Such alternatives to unsustainable lifestyles, as suggested in this chapter, do not mean the same for all and change continuously according to actual needs (Veciana 2017).

Our hypothesis is that personal sustainability is an essential condition for and simultaneously a key part of "alternative sustainable developments". We will build on intra-personal, inter-personal and group-level communication framework to study specific barriers and drivers of personal sustainability. Rather than asking how individuals in the real world are to be persuaded to act in the common interest as in the Brundtland Report (WCED 1987: 38), our inquiry searches for the preconditions for voluntary individual and collective sustainable behaviour. By theoretically integrating personal sustainability into the "alternative sustainable development" framework, we explore the key capabilities (Rauschmayer *et al.* 2011) of community-design practices for fulfilling real world sustainable lifestyles, examining specifically the relevance of conflict resolution and self-empowerment skills. Further effort will be given to scrutinizing certain perceivable crossroads of personal sustainability and "alternative sustainable development".

Three levels of personal sustainability through self-empowerment and inner conflict resolution processes

In order to examine personal sustainability in intentional communities adequately we have developed the following three levels perspective: the intra-personal (I), the inter-personal (I-You) and the group level (Me-We). The *intra-personal level* here refers to the intra-personal communication theory as applied to inter-personal competence and performance (Vocate 1994) and intra-personal communication relates to an internal process of communicating to the self as e.g. "self-talk" or "self-writing" for analysing situations or reflecting upon phenomena. At the *inter-personal level* we give particular attention to the inter-personal communication theory (Knapp/Daly 2011, Vangelisti 1994) contemplating verbal and non-verbal communication and focusing on conflict and conflict resolution. The *group level* relates to the group communication theory (Frey *et al.* 1999) concentrating particularly on communication processes and facilitation for conflict resolution.

The intra-personal level can be a crucial barrier to personal sustainability (Lauer 2015). This dimension shows up as strong psychological inner confrontation between our habituated social backgrounds versus the awareness of who we truly are and what we genuinely want. Community life commonly encourages this search for authenticity activating a process of personal sustainability. Through practices of self-empowerment an individual may cultivate more courage for facing patterns of social adaptation, interiorized norms and role expectations passed on by parents, teachers, supervisors and society. Individuals following their own value system commonly develop more self-confidence, and as a result free themselves from undesired situations like unsatisfying professional activities to pursue more fulfilling activities that serve the community.

Similarly to the intra-personal level, personal sustainability at the *inter-personal level* is also related to inner barriers e.g. on interiorized rules of conduct inhibiting following one's own authenticity. Individuals involved in any conflict are invited not to conceive the other as an exterior opponent, but to face their own limitations – for instance by transgressing interiorized role expectations. The personal sustainability process through self-empowerment and inner conflict resolution means at this level coming in authentic contact with yourself and the other. By making hidden conflicts visible inequitable structures of formal and informal hierarchy can be changed. This is particularly significant in intentional communities, where rules are usually more informal than formal.

At the *group level* personal sustainability refers to individuals being confronted to the remains of education and law systems within themselves that often create feelings of powerlessness. These feelings of lack of influence are a result of the pressure to follow strict authorities and prescribed rules. Through inner transformation, personal sustainability appears as an expression of individual authenticity in group processes regarding any social, ecological, economical or cultural matters to be addressed by the community. While the community learns listening to individual authenticity, individuals evolve their own inner process of personal sustainability, for example by self-empowerment strengthening their involvement in community processes. Following the own individual authenticity within a "group culture" or a dominant group opinion requires courage from the individual. Self-empowerment and conflict resolution processes at the group level are very complex and often bring up resistance and fears as they question our habitual patterns of behaviour. Nevertheless, the creative engagement of self-empowered individuals will transform and shape the whole group process, and may foster more mature group decisions by focusing on achieving the "best solution for the whole". Personal sustainability for the benefit of the whole can be enacted through shown leadership and creative power, but also remaining silent and "holding" the group process by creating an atmosphere for mutual listening and learning enabling a respectful and non-violent attitude. Thus personal sustainability requires a lot of experience in self-reflexivity within the group process.

In view of the above, addressing inner personal sustainability is considered the key driver for outer sustainability transitions. In the following section three case studies of community-design practices fostering personal sustainability and "alternative sustainable development" are discussed on the previously introduced distinctive levels. What kinds of community-design methods are used by ecovillagers to support self-organized structures and personal sustainability in their daily life? In which way do they configure adequate preconditions and indispensable capabilities for sustainable behaviour and a balanced use of personal resources?

Community-design practices for personal sustainability and "alternative sustainable development"

Over the last decades different types of community-design practices have emerged within the ecovillage movement. Kosha Joubert, executive director of GEN, has described them as maps, which practicality depends on the specific situation and on what is actually needed by the members of a community. She emphasizes the relevance of collective improvising for transformation: "The capacity to improvise collectively makes it possible to create something new beyond the habitual and out-dated ways of thinking and feeling" (Joubert 2010: 114). In this way, communities have become fruitful environments for different types of self-empowerment and conflict resolution practices that make a significant contribution to personal sustainability.

We have divided the community-design practices fostering among other things self-empowerment and conflict resolution into the following distinctive types:

1   *Self- and group-awareness* to gain self-empowerment and to create a deep bond between community members by giving support to overcome personal and group barriers e.g. "Forum" (Richter 2006), "Community Building" (Peck 2015) or "Conscious Discharge" (Dittmar 2014).
2   *Self-governance and decision-making processes* where community members have already developed in a shared process a high level of self-empowerment and have developed a rewarding community-owned decision-making process e.g. "Sociocracy" (Endenburg 1998), "Holacracy" (Robertson 2007) or a coordinated "Councils Circle-system" as in Sieben Linden ecovillage.[3]
3   *Capacity building for self-governance* practices help to manifest the creative power of (re)inventing and forming a community or parts of it e.g. the "Ecovillage Design Education" (EDE) developed by the Gaia Trust (GEESE 2012), the project management tool "Dragon Dreaming" created by John Croft (Croft *et al.* n.d.), or the consulting tool for business and communities called "Community Learning Incubator for Sustainability" (CLIPS)[4] generated by ERASMUS+ Learning partnership by GEN Europe.

In this chapter our research on personal sustainability focuses particularly on practices of the first type. The following discussion of specific methods is based on case studies, qualitative interviews and personal experience of the authors. In the following sections the practices are discussed by introducing the method, identifying competence advance for personal sustainability, as well as the observed socio-political-cultural impact on intentional communities. Furthermore, the potential socio-political and cultural impact on broader society, as well as awareness raising for "alternative sustainable development" are discussed. The analysis of individual cases will be followed by a comparative analysis of the community-design practices grounded on the previously identified key capabilities for personal sustainability discussing their limits and possibilities.

Case 1: Forum

In the early 1980s the Forum method evolved out of the *self-representation method* practiced regularly at the Bauhütte, a forerunner project for the Centre for Experimental Cultural Design[5] (Zentrum für experimentelle Gesellschaftsgestaltung, in short ZEGG). In the first decades Forum practice focused on performing and very expressively acting out deep emotional and inner processes. Since then the ZEGG community has developed the method further as a framework for investigating human nature through transparent communication. Nowadays Forum is used as a community-encouraging instrument: "The aim is to reveal whatever is authentic, alive and true, and to share the inner motivation behind actions" (Meyer-Stoll, Ecker 2013).

During a Forum session participants sit in a circle creating a centre or "existential stage" for a presenter willing to explore upcoming thoughts, feelings, concerns etc. While the presenter has space to speak and act, the circle supports them through their presence and active listening. One or two trained facilitators guide and serve the presenter in finding ways to express creatively whatever arises in words, gestures and/or non-verbal actions. The role of facilitators is crucial in the way they create and maintain a safe environment that helps the presenter to go beyond personal barriers, to deepen into hidden personal 'shadows', and to explore different approaches for dealing e.g. with inner conflicts. Once finished, the witnesses may mirror their feedback to the presenter in an appreciative, honest and non-judging way.

In this way, Forum reveals "the blind spots in a person's awareness and harbors the treasures that lie in our shadow" creating "a space of trust and openness" (Meyer-Stoll, Ecker 2013). As a result of this space of trust, participants risk to step beyond their usual roles in the community and to share what really moves them deeply, uncovering actual or previous experiences of rank, power and privilege.

Capabilities for personal sustainability

Practicing Forum supports sustainable lifestyles by fostering competences and inner resources for personal sustainability such as self-reflexivity, unprejudiced listening,

Figure 8.2 Forum situation in Sieben Linden ecovillage, 2015.
Photographer: Satoshi Hirsch

appreciative feedback, creativity, trust, transparency, peacefulness, self-responsibility and self-empowerment. As Forum facilitator and trainer Ina Meyer-Stoll points out: "The community sees itself as a living experiment for the establishment of new and deeply sustainable ways of living" (Meyer-Stoll 2013: 9).

At an intra-personal level presenters experience the permission to be who they are, regaining creative power and intrinsic motivation as well as feeling self-empowerment and trust. On an inter-personal level the facilitator's guidance and the witnesses' appreciative mirroring support raising self-awareness, self-reflexivity and self-responsibility. The Forum facilitator and trainer Dolores Richter assumes that the lack of appreciative feedback culture in our society is an important reason for the burnout syndrome as an expression of a non-sustainable lifestyle at personal level (Richter 2017). Learning unprejudiced listening and appreciative feedback enables changing perspectives and making blind spots visible. Moreover, creativity and feeling of self-empowerment arise as honest feedback "sets free a lot of energy normally bonded being busy with thoughts about what others think about myself or with doubts if I am good enough and other energy killers occupying our head" (*ibid.*). By way of such transparent communication, mutual support, deep feelings of connectivity, peacefulness and trust can appear within the group becoming a healing source of energy (*ibid.*) for nurturing personal sustainability and sustainable lifestyle practices/aspirations. In sum, Forum enables experiencing relevant capacities for personal sustainability at intra-, inter-personal and group levels by fostering the development of transparent communication, appreciative feedback and self-empowerment skills.

Socio-political and cultural impact on ZEGG community

While in the founding years of the ZEGG community Forum was performed on a daily basis, in the past decade there were also few periods where the community did almost not practice Forum anymore. Presently Forum is commonly used by ZEGG and other intentional communities taking place in different styles and settings: large Forums, held periodically where the entire community attends, and smaller Forums held by subgroups such as working circles, thematic groups, the youth etc. (Richter 2007: 133). Community members/practitioners have argued that practicing Forum on a regularly basis has a vital impact on the everyday community life by helping "to maintain a clear distinction between factual discussion and emotional processes" but also for developing "self-knowledge and trust within the community" (Meyer-Stoll, Ecker 2013).

On a group level Forums can ease the decision-making processes when meetings start by making feelings and conflicts visible. In this way the decision-making process can go ahead without being sabotaged e.g. by a conscious hidden agenda or by unconscious processes.

On an inter-personal level, conflicts are reduced or disappear as people learn to be more in contact with themselves, to face and take self-responsibility for their blind spots and to stop blaming others, and becoming more self-aware and compassionate in the process. Additionally Forum has contributed to a non-violent conflict culture at the ZEGG community and further communities practicing Forum regularly. As Richter pointed out:

> To transform the culture of domination we must make friends with all that is inside of us: our feelings, our loneliness, our deep wish for intimacy. Violence happens when we feel disconnected from others, nature, ourselves; non-violence can happen when we allow real contact to take place.
>
> (Richter 2007: 130)

Furthermore, Forum is a tool for transparent communication where community members get the same information at the same time, while primordially essential themes are shared. This alleviates the community significantly as it prevents problems resulting from lack of information or non-transparency as well as non-authentic or superficial communication (Richter 2017). Essentially, "Forum is part of the glue that keeps our community alive and together, it lies at the heart of the community" (Meyer-Stoll, Ecker 2013).

Potential socio-political and cultural impact on broader society

Forum is not only practiced by ZEGG and other intentional communities, but offered as part of the regular ZEGG adult education programme open to everyone

with up to 285 seminar participants of the regular ZEGG adult education programme a year and 20–30 participants in a Forum session. The aim is to transfer
their knowledge, to broader the group of multipliers and other institutions to initiate
and support the development of a culture of personal and organizational sustainability in different fields of action. Besides education, Forum is used for
community consultancy to aid new communities or communities in crisis.

Through training, Forum has spread to intentional communities and other self-
committed groups all over the world: "Forum is designed to work with people
who are living together, sharing a common vision and who are committed to
certain values such as self-responsibility, compassion, solidarity and truth" (Richter
2006: 1). As Forum requires a group of committed members with a common vision
and value system to create a safe space for deep sharing, this practice is not trans-
ferable to any context, but is particularly effective for laying seeds for lived
sustainability.

Forum can also have a significant political impact for wider society by
preventing from falling for political demagogy: "A group in which each member
works on their own uncertainty is definitely not disposed to follow demagogic
tendencies" (Richter 2017). In this regard the main political task of Forum may
consist in personal sustainability-work by creating settings that make conflicts
transparent and graspable by a deeper and more authentic communication practice.
In this sense Forum can develop safe communication spaces where personal
sustainability conflicts but also broader sustainability dilemmas can be addressed
in a transparent and non-violent manner.

Case 2: Community Building and We-Process

The use of the We-Process based on the Community Building method was
explored during several stays in Schloss Tempelhof intentional community for
this study. The Community Building process was described and developed into
an experiential workshop format by Scott Peck in early 1980s (Peck 2015). These
workshops teach how to communicate authentically at a deep emotional level,
allowing participants to experience how it feels like being in community with
themselves and the group. Two facilitators usually introduce Community Building
presenting some simple guidelines for conduct and almost not intervening after
participants begin to speak. These communication guidelines intend to hold the
freedom of an unstructured communication space and try to maintain the feeling
of confidence and to hold a safe space without judgment. For the next 2 or 3 days,
the group works through the four phases of the Community Building process:

- the *pseudo-community* stage – socially conventional behaviour using "good
  manners" and avoiding differences to build safety which becomes boring after
  some time;
- the *chaos* stage – participants explore their differences, intent to change/heal
  others, or project their prejudices, opinions and judgments on others until
  finding their own internal chaos;

- the *emptiness* stage – letting go of conventions and projections that keep them from being in community with themselves, acceptance of who they are, who the other is, and feeling gratitude for this;
- the *authentic community* stage – participants accept and even honour differences, act through collective knowledge, feel peaceful, have an experience of oneness and love.

As each participant may be at a different point of seeking community, these phases do not necessarily occur in a linear sequence, until sufficient participants archive to move into community or any other phase. After the workshop, participants are enabled and expected to go on practicing Community Building without facilitation in their own ongoing groups by taking responsibility for themselves and the Community Building process.

Capabilities for personal sustainability

Attending the workshop is the first step in developing competences such as unprejudiced listening, self-reflexiveness, authentic communication, open-heartedness, peacefulness, responsibility, self-empowerment and leadership.

One of the main aspects of Community Building is what Peck calls "the group of all leaders" and describes as a safe place, where "compulsive leaders feel free in community – often for the first time in their lives – to not to lead. And the customarily shy and reserved feel free to step forth with their latent gifts of leadership" (Peck 2015: 72). The initial "group of followers" of social norms and conventions becomes a self-empowered group of all leaders remarkably capable of tackling inner and outer sustainability conflicts and challenges. This happens through learning authentic communication by sincere listening to oneself and others. By this self-listening "I discover my own perception patterns that precondition my worldview systematically, not in theoretical terms but as interiorized knowledge which I consider evidently sustainable," a participant commented (Stiefel 2017). Likewise, participants practice following their genuine inner impulses instead of reacting precipitately to the actions of others. Developing such capabilities leads to well-ordered group-discussions without interruptions, and enables Community Building practitioners to perceive and address underlying group-tensions as they happen (*ibid.*).

Another result of practicing the Community Building method is the development of open-heartedness capable of changing attitudes and behaviours. Marie Luise Stiefel brings as an example the community dispute caused by her transatlantic flight, resulting in the introduction of a carbon offset fund:

> What I learned through Community Building is to allow to let into my heart what moves other hearts. First I felt resistance against what I perceived as a moral imposition. But realizing their hearts desire to compensate CO2-emissions, my heart opened and I became much more conscious about flight emissions.

> (Stiefel 2017)

In this way, authentic communication following one's own truth and taking self-responsibility encourages conflict resolution and self-empowerment in everyday life.

Following the Community Building Guidelines of taking responsibility for the own involvement and for the outcomes of the Community Building Process, leads the participants to stop blaming the others, explore their inner barriers and enact leadership. Concurrently, the desire for control disappears. Stiefel adds: "If I do not empower myself, nothing happens. Now I do not look for the obstacles outside anymore, but search inside for my part of responsibility" (*ibid.*). The ideas are shared without the need to interfere or manipulate anyone with arguments, but being aware of how a proposal resonates in the group: "I consider this as the basis for collective intelligence and a relevant competence gain for our community's way to do personal sustainability work" (*ibid.*). In sum, the Community Building process can be experienced at intra-, inter-personal and group levels as a method for conflict resolution, healing and self-empowerment.

Socio-political and cultural impact on the Schloss Tempelhof community

In the particular case of the Schloss Tempelhof (Tempelhof castle),[6] the initiators of the community referred to the We-Process method as the key precondition for its establishment. Members who joined the community later expressed their perception of an invisible bond between the initiators of the project, which made them very attracted to getting introduced into the Community Building framework. From the beginning the community developed Pecks' Community Building method further into a moderately different process called the "We-Process"[7] (Wir-Prozess). The whole community practices the We-Process during regular internal "intensive meetings" (Intensiv-Zeiten). Some Tempelhof community members describe it as an indispensable complementary approach to individual processes of personality development "in which I do not have to protect me, but I can trust completely" (Ratering 2015). It is also referred to as a complementary format to other regular community meetings for solving everyday problems: "After a We-process you can love everyone again. There remains a closeness that transforms ordinary life and allows to solve everyday problems in a much more effective way, mainly because there are less hidden personal barriers" (*ibid.*).

Potential socio-political and cultural impact on the broader society

By offering the We-Process in the regular adult education programmes and as a company's consultancy service, Tempelhof and other communities that have adopted the method aim to transfer their knowledge to multipliers to initiate and foster the culture of personal and organizational sustainability in their respective fields of action.

In terms of Peck, Community Building may evolve into a "laboratory for personal disarmament":

> where the gladiators have laid down their weapons and their armor, where they have become skilled at listening and understanding, where they respect each other's gifts and accept each other's limitations, where they celebrate their differences and bind each other's wounds, where they are committed to a struggling together rather than against each other. It is a most unusual battleground indeed. But that is also why it is an unusually effective ground for conflict resolution.
>
> (Peck 2015: 71)

In this laboratory personal sustainability conflicts, but also dilemmas related to the broader sustainable development challenges can be addressed. Particularly in the third and fourth stages of the Community Building Processes, practitioners may overcome the common feelings of separateness in modern life. Instead, a deep sense of connectedness to oneself, the others, nature and the world emerges becoming an ideal precondition for practicing both sustainable development and "alternative sustainable development".

Case 3: Conscious Discharge

Vivian Dittmar introduced the Conscious Discharge practice in Sieben Linden ecovillage[8] in 2016 combining her training in "present healing" with her research on feelings and emotions, particularly the focus on discharge of the co-counseling (Harvey 1970) movement. Conscious Discharge works with the basic assumption grounded on Dittmar's observation that emotional baggage is increasingly accumulated over lifetime (Dittmar 2017). She argues that this is due to the fear of not being able to cope with feelings and holding them back for posterior processing. Nevertheless controlling feelings can be adequate, and the problem appears when not having learned to consciously discharge the previously contained feelings sometime later (*ibid.*).

Practicing Conscious Discharge raises the ability to sense unconscious emotions and prevents emotions from being discharged on somebody thus creating rejection, confusion and pain. Instead of continuing such a hurtful habit, emotions are discharged in a designated space where the "space holder" actively listens to the "speaker". Thereby the speaker may deepen in present feelings and become aware of unconscious emotions without being overwhelmed by them. The speakers do not want to get rid of feelings – on the contrary, they speak from the emotions, not about them. Learning to "give feelings a voice" in such a way may take some time for dealing with the situation of not getting any response e.g. (dis)approval from the space holder (Dittmar 2017). Once learned, the process of discharge may happen on itself in a very short time frame. The Conscious Discharge setting is agreed beforehand ranging from 5 to 15 minutes and it also requires an agreement on confidentiality. The space holder commits not to speak about what was shared with neither the speaker nor the others. The discharge becomes meaningful if the experience attached to the emotional baggage is integrated into everyday awareness, thus the integration becomes part of personal sustainability.

Capabilities for personal sustainability

In the present times work-life balance is increasingly difficult to sustain. Proper physical, emotional and spiritual self-management and self-care methods are needed. Dittmar describes Conscious Discharge as a sustainable way of dealing or even transforming emotional baggage into wisdom to keep personal resources and prevent burnout (Dittmar 2017). If such a practice is missing, inter-personal relationships and personal well-being and even health can suffer. Dittmar details numerous competences to be gained by Conscious Discharge practice to nurture inner resources continuously, such as sincere listening and "speaking from feeling", "being in contact" with ourselves and our intuition, "early recognition of emotional distress" and openness to the beliefs or values of the others, taking responsibility and self-empowerment (ibid).

The key competence for personal sustainability according to Dittmar is learning active listening, a competence that is scarce in the western culture inciting more active expression. Active listening means opening to others and letting their world inside without judging (Dittmar 2017). This capability deepens intra- and inter-personal connection, thereby cultivating empathy and compassion. By enabling to remain in touch with oneself it helps, e.g. not to react aggressively but being relaxed in stressful situations. In this context, the skill of recognizing early warning signals for emotional distress helps to manage emotions and take appropriate decisions in time. Accepting the other's truths is another competence supporting conflict resolution and personal sustainability work. Instead of rejecting differences and trying to convince, Conscious Discharge practitioners learn to relate to others and deal with their truths, appreciating communalities as well as differences (ibid).

Besides, Dittmar describes Conscious Discharge competences in terms of qualities of maturity by taking responsibility for the personal emotional baggage, and self-empowerment grounded on self-acceptance and self-confidence. These capabilities arise out of the space of discharge created in Conscious Discharge, as a singular space of trust to listen and feel oneself:

> There is no therapist who tells you what you should be thinking or feeling. It is a space of expression of trust where you will hear in yourself and work out your challenging emotions or not. You may get lost in personal drama or just try to make sense of personal experiences (*ibid.*).

Socio-political and cultural impact on Sieben Linden ecovillage

In Sieben Linden ecovillage Dittmar introduced the Conscious Discharge method in March 2016 during an internal community meeting (Intensiv-Zeit) with the aim of providing the community with an everyday tool for working with emotional conflicts on a regular basis. Previously, the preferred regularly used socially binding format with a similar function was the Forum, but at that point it was only practiced at a few yearly community meetings. Dealing continuously with emotional baggage is vital in communities as people have a lot of daily contact where they can trigger each other and the accumulated baggage may be causing quite unhealthy relations. "I dream of the time when emotional hygiene will be considered equally normal as physical hygiene today, comparably to 200 years ago when brushing teeth everyday was not a common practice," says Dittmar (Dittmar 2017). Half a year after the introduction in Conscious Discharge an internal evaluation meeting of the Conscious Discharge practice in Sieben Linden took place. It revealed different variations of agreements between practitioners e.g. about speaking or just remaining silent and a shared openness for experimenting with the approach. While finding the most appropriate way of deepening into their experience, practitioners described the experience as becoming a researcher of themselves and the human nature.

Potential socio-political and cultural impact on the broader society

Emotional hygiene can be applied in any social context. For example in school education the teacher usually prevents children from discharging, lowering their self-confidence and inherent capacity for authentic communication. Following Dittmar, the potential of upscaling Conscious Discharge to the broader society has several dimensions. First, regular Conscious Discharge practitioners are able to connect through their intra-personal baggage with the collective baggage and thereby discharge emotions for others, giving them a voice. Second, Conscious Discharge can be practiced in larger groups from 30 up to 100 people, multiplying the experience exponentially. Thereby the whole group converts in one "space holder" for the speaker, who becomes a human representative for all leading to a profound connective experience. Third, Dittmar is clear to point out that Conscious Discharge is not bound to one particular method and that many traditional cultures have collective practices in place that foster discharge. Dittmar explains: "It is not about creating a new globalized way of doing 'emotional hygiene' that can only be practiced in one particular way, but about mutual learning, filling gaps of our own culture, and valuing practices that are already in place" (Dittmar 2017). Fourth, emotional hygiene serves as a tool for "alternative sustainable development" preventing violent social transformations by addressing emotional baggage mismanagement. An example here is the emotional manipulation on the political level as the lack of awareness of personal or collective emotional baggage comes along with vulnerability towards absolute truths promising easy solutions for any problem. Contrarily, practicing emotional hygiene leads individuals and groups to more self-confidence and self-empowered actions.

In this way, Conscious Discharge is a key practice in terms of emotional integration and addressing personal conflicts as dilemmas related to sustainable development.

Comparative analysis of community-design practices and their key capabilities for personal sustainability and "alternative sustainable development"

The three previously discussed community-design practices exemplify similar and different qualities that are relevant for developing personal sustainability in the context of intentional communities. The comparative analysis of those methods and practices discloses the key capabilities to be learned and developed as communication skills, conflict culture and self-responsibility, self-empowerment and leadership. Out of the comparison of these methods and their specific limits and chances, we finally review their potential impact on personal sustainability, and unfold the argument of personal sustainability being simultaneously a precondition for and part of sustainable development.

Following the interviewees, all chosen methods distance themselves from therapy approaches and from being considered a well-defined or fixed method for different reasons related to different notions of communication. The interviewees specify different notions of *communication* that differ from our conventional idea of communication as interaction or dialogue between participants. For instance Forum "is not therapy, nor is it a method in itself; rather, it is a ritualized form of communication designed to enhance transparency, spiritual growth and community" (Richter 2007: 129). It works with an expression-oriented communication using all possible means for performativity as body movement, non-verbal action, voice, etc.

Likewise, Conscious Discharge is not bound to one particular method but there are many traditional cultures with collective practices in place which foster discharge. Conscious Discharge aims to process emotions at a personal level without communicating in the sense of conveying. Words are not directed to the space holder to communicate anything, but serve the speaker to express and digest the discharge. More than a communication method, Conscious Discharge is described as an open cultural practice of personal emotional hygiene with practitioners serving each other (Dittmar 2017).

Community Building is also very far from the guiding therapeutic approaches. One Community Building Guidelines explicitly instruct not to give advice. The aim is to self-empower by learning to cope with one's own and others difficulties wholly through the shared process. Crucial is the experience of authentic communication by sincere listening, and following inner impulses rather than reacting to others. The transformative flow of an honest and open communication allows getting rid of personal masks and defences, and helps to connect to the hidden within and between the participants. The process leads to a strong inner bond among all participants. What all practices have in common regarding communication is the focus on an inner and outer contact based on honesty and transparency.

While all practices are effective in dealing with conflict and conflict resolution for personal sustainability-work, each one has its own 'conflict culture': Conscious Discharge has deep listening and emotional hygiene, Community Building has open-heartedness and shared leadership, and Forum has true contact and a culture of non-violence. As an effect the non-violent culture of Forum aims to bring essential personal and group issues on the surface more than solving conflicts or problems directly. It makes conflicts visible by exploring the performer's own implication and view, by taking self-responsibility for one's own thoughts, feelings and emotions coming up and by making a true contact to oneself, the others, nature, etc. The urge to blame others disappears out of this attitude of self-responsibility creating the right precondition for a non-violent, peaceful communication culture and conflict resolution.

Similarly, Community Building creates deep contact and open-heartedness. In this inner stage participants are able to change attitudes and behaviours while experiencing a conflict situation in everyday life. As a way of personal sustainability-work in Community Building participants may discharge emotions, but not with the intention of personal hygiene as in Conscious Discharge, but of emptying oneself in order to be really able to accept and listen to others. In the state of emptiness, obstacles are not searched outside and the desire of control disappears. In Forum the emotional clearing is enacted through performative expression and creation.

In terms of conflict resolution Conscious Discharge aims to take care of emotional baggage and recognize emotional distress before entering a conflict situation. This helps conflicts to disappear or be solved more effortlessly. In the way the Conscious Discharge practitioners do not accuse or criticize others while being emotionally activated but try to recognize personal triggers, they learn to take responsibility for emotions as they emerge. Along with an advanced conflict culture comes the recognition of self-responsibility. All practices work with the unconscious or 'inner shadow' at the individual and collective level. Whereas in Conscious Discharge responsibility is taken for the personal emotional baggage by trusting in listening and feeling oneself, Forums' responsibility approach often evolves out of a creative process for instance by trying out new behaviours, while the Community Building practitioners make themselves responsible for their involvement focusing on shared leadership.

By way of enriched self-confidence in Conscious Discharge, creative self-expression in Forum or shared leadership in Community Building, all practices address self-empowerment for sustainability transitions at the intra-personal, the inter-personal and the group level. The notions of leadership and the "group of all leaders" is what particularly distinguishes Community Building from other practices. Peck describes this process as a "flow of leadership" where members feel free to express themselves, offering their individual gifts at just the right moment in the decision-making process (Peck 2015: 74). In Forum a trained and experienced facilitator is required to guide the creative resources of the presenter and the group through mirrors giving feedback. On the contrary, in Community Building no guidance in workshops is to be expected from facilitators aside from their presence, as the group of all leaders drive the process. There is also no mirroring from the other participants. In Conscious Discharge by following one's own way, self-confidence is gained. However, similarly to Forum each participant is resonating with and understanding the difficulties and pain of the others as a common human experience, co-creating a common space for shared vulnerability and intimacy. Herby the circle is enabled to understand and support the experience and further changes of the performer, as they have witnessed the whole Forum process.

Obviously, community-design practices do have their limitations and demand certain preconditions from their practitioners. Preconditions for the Community Building method to work are e.g. participants willing to participate and stay during the whole process, and be prepared to face blind spots or underlying feelings. Forum requires, besides its particular setting, also a clearly formulated research question by the performer, and to be grounded to a wider common worldview. As a limitation to Conscious Discharge practice it is important to note that the discharge cannot be practiced with the conflicting person itself. Only after having discharged with someone else, a fruitful outcome with the conflicting person can be expected. In this way, Conscious Discharge creates the adequate circumstances for an easy conflict resolution. For all practices the main challenge may relay at the intra-personal level to learn the distinction of feelings and emotions, to be in touch with oneself and practice authentic communication.

Conclusions

Grounded on a multi-level communication framework, we have explored the limits and potentials of three community-design practices and exposed the key personal capabilities relevant for cultivating personal sustainability. Out of the comparative analysis we highlight conflict resolution and self-empowerment as the core capabilities needed for personal sustainability, sustainable behaviour and alternative paths of sustainable development. First, the capability of inner conflict resolution based on transparency and self-responsibility is the key for personal sustainability as it sharpens the awareness for potential conflicts and supports clearing problems in daily community life. Besides, this kind of conflict approach enables collective personal sustainability-work within processes of vaster social transformations by converting feelings of separation and violence coming up in situations of existential uncertainty into processes of mutual learning. Second, our study shows that the experience of strength resulting from following one's own path accelerates processes of self-empowerment for both inner and outer sustainability. Through feeling connected to oneself patterns of consumption that substitute real needs are overcome and personal resources for further steps towards personal sustainability become available. While community-design practices are not primarily trained with a political intention for instance to fight for sustainable government policies, their practice may have significant political impact on outer sustainable development processes. In the way these practices lead individuals and communities to more self-confident and self-empowered actions towards sustainability transitions, governmental or societal control measures are increasingly less required.

Within the value-oriented context of intentional communities, personal sustainability approaches prove to be crucial preconditions for achieving/realizing "alternative sustainable development". Simultaneously, outer sustainability may condition inner sustainability. More in-depth research is needed into how community-design practices may be integrated in a lifelong education system fostering lifelong sustainable behaviours and lifestyles. In sum, the study evidences the need for further research on other community-design practices and corresponding competencies as individuals have different entry points to sustainability and differing needs towards practices fostering sustainability transitions. Moreover, knowledge is required to uncover the complex interdependencies between the inner and outer sustainability, for instance the relations between an unsustainable professional environment and personal stress. Likewise, a better understanding is needed about the implications of personal sustainability on researchers, about researcher-practitioner relationships and about what kind of capabilities are required for the transitions research practice itself.

Notes

1 Robert Gilman defines an ecovillage as a human-scale, full-featured settlement in which human activities are harmlessly integrated into the natural world in a way that is supportive of healthy human development and can be successfully continued into the indefinite future (Gilman 1991: 10). The term "ecovillage" covers varied forms of communities from traditional villages and intentional communities to sustainable urban neighbourhood projects, which are becoming increasingly networked (Veciana, Neubauer 2016: 39).
2 GEN works through five regional networks: GEN-Oceania and Asia (GENOA), GEN-North America, GEN-Latin America (CASA), GEN-Europe, and GEN-Africa. Additionally, GEN-Middle East is an emerging network and NextGEN is a global network engaging and empowering youth in the ecovillage movement. More: http://gen. ecovillage.org/en/page/about-gens-work (accessed 7 June 2017).
3 More information here: https://siebenlinden.org/de/oekodorf/soziales/entscheidungs findung/ (accessed 1 June 2017).
4 More information here: http://clips.gen-europe.org (accessed 1 June 2017).
5 More information here: www.zegg.de/en/ (accessed 1 June 2017).
6 More information here: www.schloss-tempelhof.de/ (accessed 1 June 2017).
7 More information here: www.schloss-tempelhof.de/wp-content/uploads/2013/05/WIR-Prozess_Zukunftswerkstatt_Tempelhof.pdf/ (accessed 1 June 2017).
8 More information here: www.siebenlinden.org/ (accessed 1 June 2017).

References

Croft, J., Blanke, C., Prado, M., Koglin, I. (n.d.): Dragon Dreaming Project Design. Retrieved 20 February 2017 from www.dragondreaming.org/wp-content/uploads/Dragon Dreaming_eBook_english_V02.09.pdf.
Dittmar, V. (2014): *Gefühle & Emotionen – Eine Gebrauchsanweisung: Wie emotionale Intelligenz entsteht*. München: Verlag VCS Dittmar, Edition Est.
Dittmar, V. (2017): Telephone interview by Veciana, S. and Ottmar, K., 15 February 2017.
Endenburg, G. (1998): *Sociocracy: The Organization of Decision-Making*. Delft, Netherlands: Eburon Academic Publishers.
Frey, R. L., Gouran, D., Scott Poole, M. (Eds) (1999): T*he Handbook of Group Communication Theory and Research*. Thousand Oaks, CA: SAGE Publications.

Geels, F. W. (2002): Technological transitions as evolutionary reconfiguration processes: A multi-level perspective and a case-study. *Research Policy* 31(8/9), S. 1257–1274.

Geels, F. W. (2011): The multi-level perspective on sustainability transitions: Responses to seven criticisms. *Journal of Environmental Innovation & Societal Transitions* 1 (1), 24–40. Retrieved 15 September 2017 from www.clips.gen-europe.org/.

GEESE (2009): *Ecovillage Design Education. A Four-week Comprehensive Course in the Fundamentals of Sustainability Design.* Findhorn, UK: Gaia Education.

GEESE Global Village Educators for Sustainable Earth (2012): Ecovillage Design Education. Retrieved 20 February 2017 from https://gaiaeducation.org/shop/wp-content/uploads/2017/02/EDE-Curriculum-English.pdf.

GEN (2015): *GEN Ecovillage Transition Strategy 2015–2020*, presented at the GEN +20 Summit taking place in Findhorn in July 2015. Retrieved 20 February 2017 from https://gen.ecovillage.org/sites/default/files/files/6_gen_future_strategy.pdf.

GEN Europe (n.d.): ERASMUS+ Learning Partnership CLIPS (Community Learning Incubator for Sustainability). Retrieved 20 February 2017 from www.clips.gen-europe.org.

Gilman, R. (1991): The Eco-Village Challenge. In *Living Together, Sustainable Community Development.* In *Context* No. 29, pp.10.

Gudynas, E. (2011): Desarrollo, extractivismo y buen vivir. Debates sobre el desarrollo y sus alternativas en América Latina: Una breve guía heterodoxa. In *Más allá del desarrollo.* Report from the Permanent Working Group Grupo For Alternatives To Development. Abya Yala (Ed.), pp. 21–54. Quito: Rosa Luxemburg Foundation.

Harvey, J (1970): *Fundamentals of Co-counselling Manual.* Seattle, WA: Rational Island Publishers.

Joubert, K. A. (2010): *Die Kraft der kollektiven Weisheit. Wie wir gemeinsam schaffen, was einer allein nicht kann.* Bielefeld: J. Kamphausen Verlag.

Knapp, L. M., Daly, A. J. (2011): *The Sage Handbook of Interpersonal Communication.* Thousand Oaks, CA: SAGE Publications.

Lauer, P. (2015): *Mein Klimawandel: Die inneren Konflikte der Nachhaltigkeit*, Norderstedt, Germany: Books On Demand.

Maassen, A. (2012): Heterogeneity of lock-in and the role of strategic technological interventions in urban infrastructure transformations. *European Planning Studies* 20 (3), 441–460.

Meyer-Stoll, I. (2013): ZEGG Community. In *Inspiring stories from Ecovillages: Experiences with ecological technologies and practices.* A. Palojärvi, J. Pyysiäinen, M. Saloranta (Eds), pp. 9–10. Vilnius, Lithuania: BMK Leidykla.

Meyer-Stoll, I., Ecker, A. (2013): Grassroots Economic Organizing (GEO) Newsletter, Volume 2, Issue 16.

Meyer-Stoll, I., Ecker, A. (n.d.): *ZEGG-Forum – A Journey through the Heart of Community.* Retrieved 20 February 2017, from http://zegg-forum.org/en/background-info.html.

Peck, S. (2015): *The Different Drum: Community Making and Peace.* New York: Random House.

Ratering, W. (2015): Group interview by Veciana, S. and Ottmar, K., 29 February 2015.

Rauschmayer, F., Omann, I., Frühmann, J. (Eds) (2011): *Sustainable Development: Capabilities, Needs, and Well-Being.* London: Routledge.

Richter, D. (2006): The Forum – A Way of Group-Communication with the Aim of a Culture of Non-violence. Retrieved 20 February 2017 from www.zegg-forum.org/images/PDF/Texte-Englisch/FORUM-For-Nonviolence.pdf.

Richter, D. (2007): *Beyond You and Me*. East Meom: Permanent Publications.

Richter, D. (2017): Telephone interview by Veciana, S. and Ottmar, K., 23 January 2017.

Robertson, J. B. (2007): Organization at the Leading Edge: Introducing Holacracy. Retrieved 20 February 2017 from www.integralesleben.org/fileadmin/user_upload/images/DIA/Flyer/Organization_at_the_Leading_Edge_2007-06_01.pdf.

Steinhilber, S., Wells, P., Thankappan S. (2013): Socio-technical inertia: Understanding the barriers to electric vehicles. *Energy Policy* 60, 531–539.

Stiefel, M. L. (2017): Telephone interview by Veciana, S. and Ottmar, K., 9 February 2017.

Vangelisti, A. (1994): Family secrets: Forms, functions, and correlates. *Journal of Social and Personal Relationships* 11(1), 113–135.

Veciana, S. (2017): Shared Spaces als Orte der Wissensintegration und künstlerische Experimentierräume für eine partizipative Forschungspolitik. In *Gesellschaftliche Transformation und neue Governance-Formen. Herausforderungen des Wandels in Richtung nachhaltige Entwicklung*. Berlin, Germany: ISInova e.V., VS Verlag Springer.

Veciana, S., Neubauer, C. (2016): *Demokratisierung der Wissenschaft – Anforderungen an eine nachhaltigkeitsorientierte partizipative Forschung*. Berlin, Germany: Stiftung Mitarbeit Bonn, Vereinigung Deutscher Wissenschaftler.

Vocate, D. R. (1994): *Intrapersonal Communication: Different Voices, Different Minds*. Hillsdale, NJ; Hove, UK: University of Colorado at Boulder Publishers.

World Commission on Environment and Development (WCED) (1987): *Our Common Future*. Oxford, UK: Oxford University Press.

9 Awareness as the new paradigm for personal sustainability

A practitioner's perspective on the sustainability transition

Ingvar Villido

Introduction

The consequences of human actions consist of the sum total of individual actions. The processes of the inner world inform and guide human actions in the outer world. Still, nowadays we pay immeasurably more attention to, and consequently know much more about the outer world than the inner dimensions of human life. This also applies to discussions about achieving sustainable development. The anthropologist and ecologist Paul Maiteny has expressed this in the following way:

> Environmental policy and social research tends to neglect the inner, experiential dimensions of human life. Yet, the ways in which individuals seek to achieve (. . .) well-being in their lives is inevitably expressed in behaviour that impacts on ecological (and social) processes.
>
> (Maiteny 2000: 339)

Thus, this chapter suggests that in order to make sense of the current sustainability crisis on the societal level, it is necessary to take a deeper look at the processes taking place on the individual level.

In this empirical chapter I share with you my personal practical experience of 30 years of studying and teaching the phenomena of the inner world enabling or hindering personal sustainability. I suggest that the key role of awareness in processes fostering or hindering sustainability transition has been largely overseen. Furthermore, if we wish to foster transition towards more sustainable ways of life, much more attention needs to be paid to learning to understand and deal with inner processes and issues. The resulting increased understanding about the inner processes will subsequently support the external transition. The relevance of not following blindly the socially learned values, norms and habits, but accepting different ways of knowing and making personal experiences based on the here and now is suggested as a way for exiting the automatic behavioural patterns, which are often harmful for the individuals as well as communities and the environment.

More precisely, two basically different behavioural and perceptual strategies are outlined and discussed in this chapter: the currently dominant mental-emotional paradigm, and awareness as the new paradigm. The view of human being as a biological robot or survival machine in the Western world is limiting and has proven insufficient in supporting sustainable human development. This view of human identity, role and abilities rests on the mental-emotional paradigm, which often does not adequately reflect the reality and can be considered one of the main sources of problems and conflicts in the inner and outer worlds (Villido 2014, 2016). A gradual shift to the new paradigm is suggested as a solution for coming to terms with the sustainability challenges on the personal and on the long run also on the societal level.

To clarify several points, some practical experiments to foster personal experience are suggested throughout the chapter.

The relevance of accepting different ways of knowing

A shift from focusing on the outer aspects of development to giving more and more attention to inner processes requires more openness to different modes of knowing and development of new types of education and training, which are able to encompass this broader spectrum of human experience.

The need for more extensive study of ourselves to understand and better predict human affairs has been suggested also by many academic authors with diverse backgrounds, such as biologist Brian Goodwin (1995, Brockman 1997), philosopher Noam Chomsky (1999) and folklorist Marilyn Motz (1998). Chomsky has argued that humans "have only limited understanding of human affairs and human potentialities. We can learn about ourselves and others by imaginative exploration and experiment, which should be encouraged" (Chomsky 1999). Goodwin and Motz have argued for the relevance of accepting the still often sidelined qualitative and intuitive knowledge called "contextual knowledge" by Goodwin (Brockman 1997) as equally relevant aspects of human experience and world-making. Motz has stated that intuitive knowledge is one legitimate way of knowing, intrinsic to human societies and the fact that it cannot be evaluated with measuring sticks of modern science does not undermine it (1998: 340). On similar lines, Goodwin has maintained that science has denied subjectivity for the past 400 years, creating the basis for a very one-sided development along with a devaluation of values and general commodification. This has led to perceiving human beings themselves as commodity storage consisting of blood cells, skin, genes, hair and various organs with a possible market value (Brockman 1997). Furthermore, Goodwin has suggested that the rejection of this commodifying and reductionist approach is the reason for the keen interest in the Eastern non-dual cultures and practices in the recent decades (*ibid.*). In short, these authors stand for a more holistic way of understanding the human being.

This chapter also argues for a more holistic way of understanding human being and for the relevance of accepting and learning to use new ways of knowing as relevant sources of innovation. The roots of the perspective outlined here are intimately connected to non-dual practices and my personal practical experience of three decades of intense study and teaching of the phenomena of the inner world. More precisely, the roots of my approach are in the Saiva Siddhanta tradition that has been practiced in an uninterrupted manner for thousands of years in Southern India (Shomer, McLeod 1987, Ganapathy 1993, White 1996). Particularly the tradition of Kriya Yoga (Govindan 2005, Villido 2014, 2016) has been instrumental for providing insights relevant for this chapter. For the sake of clarity, two paragraphs are added below to open the context, as I consider it relevant to distinguish the way "yoga" is discussed in this chapter as a systematic process of self-study and transformation from the widespread practices under the same name focusing of achieving physical and emotional wellbeing and relaxation. However, rather than discussing one particular tradition, or specific yogic practices, this chapter focuses on relevant insights stemming from inner research for achieving and improving personal and consequently communal sustainability.

When talking about broadening the spectrum of legitimate knowing I suggest that we can roughly distinguish between three groups of researchers: the ones studying the outer world, the others studying the inner world, and the ones studying both worlds and their interrelations. Based on the depth of their knowledge and the relevance of their insights in the current context I suggest that also many yogis and sages over millennia can be considered researchers. Kriya yogis belong to the latter group – researchers studying both inner and outer worlds and their interrelations. They also choose a field of interest, be it medicine or linguistics, raise questions and make systematic experiments to find out how the processes work and which are the interconnections between the inner and outer worlds. The systematic approach and depth of research gives a ground for calling certain types of yoga "the science of yoga" (Villido 2014: 20).

The science of yoga has never belonged to the masses, even in India. Ancient wise men left behind a huge amount of studies, written on palm leaves. For somebody not familiar with the tradition, these texts may appear enigmatic and theoretical, but for practitioners of yoga they contain practical instructions for putting the words into action. I argue that their method is actually an instructive one: creating a dilemma for the reader and through that opening an opportunity for new insights (Villido 2014: 20), a method also practiced in Zen Buddhism. In similar lines to what Goodwin and Chomsky suggested when highlighting the relevance of contextual knowledge and experimental approach for studying ourselves, also the Kriya Yoga approach is based on gathering experiences by testing and finding out what works and how. Its aim is lessening the proportion of automatic unconscious decisions and actions and increasing the amount of conscious actions to minimise unwanted results and consequences that can be harmful for oneself and the surrounding people and environment (Villido 2014: 15).

The role of automation and disconnection in unsustainability

Looking at the root problems causing unsustainable inner and outer processes disconnection from nature and oneself, automatic character of human behaviour and ignorance of the inner sphere count among the key issues.

The way a human being understands oneself and the surrounding world, and the way a society is regulated and self-regulates are intrinsically connected to culture. In this chapter culture is understood as the sum of practices, knowledge and beliefs, learned by each individual from their social and physical environments. Cultural transfer can be described as the process of social learning – socialisation. Each individual takes over certain cultural patterns or practices shaped by preceding generations and modifies and reproduces them before giving them further to their offspring. Thus the sustainability or unsustainability of an individual and broader society depends very much on what has been taught since the early childhood.

In our everyday life we conduct a tremendous amount of actions which all have consequences in both our inner and the outer world. People have many emotional and mental automatic complexes. The expression of these complexes depends on both inner and outer triggering factors and as it is not possible to fully control the activating factors, essentially all humans are dependent on automatic reactions. Such automatic reactions are based on memory and are often disconnected from the current situation and immediate environment. This increases their likelihood of creating problems instead of providing solutions. Such sets of emotional-informational complexes make up the main differences between cultures. They can be both more or less favourable to sustainable development aspirations.

Today Western societies are mostly regulated by written laws and unwritten norms based on the principle of avoiding pain.[1] Everyone needs to act according to these regulations to avoid punishment. The specific regulations in societies that are internalised by individuals in the socialisation process can be very different depending on the countries and cultural spheres. Sustainability based on reactions and regulated by societal norms and sanctions is possible. Humanity has used this way for thousands of years to survive with more or less success. However, regulating human behaviour in such a way based on the principle of carrots and sticks requires massive control structures and making changes is very time- and energy-intensive.

The understanding of who is a human being, what is our purpose and how we function, can also be very different across cultures. When we leave aside the culturally-shaped mental spheres based on ideas and emotional spheres based on habit and look at the empirical experience, there are some universal similarities all people share: people experience that they have a physical body, emotions, thoughts, memories and imaginations, the ability to notice and become aware. The differences of physical bodies are marginal, their functions similar. The same applies to the functioning of emotions: emotions themselves, such as anger, compassion, sadness or pride, are similar across the cultures, although what triggers them and how they are expressed, is culturally and individually dependent. What is more different is the mental sphere, the mind, which is based on memory as it contains all the learned culturally shaped information.

Acquiring legitimate knowledge in Western societies is nowadays connected to institutionalised educational systems based primarily on the repetition of theoretical knowledge. The knowledge learned from others is often considered more valuable than the knowledge stemming from personal experience, making practical knowledge secondary. Thus in daily life the knowledge we are used to using primarily comes from memory, not from empirical experience of the reality around us and is thus more or less disconnected from it. Disconnection from nature – both from our inner human nature as well as the surrounding environment – can be considered one of the root causes of multiple problems, especially in well-developed societies.

Growing up, we learn certain sets of behaviour for acting and solving problems in this world, which often result in conflicts causing personal and social unrest and consequences that can be described as unsustainable processes. Learning new information does not provide any guarantees that conflicts based on such cultural differences will be diminished or avoided. Looking deeper at whatever human sphere of action most of the problems seem to be created by repeating historically developed and socially learned reflex complexes. Actions based on this kind of reactive reflexes are often not very smart. Thus, being prone to conflicts is socially learned and acquired, just as the values and behavioural patterns that do not cause conflicts.

Human life is based on actions, and these are either automatic or conscious. The yogic experience tells us that no one can be without actions and consequences (karma[2]), because also seeming inaction is an action. Observing how we act, we may discover two different ways. One way is acquired through repetition and runs automatically. The other is action with awareness. In this case one is aware of the process while acting. For example you are washing the dishes and at the same time talking on the phone about something important. Washing the dishes is an automatic activity which happens almost by itself. But if the phone call is about something important, the conversation is controlled with awareness: you know what you hear, and know, what you answer. This is action with awareness (Villido 2014: 16). Everybody has such moments of being aware. But usually this awareness is rapidly replaced by mental or emotional automatisms.

There is nothing wrong with automatic processes – they often make our life much easier – we do not have to control how our organs work or relearn how to walk each day. The problem is that automatic actions make up the main basis for human actions. In yoga, it is estimated that about 95 per cent of our (re)actions are unconscious and automatic and only about 5 per cent are conscious and intentional (Villido 2014: 17). To choose the right action, it is relevant to orientate in the inner world and awareness is a much better basis for that than automatism. The solution lies in relearning, i.e. revising and changing the patterns of behaviour, values, prejudices and habits acquired blindly and without reflection in the process of socialisation.

Shared and individual reality

We are surrounded by physical objects, we have lots of different emotions and an infinity of thoughts, imaginations and memories. In yogic terms this means that we have three different realities: physical, emotional and mental. Whereas the physical reality is shared and visible, the emotional and mental realities are invisible and individual.

Problems arise not because we have three different realities to deal with on the daily basis, but because we perceive them as mixed. Often people do not realise that although the physical, emotional and mental reality seem to merge on the individual level, they are not the same. Physical reality is shared, although our mental interpretations of it as well as emotions we feel in certain situations might completely differ from others. The thoughts and emotions we are experiencing are often not related to the physical reality, and the experienced emotions and thoughts can even be contradicting. For example: if you look at a glass while thinking about a glass that you used in your childhood, it seems normal – you are thinking about glass. But the glass in your imagination is not the same as the physical glass that you see; so through the mental process of remembering you become disconnected from the physical glass. If you have emotions related to the childhood memory of the glass, for example sadness, they surface and influence the behaviour in the current situation in a way that is not related to the shared physical reality. This creates a situation where the realities don't match.

This is also connected to illusion, something that everyone experiences in their life. It is created by thoughts and imagination, and when supported by emotions, one starts to believe and live according to it. For example, there is a situation that has passed. But one is still thinking about it, reliving it. That is an illusion. Illusion-based activity has direct influence on that person's life. The amount of such activities is usually large. This means we spend a big part of our time reliving such past experiences – or when using imagination, creating future illusions. As a result, we lose orientation and mix shared reality with personal illusions. In such a way people live their daily lives more or less in illusion and disconnection, resulting in confusion, disappointment and harmful actions for oneself and the surroundings.

Sometimes we hope that when we change the physical reality, for example move to a new location, the other dimensions are also changed. For example, over the years I have visited several intentional communities and ecovillages. People come together there with lots of good ideas. They start living together and everything is nice – like marriage in the beginning. But after some time conflicts start appearing. Fights start over positions and rights and people are again faced with problems they had hoped to leave behind. This shows that changing the outer setting does not necessarily mean getting rid of the mental and emotional problems that people tend to carry along. When the outer situations change, these patterns tend to resurface.

The mental-emotional paradigm

The process of changing something on the societal level can be very time- and energy-consuming. It can take generations. But also on the individual level change can be slow and difficult to achieve. This is due to people having many contra-dictory opinions, doubts, thoughts and emotions about things – some conscious, some unconscious. Becoming aware of them and changing them takes a lot of energy and time.

Human subconsciousness[3] functions on the principle of avoiding both physical as well as psychic pain and finding both physical as well as psychic pleasure. I call this emotional-mental basis for actions the old mental-emotional paradigm. "Old" because this paradigm has been widespread and used internationally regardless of skin colour or language for a long time. I advise people to take time to look at their life and find their strongest driving forces. Most often, they find that their decisions and choices are made based on likes and dislikes. All humans have deep dislikes and preferences, even if they prefer to think that they don't care. What you try to avoid drives your life. The same goes for what you like in your life. Reactive persons base their actions on likes and dislikes, aware persons use conscious action with awareness.

Let us make an experiment. Think about something and pay attention to your vocal chords – they become a little tense when you think. You can use some letters and observe – your vocal system becomes tense. Did you find it? You can relax those muscles. Do it and look what happens. The more you relax, the less you think – in fact your thinking stops. This shows that our thinking is in essence talking with voice, which we have learned to silence as we grow up. The talking that little children do when they comment what they see becomes silent, and grownups continue to comment in a silent fashion. Whatever happens in your life is described by your mind. The yogic experience tells us that thoughts are not only thoughts – they shape our reality. So choosing descriptive mind or ever-changing emotions which are often disconnected from current reality as the basis of your life is not a smart decision suitable for *homo sapiens sapiens*.

Following positive ideas like loving kindness is nice, but there are still emotions and thoughts driving your life, limiting the perspective and clouding the judgement. Not using such emotional or mental "lenses" leads to becoming much more realistic and open to what is currently happening around you.

Change-making: exiting the old paradigm

Let's see if you can recognise your thoughts. Let the mind say your name and just recognise – is it you who is aware of thoughts and the name given to you? Your thoughts are always talking in your name: I am an "emotional person" or "tired" or "intelligent" or "old". Are all those "you's" in your thoughts the same as the one who is aware of them? It's the same with physical body and emotions – you experience that you have the body and different changing emotions. The phenomena you can recognise in the inner or outer world are visible and invisible objects. You are the subject that can recognise and experience, follow, suppress or ignore. It's a common misconception that you are an "emotional person" or "fat" or "intelligent" – because you are not that, these are objects that you use. Or more often – that use you.

My experience both as a practitioner and a teacher has shown that receiving knowledge and short experience of something new is not enough to change something in the long run. If you really want to change something, consistency is needed. Overcoming the autopilot takes a lot of time, patience and practice.

What is also needed is openness for looking beyond the learned truths and reactions offering themselves readily and finding out what really works and what would be the best way to act. In order to exit the old paradigm you need to ask questions and gather your own experiences and find you own answers. This means learning anew through conscious and systematic experimenting. From the consequences, results, we see if our idea works. If needed, adjustments can be made and tested again. This helps to overcome the automatic processes, cultivate awareness and find innovative solutions.

Awareness with its abilities to receive insights, intuition and inspiration is not mind or emotions, it is different. It is the fourth dimension of reality, a different layer.[4] Self is the fifth. So we live a multidimensional life. Many processes in emotional and mental levels do not support physical life, the shared reality. The yogic experience tells us that for the best results for the person as well as their surroundings, the realities need to be aligned. To do this, it is necessary to take the shared reality as the basis. Yoga, as discussed in this chapter, focuses on aligning the dimensions so that they would not contradict each other. It is not always easy because by aligning the dimensions you oppose the automatic tendencies. In a way you are fighting a non-violent fight for your right to be the driver of your life. Otherwise emotions and thoughts take over and you function on the autopilot.

In order to learn to orientate in the realities and align them, we need to deepen our ability to be aware. This starts with using the neutral ability to notice, to observe. All people have this ability, but the majority is unaware of it and thus this quality is not intentionally used. Being consciously aware, or aware of awareness, differs qualitatively from the ability to feel bodily sensations and emotions, to think, remember and imagine. Using awareness as the primary tool to relate to the surrounding provides adequate information about the circumstances, and creates a sound basis for actions. Learning to reconnect and realign in this manner also means exiting the old paradigm.

What is awareness?

The essence and even the existence of awareness is still contested in science (cf. Varela *et al.* 2016). However, in daily life everyone uses this quality we call awareness in this chapter to differentiate between visible and invisible, inner and outer objects and phenomenon. On the practical level, for example in Kriya Yoga, there is no doubt that awareness exists.

Action with awareness includes knowing what I do, why I do it and how I do it. If this control does not require emotional and mental effort, but comes naturally, then work gets done fast, activities go smoothly and the results are rewarding. When you analyse what you used when you acted that way, you might discover that it wasn't thoughts or emotions, but a phenomenon different from both of them – the intellect (Villido 2014: 16). The meaning of intellect in yoga differs from its everyday meaning. It does not mean knowing much and being well educated. Instead it is comprised of the abilities to differentiate, be aware, and have insights, use intuition and inspiration. Everybody has these abilities, but they are rarely used because people generally don't know how to access them. Instead they are often confused with mental or emotional phenomena.

We need to use awareness intentionally and practically to discover it for what it is. Look around you, choose one object and concentrate on it, exploring it slowly. Choose another object and repeat. Recognise that if you touch something with your attention there is a small gap – perhaps half a second – before commenting thoughts arise. During this gap you are connected to this object in silence: you are aware of it. That is the way to connect directly to physical reality. After that short moment your awareness jumps to your thoughts and you find thoughts describing and commenting those things that were touched by your awareness. Thinking is the description of your mind that follows the recognition. You can prolong this half a second of being aware. Awareness can be very useful because if you are aware of something you are directly connected to it and can influence it in a more effective way. Awareness is like a tool and you can be more or less skilled in using it.

Let's carry out one more experiment to find out what awareness is. There are two ways of speaking – spontaneously and with control, being attentive to what you say. In the latter case you cannot say everything that comes to your mind, you must control it. Please think with control and recognise two things: thoughts and that part that controls thoughts. And recognise – are they the same or not?

Awareness is not the same as thinking, emotions or physical body, it is the ability to be in contact with thoughts, emotions and physical body and understand these processes. So it is something qualitatively different. Normally people don't give enough relevance to that tool. In our inner world there are lots of processes that become automatically activated and switch us off from physical reality, because they draw our attention to themselves. By noticing how difficult it is not to think about the objects, you find out how good a driver of your awareness you are.

Over the decades I have taught thousands of people and my experience has shown that although awareness is a simple natural phenomenon, people rarely find it – and even if they do, almost never keep using it as they simply forget it. Cultivating awareness of awareness[5] enables to adopt a more sound way of orientating in and directly relating to the inner and outer processes. I suggest that starting to cultivate awareness of awareness as a primary tool instead of the current emotional-mental paradigm can significantly accelerate the needed sustainability transition.

New paradigm

Humanity has developed into "keepers of things": we are used to focusing on visible outer and invisible inner phenomena without paying attention to the fundamental quality that enables us to discover them: awareness. Noticing these "things" is made possible by awareness, which should be considered primary. So we as humanity are well versed in the old paradigm and using secondary phenomena. The new paradigm is based on starting to use what is primary – awareness.

Awareness is the tool that enables us to be aware of the objects, both inner and outer, but also of itself. Awareness of awareness does not only bring the ability to differentiate, but also allows letting go of disturbing emotions and mental patterns which are very limiting. By doing that, more and more inner space opens up, allowing for more freedom. Once you start using more awareness in your daily life, you will notice that it is indeed like space, surrounding and encompassing everything. So it is not possible to lose awareness. It is only possible to forget about it. This means placing exclusive emphasis on inner and outer objects instead of remaining aware of both objects and awareness itself. To set it right, you can use your senses. Become aware of some phenomenon or object – this can be a thought, a feeling or a physical object, as you wish. Be aware both of the object, and the invisible connection that connects you to it. In this way you not only know the object, but also your awareness: you are aware of awareness. It is a small, but fundamental difference.

Being aware of the awareness binding subject with objects makes it possible to combine, recombine or dismantle the acquired automatic habits and achieve direct contact with the shared reality. This enables us to change from a socio-culturally shaped reflex-driven unit to a smart realist who uses awareness as the primary tool and is able to open their potentials. Such a human being is naturally efficient, benevolent, smart, spares resources, has good concentration, does little, but achieves a lot. I suggest calling a human acting on the basis of awareness of awareness a user of the new paradigm.

When you start to learn something, you always use action with awareness, because otherwise it would be impossible to essentially understand what you learn. Due to repetition, what we learned inevitably turns into unconscious activity and the conscious part gradually retires to the background. Learning by repeating is considered normal today, but it has certain shortcomings – it does not consider the current context. Many reflexes are necessary. However, the situation where they are the main drivers of human lives is not good because it makes us reactive and decreases our ability to respond adequately. In Kriya Yoga the conscious control of action with awareness never disappears. It is shaped into a new habit of being aware.

About a person who uses awareness we can say that they are awake, while a person who follows unconsciousness can be described as sleeping – dreaming with open eyes, following an illusion created by the mind and supported by the emotions, which they mistake for reality. Instead, a conscious person is guided by what is happening now in reality. This is the crucial difference.

Adopting the new paradigm teaches people independence by showing how to change one's life by themselves. It suggests that the root causes of problems as well as the solutions are always inside the people. In such a way it teaches taking responsibility for one's life and actions.

Awareness as the key to inner and outer sustainability transition

If you look at your actions – how do they look like? Are they hectic? Are they driving you, or are you driving them? How big is your role here? You will see it is probably relatively small. There are a tremendous amount of actions happening in your inner world – ideas, imaginations, remembering, thinking, feelings and emotions, listening to sounds, looking, thinking, bodily sensations – which makes up a big mess. That mess, in turn, makes up your life. It is very hard to drive that mess. For making some changes it is not enough to just think about it or feel some emotions. There is a specific tool for orientating in this mess – awareness. Starting to orientate in that mess you will start to exclude things that do not make sense. Excluding unnecessary habits and patterns is like an inner clean-up: you are reducing the amount of unnecessary inner processes and making more space for the things you need in your life. Awareness is the tool that helps you to orientate and recognise what is important in your life. Practicing awareness improves your ability to orientate in your inner mess. The key for more awareness is: less is more. Finally through this practice you reach an absolutely practical life based on awareness and actions. It means becoming practically smart – you can learn everything by practicing it, by doing it yourself. That knowledge becomes yours through real understanding acquired by your independent learning process. There lays your individual responsibility: you are the only one who can free your inner space from unnecessary clutter. Each individual can do it in their own inner world, step-by-step. Here the knowledge is not based on memory, but practical experience and learning through reality. This is absolutely another paradigm of independent self-learning humans.

Awareness also enables the intentional use of inspiration and intuition. Have you ever discovered something? Probably you looked at something, examining it, or posed a question and – heureka! – had an insight.[6] Scientists basically do the same, delving deeper into the details of nature or other specific problems in search for answers. New discoveries are often due to insights. Along the same lines Goodwin has argued that intuitive knowledge is a specific way of knowing necessary for insights; the problem being that only few acknowledged experts have been courageous enough to admit the role of intuition enabling them to have insights, make new connections and realise the whole in a different manner (Brockman 1997). What is understood through insight will then be verified in practice and elaborated upon.

If I were to ask you if thinking is the same as having an insight, the answer would be no. Insight can come during thinking, but insight itself is not a thought. Insight gives new knowledge and takes place in all people with varying frequency. It is also possible to examine insight itself: how does it arise? What is its source? What makes insights special is the proportion of the use of awareness, and that they enable learning about the formerly unknown (Villido 2014: 19).

Human identity in the new paradigm

One more dimension of being human deserves attention here. It is always present, yet still somehow hidden. Each person is able to become aware of the physical environment, physical body sensations, the existence of emotions and thoughts and the process of being aware. Everything we are able to become aware of is an object in relation to us as an observer, the subject. The difference of subject from object is that humans experience themselves as subject that has or perceives objects. Where is the subject?

Let's take an example. Notice your thoughts. Do you recognise that in your mind someone is talking in your name? While the real you is observing it. You are not that. The problem is that today generations of people are taught differently. They are taught that they are the physical body, they are the character and thoughts and emotions and past, and people really believe it. But if you understand that you are a user of these means – that you have a body, that you have a mind, that you have emotions, without being identified with them, you achieve a certain freedom. And you will see that a false "you" that is not you is living your life and you are sitting in the back seat, letting it drive your life. So the truth is that people not only don't know who they are, but they don't live their lives. That is a tragedy.

Identification with objects is a misunderstanding. We are the subject, the one who has awareness. However, people tend to forget it, and if we forget it, we begin to suffer: the freedom fades and we become identified with the mental-emotional paradigm. We become involved in trying to fulfil three basic needs: to be somebody, to know and control, and to be happy. In this way we have lost our freedom.

As mentioned at the beginning of this chapter, Kriya Yoga practitioners consider yoga an empirical science – a systematic path of learning about oneself and the surrounding reality through asking questions and making real life experiments to find answers that are not predetermined or socially learned, but stem from the current situation and context. Kriya Yoga means action with awareness and is an empirical approach for exploring one's inner world and investigating the relationships between the inner and outer processes (Villido 2014: 20). The yoga science does not agree with the modern science that often considers humans as biological machines. Yoga is a holistic science of us – human individuals. And about how we live in our many-dimensional surrounding while simultaneously inhabiting different dimensions. Each human being has a physical dimension, an emotional dimension, a mental dimension, the dimension of awareness, which we call intellect, and the dimension of existence, which we call the Self. Awareness is the main tool for finding the Self.

Understanding the central relevance of the individual dimension of existence is not egoistic. Ego is the part that talks in your name, accompanied by emotions. Ego is that taxi driver that keeps you sitting like a silent observer in the backseat. Mostly the subject takes the back seat and observes how the complexes drive their life.

To be human means finding an answer to the questions "who am I?" and "what am I doing here?" For that I use the following technique. Imagine a green apple one meter in front of you. Find that you are looking at it without using your physical eyes. There is an invisible connection between you and that imagined apple – it is awareness. Following the beam of awareness, bring your awareness from the apple back to the source, to you. And change the ability to see to the ability to feel, to experience yourself. If you get distracted or start to look outside, just bring your awareness back in to the ability to feel your existence. Being identified with yourself as Self feels calm and stable. That is how you become the taxi driver. In this state you are truly *homo sapiens sapiens*.

Conclusions for achieving personal sustainability

This chapter has argued that the currently dominant mental-emotional paradigm, called "the old paradigm" in this chapter, has proven insufficient for dealing with the sustainable development crisis humanity is facing. Sustainability based on automatic reactions and wish to avoid punishment is to a certain extent possible. Mankind has used this way for thousands of years to ensure survival. However, regulating human behaviour based on the principle of carrots and sticks is very energy-intensive and the changes in the systems happen very slowly.

In terms of fostering sustainability, my practice and work with students has shown that the change that does not require carrots and sticks starts from each person – it is a very personal matter. The best way to foster sustainability transition is to create practical understanding about what is happening and why we are reacting in this or that way. This means acquiring personal experiences about the development of the processes in direct contact with the present situation. A more holistic approach to being human needs to be adopted and the often side-lined empirical and intuitive knowledge also needs to be accepted as relevant parts of human experience directly influencing the success or failure of the sustainability transition.

To exit the automatic habitual behavioural patterns it makes sense to make experiments, but we must be sure to base our actions on reality, not illusions. There is a lot of wrong information and many harmful habit patterns in our inner systems, giving ground for saying that the old paradigm is largely based on illusions. How can we expect to create sustainability 'out there' if we are full of lies and half-truths about ourselves and others? If you want to foster sustainability you need to take responsibility to change your inner landscape and move towards the new paradigm.

An alternative path to sustainability in comparison to the logic of carrots and sticks is presented by placing emphasis on awareness itself. This does not mean thinking about things, or feeling them, but an essential ability to notice and intentionally influence objects. To achieve personal sustainability, which can serve as a basis for a broader sustainability transition, it is necessary to become aware of the inner processes and learn to manage them. This cannot be done by emotionally fighting or mentally suppressing or theorising. Transition from the old paradigm to awareness as the new paradigm starts with noticing what is relevant in your life. The things that are relevant to you tend to drive your life, as well as the things you would rather avoid.

We are usually unaware of our awareness because we are limited by our habits that occupy our inner space. Being constantly engaged with changing emotions and thoughts, we are too busy to notice the space where they occur. Becoming a skillful user of awareness means discontinuing the automatic habits to free more inner space. This is the yogic way towards freedom. On that path, the principle of "less is more" applies: the quality of techniques that reduce the amount of automatic reactions is of greater importance than the quantity of mere knowledge and experiences. The space of awareness is characterised by silence, which is already present – just become aware of it.

Using awareness as the primary tool when relating to the inner and outer worlds provides adequate information about the circumstances, which creates a sound basis for acting purposefully. A creative and insightful individual can function sustainably in the long run only when the automatic emotional and mental complexes are reduced and substituted by increased use of awareness. Awareness of awareness is the standard of the new paradigm. From this state, personal sustainability can start to enfold. The resulting personal transformation will support the necessary transformations in the outer world.

Notes

1 Pain can be physical or psychological including mental discomfort and painful emotions.
2 The concept of *karma* signifies the interdependent relationship of action and result.
3 Subconciousness is understood as the part of your mind that notices and remembers information when you are not actively trying to do so, and influences your behaviour even though you do not realise it (*Cambridge English Dictionary* http://dictionary.cambridge.org/dictionary/english/subconscious, accessed April 2017).
4 The physical body being the first, the emotions the second and the mental level with memory, thinking and imagination the third dimension.
5 *Awareness of awareness* means being aware of where your awareness lays.
6 Insight is understood as a *clear, deep,* and sometimes *sudden understanding* of a *complicated problem* or *situation* (*Cambridge English Dictionary,* http://dictionary.cambridge.org/dictionary/english/, accessed April 2017).

References

Brockman, J. (1997): *A New Science Of Qualities. An Interview with Brian Goodwin.* In: Edge, 29 April 1997. Retrieved May 2016 from: www.edge.org/3rd_culture/goodwin/goodwin_p2.html.

Chomsky, N. (1999): On Freedom of Press and Culture: An interview with Noam Chomsky. Interviewed by N. Raptis, T. Fotopoulos. In: *Democracy and Nature.* Vol. 5 (No. 1), pp. 17–26. Retrieved December 2016 from www.inclusivedemocracy.org/dn/vol5/chomsky_press.htm.

Ganapathy, T.N. (1993): The Philosophy of the Tamil Siddhas. Indian Council of Philosophical Research. New Delhi, India: Affliated East West Press.

Goodwin, B. (1995): Neo-Darwinism has Failed as an Evolutionary Theory. In: *The Times Higher Education Supplement,* 19 May 1995.

Govindan, M. (2005): *Babaji and the 18 Siddha Kriya Yoga Tradition.* Quebec, Canada: Kriya Yoga Publications.

Maiteny, P. (2000): The Psychodynamics of Meaning and Action for a Sustainable Future. In: *Futures.* Vol. 32, pp. 339–360.

Motz, M. (1998): The Practice of Belief. In: *The Journal of American Folklore.* Vol. 111, (No. 441), pp. 339–355.

Shomer, K., McLeod, W.H. (eds) (1987): *The Saints – Studies in a Devotional Tradition of India*. Berkeley, CA: Berkley Religious Studies Series.

Varela, F.J., Thompson, E., Rosch, E. (2016): *The Embodied Mind: Cognitive Science and Human Experience*. Cambridge, MA: The MIT Press.

Villido, I. (2014): Eessõna. In: Satchidananda, Govindan, *Patandžali joogasuutrad: kriya jooga õpetaja Marshall Govindani tõlge ja kommentaar*. Lilleoru, Estonia: Lilleoru Keskus OÜ, pp. 15–21.

Villido, I. (2016): Awareness as the Key to Sustainability Transition. Transcription of the lecture by Ingvar Villido at the Research Seminar on Personal Sustainability, Karlsruhe Institute of Technology, Germany, July 2016.

White, D. G. (1996): *The Alchemical Body: Siddha Traditions in Medieval India*. Chicago, IL: University of Chicago Press.

10 Reflexivity

Exploring the metanarratives of sustainable development

Kaidi Tamm

Introduction

Despite inhabiting the same physical world and living next to each other, we tend to have diverse impressions and interpretations of it because we use different meaning constellations for making sense of the world. Understanding the present situation, acting in the world and planning the future are directly dependent on our intangible meaning-making structures determining what is considered "good" or "bad", what should be sustained and continued into indefinite future and what should be stopped, and whose interests should be primarily considered when choosing a development direction.

Such inner meaning structures have developed in the course of socialisation and are both individual and culturally dependent. In the same vein, the complex concept of "sustainable development" encompasses different perceptions of the current situation and development directions, and is both a culturally dependent and individually interpreted concept. In the context of this chapter, culture is understood not in the narrow sense of high or indigenous culture, but in the broader sense as a human meaning-making system. As Clifford Geertz puts it:

> The concept of culture [. . .] is essentially a semiotic one. Believing, with Max Weber, that man is an animal suspended in webs of significance he himself has spun, I take culture to be those webs, and the analysis of it to be therefore not an experimental science in search of law but an interpretive one in search of meaning (1973: 5).

Despite the relevance of such individually and culturally dependent factors, they have received surprisingly limited scholarly attention so far.

This chapter is concerned with "anthroposemiosis" (Deely 1993) – the way human beings create and orientate in meanings, which translates into actions shaping personal and social reality in a manner that can be described as more or less sustainable. What is considered worthy of being sustained is not unambiguous. Based on empirical and theoretical analysis (Tamm 2017),[1] this chapter argues that it is a widespread misconception to believe that a consensus exists about the meaning and relevance of sustainable development. When looking more closely, a plurality of attitudes, including much ignorance, becomes evident. Even among those who see the need for sustainability transition, the directions of change envisioned and worked towards under the same notion are very diverse. Therefore, "sustainable development" is understood in this chapter as a kind of container concept filled with different meanings, hopes and fears by different groups, expressed in different narratives about reality.

Next, the relevance of narratives for human understanding of oneself and the surrounding world are discussed. The role the narratives assign to individuals and ways for dealing with the crisis are discussed by exploring the three core dichotomies characterising the sustainable development metanarratives.

The popular solution, namely creating a new narrative, is discussed as one option. The currently dominating disconnection metanarrative has led to multiple problems that could be mitigated by balancing it with elements from the reconnection approach. Alternatively, building capacity for increasing individual reflexivity is suggested as a way for becoming aware of and transcending the narrative limits. Empowering individuals by legitimising research on intangible aspects influencing sustainable development and building up educational structures supporting qualitative growth in awareness and reflexivity can result in a new type of society of lifelong learners. It would facilitate the transformation into a more sustainable society characterised by greater meaning-making freedom, innovation capacity and respect for the limits to growth.

The multifaceted concepts of sustainable development and sustainability

"Sustainability" and "sustainable development" are fuzzy concepts, understood by different social groups in different ways. Numerous researchers in the broad field of sustainability studies have acknowledged this confusion and criticised these concepts as semantic gold dust, empty signifiers, oxymorons, utopia or greenwashing tools (e.g. Sachs 1997, Sebaldt 2002, Faber *et al.* 2005, Goggin 2009, Jäger 2009). The diversity of views on what these concepts mean and aim at testify to their normative and contested nature.

In the context of this chapter, "sustainability" is understood as an open concept with its meaning depending largely on the context it is used in and by whom it is used. The "sustainable development" concept, on the other hand, is intentionally created (WCED 1987), referring to the balanced development of ecological, social and economic dimensions to ensure intra- and intergenerational equity, which is considered when using this concept. In the context of this chapter, culture as the fourth development dimension and explicit attention to the micro-level developments are added to this understanding.

The approach called "personal sustainability" is only emerging and is consequently relatively open. "Having personal sustainability" can mean different things to different people – but in any case it refers to a state of balance and wellbeing that can be maintained in a viable manner over a longer period of time.

It explores aspects that allow individuals to live and develop in a sustainable manner. For achieving personal sustainability, the surrounding environment and socio-cultural settings as well as intangible inner aspects play a relevant role. According to this approach the inner and outer worlds are not seen as separate, but interconnected dimensions.

Thus, in the context of this chapter, these concepts are not fixed and finished, but dynamic, used by different societal actors for conveying their ideals of a better future. In the sense of an ideal towards which groups of people are striving, they can be compared to a utopia. As Oscar Wilde once put it:

> A map of the world that does not include Utopia is not worth even glancing at, for it leaves out the one country at which Humanity is always landing. And when Humanity lands there, it looks out, and, seeing a better country, sets sail. Progress is the realisation of Utopia.

(Wilde 1891)

Development of disconnection: a shift from "nature" to "environment"

Sustainable development might be a relatively new concept, but its message of balancing human ways of life with ecological limits is far from new. Different sources trace collective human efforts to shape nature back as far as 8,000–15,000 years. Occasionally these attempts led to severe pollution and social collapse toppling some great civilisations, like in Mesopotamia, where a poorly designed irrigation system slowly poisoned the land with salt, or on the Easter Island, where neglect of resource limits led to their depletion and societal downfall (Prugh, Assadourian 2003, Diamond 2005). By the turn of the seventeenth and eighteenth century, various voices were calling for greater efforts to preserve, conserve, and manage natural systems with more care (Sebaldt 2002).

However, until a couple of hundred years ago, human-inflicted environmental problems were primarily local, or at worst, regional. Human activities started to cause noticeable global damage since the industrial revolution began, accompanied by a significant increase in using fossil fuels. It was only at the turn of the twentieth century when the pollution resulting from increasing industrial production and consumption of natural resources, along with a growing population, created enough pressure to motivate the first governments to implement stricter resource management rules to lessen unwanted consequences (Dauvergne 2009).

Next, two lines of thought about the causes of the current crisis, relevant for this chapter, are briefly introduced. The first strand of thought pondering the human-nature relationship is the "limits to growth" line. Thomas Malthus started it back in 1798 by discussing the ability of the Earth to sustain its growing population (Malthus 1826). In 1968 this line was prominently continued by Garrett Hardin and Paul Ehrlich and reached more visibility with the controversial text *The Limits to Growth* by Donella and Dennis Meadows, Jörgen Randers, and

William Behrens III in 1972. In this text, the authors argued that economies would one day crash due to Earth's finite resources, motivating many people to question the sense of unrestrained economic growth. A number of authors and social movements linked with the reconnection metanarrative discussed in this chapter carry this line of thought further.

Another prominent strand of thought considers certain Western mind-sets as causes for the change in human-nature relationship, triggering the current disconnection from nature and the resulting crisis. Witnessing the negative impacts of human actions on nature already back in 1940s, the conservationist Aldo Leopold called for understanding the role of *homo sapiens* not as a conqueror of the land-community, but as its plain member and citizen that needs to respect his fellow-members (Leopold 1992: 151). This line of reasoning echoes that of many indigenous nations and social movements worldwide, including strong sustainability and deep ecology stances, discussed below. In 1967 the historian Lynn Townsend White Jr. suggested that the deeper causes of contemporary environmental problems lay in a historically developed worldview of the industrialised North (White 2008: 15). Also the historian Hayden White and the philosopher Jaan Kaplinski locate the roots of the crisis in the change of relationship between man and nature. Even though humans live in the midst of nature, and are themselves a phenomenon of nature, the view of being distinct from it has become dominant in the West. White sees the cause in Christian culture coupled with the novel "marriage" between science and technology since the 1850s leading to seeing humans as separate and higher compared to the rest of nature. This, in turn, led to lack of respect for nature – a change he describes as the greatest psychological revolution of our Western culture (White 2008: 43). In short, White suggests that the ecological crisis is the result of an entirely new science and technology oriented culture, and the main question is, if it is able to survive its own influence. He argues that unless we adopt a new set of basic values characterised by respect for nature as a new paradigm, the survival of the democratic culture is highly unlikely (White 2008: 37).

Along similar lines, Kaplinski has reasoned that the gradual shift in the mid-twentieth century from talking about "nature" to talking about the "environment" across languages reflects not only a linguistic change, but also a change in the way people in the West relate to their surroundings (Kaplinski 2003). This observation is supported by literary scholar Leo Spitzer who argues that the English "environment" was first used in 1827 to translate the German word *Umgebung*, whereby the expression that signified both the material (outer, visible) as well as the spiritual (inner, invisible) surrounding, lost the latter in translation (Spitzer 1942: 204–206). Pondering on the consequences of this rhetoric shift, Kaplinski considers the resulting anthropocentrism almost inevitable, arguing that for our ancestors in pre-Christian times "nature" primarily meant a self-organising system, which people were a part of and which did not have a centre, while "environment" has a centre – the living being that is environed:

> The more we talk about the environment instead of nature, the more we empha-sise – willingly or unwillingly – that we are in the centre of this environment.

This emphasis does not help us in reflecting on our place in the big natural system.[2]

(Kaplinski 2003: 9)

This shift does not support seeing beyond our species-centeredness. Next, let us look into the relevance of narratives for human world-making.

Homo narrans: the relevance of narratives in human world-making

This chapter discusses the role of narratives as legitimising and action-shaping tools in human world-making, in this context influencing the way sustainability is understood and practiced. Using the intrinsically qualitative narrative approach allows developing a more integrated view of the sustainable development situation by considering humans not only as rational consumers, but also as habit-, idea-, emotion- and intuition-driven beings pursuing useful as well as useless, and at times, even irrational or detrimental aims.

The relevance of narratives as basic human cognitive instruments for building identity and making sense of the world has been suggested by a number of researchers including Hayden White (1980), Alasdair MacIntyre (1984), Carolyn Merchant (1995), Thomas Berry (1998), Elisabeth Sahtouris (2000) and Karen Liftin (2003). White has commented on the intimate link between narratives and culture suggesting that raising the question of the nature of narrative means inviting reflection on the very nature of culture and possibly even on the human nature itself (White 1980: 5). He considers narratives essential for communicating meanings from people to people and (sub)culture to (sub)culture:

> Far from being a problem, then, narrative might well be considered a solution to a problem of general human concern, namely, the problem of how to trans-late knowing into telling, the problem of fashioning human experience into a form assimilable to structures of meaning that are generally human rather than culture-specific. We may not be able fully to comprehend specific thought patterns of another culture, but we have relatively less difficulty understanding a story coming from another culture, however exotic (*ibid.*).

In a similar manner, MacIntyre described narrative as a cognitive method for understanding both personal actions as well as the actions of others: "Because we understand our own lives in terms of lived narratives, the form of narrative is appropriate for making sense of the actions of others" (MacIntyre 1984: 212). Hence, narrativity as a human way of world-making undergirds human science, literature, philosophy, everyday thinking and the way we understand the others and ourselves.

What makes narratives matter, is that they carry information and meaning con-stellations. From the perspective of semiotics, understanding something means becoming aware of it and contextualising it in existing knowledge. We are in a relationship with all the objects we are aware of, both in the outer and in the inner world, interpreting and contextualising them. John Deely has suggested that the essence and uniqueness of human meaning-making process (*semiosis*) lays in its ability to bring through understanding into the objective world such relationships which are not based on the information that comes through our five senses and are thus not predetermined by our biological legacy (Deely 2005a: 92). Thus, the uniqueness of human semiosis lays in its relatively greater interpretative freedom in comparison to other known sign users such as animals. The use of signs enables language, which in turn enables a certain disconnection from the physical world, and the rise of the abstract cultural world. This mechanism also enables creating narratives, which start shaping our experiences of the world and which we co-create based on our experiences and interpretations of the world. It has been hypothesised that the emergence of the narrative function is the starting point of the emergence of language and seeing human as *homo narrans* helps to understand the development of a species-specific level of organisation in which socio-cultural laws replace, to a large extent, the socio-biological constraints governing the rest of the animal kingdom (Victorri 2007). For humans, such a use of signs enables more interpretative freedom, but also more possibilities to get confused when distinguishing between the physical outer world and the abstract cultural inner world. In the face of such meaning-making freedom it is no wonder that millions of narratives for making sense of the world have developed.

Creating a new narrative has been suggested as a way out of the sustainability crisis by a number of researchers (e.g. Merchant 1995, Berry 1998, Sahtouris 2000, Liftin 2003, White 2008), as well as by civil society and governance actors (Tamm 2013, 2017). Elisabeth Sahtouris and Thomas Berry have suggested that the current situation has reached a crisis due to being between narratives and not having a good story (*ibid.*). According to this perspective, a new way of thinking about oneself and one's surrounding is needed for changing the outer world.

End of metanarratives?

For exploring the different overarching approaches to achieving sustainability, the concept of "metanarratives" is used in this chapter. The concept was first brought to broader public attention by the postmodern thinker Jean-Francois Lyotard, who criticised metanarratives as legitimising all-encompassing stories of reality whose time is over (1979). In the same way, Michel Foucault criticised them as legitimising tools generated and supported by the power structures, dismissing the natural variety of things (Gutting 2005). Anthony Giddens suggested focusing instead on the small narratives that people can directly affect at their home, workplace or local community (Halpin 2003). "Metanarrative" is understood here in a similar manner to these postmodernists as an overarching, often unconscious legitimising narrative shaping the way humans make sense of the world, understand their identity and behave. However, whereas they rejected metanarratives and suggested the use of more democratic "small narratives", this chapter argues that neither small nor big narratives can be ultimately rejected as they form an intrinsic part of the human world-making system.

In fact, the empirical research informing this chapter (Tamm 2013, 2017) began by analysing 45 small sustainability-related narratives across nations, genders, social classes and sectors.[3] The underlying patterns forming distinctive metanarratives emerged in the course of analysis: gradually and cumulatively the individual stories merged into narratives with distinct reoccurring patterns and storylines. As the analysis reached a saturation point, two invariable metanarratives with strong legitimising power emerged. After contextualising these European metanarratives in international research, it became evident that they indeed transcend individual and group discourses as well as cultural, geographical and national borders, uniting people with diverse backgrounds to similar ways of thinking and acting to achieve sustainability. Thus, this chapter argues that the often unquestioned normative power of the metanarratives, shaping the individual and collective attitudes and perceptions of the best development paths, is still very much at work, making the claim about the end of metanarratives inaccurate. Understanding narratives as facilitators of mutual understanding across people and (sub)cultures serves as a good starting point for exploring the two metanarratives about sustainable development .It is not suggested that the two metanarratives discussed in this chapter are the only ones concerning the situation. Furthermore, there are also actors that are not aware of the sustainable development related challenges or are sceptical about them, not seeing the current situation as a crisis needing to be addressed at all.

Metanarratives of reconnection and disconnection

The empirical research on sustainable development-related rhetoric and practices of the civil society initiatives and networks and governance level in the European Union over the period of 2000 to 2015 clearly indicated that despite the seeming consensus on the necessity of sustainability transition, there are distinct differences in the underlying logic directly influencing the way sustainable development is understood and practiced. As a result of the analysis, two metanarratives emerged with "taking responsibility" as the central solution of the civil society approach, and "green growth" as the central solution of the governance level (Tamm 2017). The results of the empirical research on the European context were related to prior research on dualistic development models on the international level. Table 10.1 offers an overview of the results.

Table 10.1 Dualistic development perspectives of civil society and governance

Civil society "taking responsibility" metanarrative	Governance "green growth" metanarrative	Tamm 2013, 2017
Strong sustainability	Weak sustainability	Beder 1996, Khalili 2011
Deep ecology	Shallow ecology	Naess 1973, Devall 2001, Macy, Johnstone 2012
Sufficiency	Efficiency	Huber 2000
Postmodernism	Modernism	Giddens 2000
Organic and holistic	Mechanistic and reductionist	Sahtouris 2000, Liftin 2003

The different development models boiled down to the way the role of a human being and its relationship with nature/environment is interpreted: being a connected part of a complex self-regulating system or organism, or a disconnected manager of a mechanism which can be fixed by experts when needed. Nature is respectively regarded as a self-regulating meaningful and valuable entity that requires respect, or as environment that has to be designed and used in the best and most effective way to benefit people, meaning that the resources can be depleted as long as substitutes are found. Faith in human abilities and knowledge is strong in both metanarratives, but whereas the governance approach trusts in human inventiveness, the civil society perspective also trusts in the wisdom of nature, considering it a master of complex homoeostasis humans can learn from.

The analysis of the core aspects of each development perspective resulted in the emergence of three core dichotomies explaining the central differences between the development approaches: disconnection-reconnection, upscaling-downscaling and tangible-intangible. All these processes and qualities are natural and inevitable parts of life, what determines their impact is the context and extent to which they are used. The analysis resulted in disconnection and reconnection emerging as the central dichotomy differentiating between the metanarratives, which is why they are called the metanarratives of reconnection and disconnection.

Disconnection – Reconnection

The unpredictability and uncontrollability of the modern world has made it a "runaway world" (Giddens 2000). To deal with this uncertainty, the metanarratives use different strategies: disconnecting or reconnecting.

Disconnection is characteristic to a reductionist and mechanistic approach that tends to tackle events and processes in a manner separated from each other. While this can be faster, easier and more efficient, it leaves many aspects unnoticed. Disconnection implies ending a connection that has existed and creating a certain distance between oneself and the world. Anthony Giddens has used the disembedded (abstract) vs. embedded (practical) dichotomy to describe this phenomenon (1991). When something is disembedded, it is moved from a concrete, local context to an abstract or virtual state. Giddens argues that the process of disembeddedness is characteristic of modernisation and globalisation, where social actions have become increasingly spread across time and space, loosening the traditional social ties.

Caroline Merchant has described the disconnection process as "the death of nature", changing the perception of the living Mother Nature from a respected entity to dead matter: "If nature is dead, and humans are external, humans are engineers [. . .] Then people can manipulate and manage nature, without having to propitiate nature, and without nature retaliating" (Schoch 2002). The disconnected worldview gives permission to exploit and dominate nature, resulting in the present ecological crisis (*ibid.*). The disconnected approach shares weak sustainability stance when it comes to ensuring that the present and future generations can fulfil their needs. As long as the total capital does not decrease over time in quantity, the substitution of natural capital with manmade capital is allowed (Beder 1996).

The opposite process to disconnection is reconnection. The concept of reconnecting indicates restoring a connection that was lost for some reason. Reconnecting can happen on different levels starting from self, nature, community, places and cultures and involves re-embedding in the concrete, local context. The basis of the reconnection approach is well described by the physicist Fritjof Capra: "All living systems are networks of smaller components, and the web of life as a whole is a multi-layered structure of living systems nestling within other living systems – networks within networks" (1996: 209). In line with strong sustainability, the resources are considered non-substitutable and each type of capital must be maintained in its own right for sustainability to hold (Khalili 2011).

When studying the effects of social connection and disconnection on the personal level, social scientist Brene Brown has discussed fear as a cause for disconnection (Brown 2010, 2012). She identifies two ways of living: with control to avoid shame and fear, leading to disconnection; and without attempting to control the processes resulting in connection. Brown claims that daring to be connected, which requires being vulnerable, allows creativity and innovation. On the other hand, fear of not knowing and not controlling creates the feeling of scarcity, constant comparison with others, anxiety, uncertainty, self-doubt and a sense of shame for not being good enough, resulting in disconnection. Thus, she argues that when we armour up against vulnerability, we also shut down to love, belonging, joy, empathy, creativity and innovation – which give purpose and meaning to human lives – and then need substitutes such as drugs, or excessive food to feel all right (*ibid.*).

This chapter argues that in many ways, disconnecting from the world is an illusion: as animals living in ecosystems, humans are intimately connected with nature and other living beings. The disconnected approach has become too dominant and the balance between the natural processes of (re)connecting and disconnecting has been lost. Excessive fragmentation has led to multifaceted problems. Moving towards a more interrelated and systemic approach is beneficial because the seemingly separate problems cannot be effectively addressed in isolation.

Upscaling – downscaling

What is the direction of change that grants us sustainable development: scaling up or down? In both metanarratives the growth of human wellbeing is relevant; it's just that the nature of desired growth differs. Whereas the reconnection approach considers downscaling as the key to stopping environmental degradation, mitigating climate change, reducing poverty, inequality and social isolation, revitalising the economy and ensuring long-term wellbeing for the present and future generations, the disconnected stance sees upscaling as the key.

The Western economies have developed towards global dependency from the international financial networks. At this level of embeddedness, it is quite difficult to transition towards no-growth economy or even to imagine alternatives (Schoch 2002). For the representatives of the disconnection metanarrative, no economic growth means poverty and major collapse. This suffices to reject alternatives to growth without much further reflection.

In the downscaling metanarrative, the focus is on the qualitative growth, meaning that also no growth or degrowth are considered realistic development options, allowing to return to the human scale and to live within the natural limits. This also means that the focus is placed on relocalising not globalising economic loops, including local production, consumption and disposal.

Supporting downscaling or upscaling depends on the vision of the future. The people living according to the reconnection narrative tend to presume that the current petroculture societies cannot continue in the long run due to the peaking of resource reserves and prepare for a gradual energy descent and simpler way of life to avoid chaos. This involves willingly 'sacrificing' their comforts to lessen the burden on the environment and live according to their values. The proponents of the disconnection approach do not consider adopting a simpler way of life reasonable or necessary. They presume that new energy sources will be found via technological innovation, and these will enable avoiding a low-energy future. On the personal level one is not expected to consume less, as this would be detrimental to economic growth – consumption, production and waste disposal should just become greener and more efficient. This links to the sufficiency-efficiency distinction. Whereas the sufficiency approach tends towards "self-limitation of material needs, withdrawal from the free world-market economy and an egalitarian distribution of the remaining scarce resources" (Huber 2000: 269), the efficiency approach stands for "further economic growth and ecological adaptation of industrial production by improving the environmental performance, i.e. improving the efficient use of material and energy, thus increasing resource productivity in addition to labour and capital productivity" (*ibid.*).

Next to relocalisation, downscaling also involves other re-s, for example reconnecting to the local place, nature, culture and community, or reskilling to become more self-sufficient and independent from big-scale systems. On the personal level, the imperative of growth demands high efficiency and continued success to feel valuable. Having to live up to these high standards on the long run can easily result in weariness, depression or burnout – the opposites of personal sustainability.

The core strength of the downscaling approach is that it counteracts the disembeddedness of the Western way of life and lends a sense of belonging, meaningfulness and security. Focusing on the local scale encourages participation and facilitates taking responsibility not only in rhetoric, but also in practice. Things that are overwhelmingly complex on the global or national scales are much more manageable on the local scale and because they take the local settings into consideration, they are also more likely to succeed. Local initiatives also enjoy a stronger sense of ownership among participants, who act because they need the solutions rather than carry out someone's orders.

Tangible – intangible[4]

The disconnection metanarrative has a specific understanding of what should be developed in a sustainable manner. It focuses on the tangible aspects, leaving little room for considering the intangible aspects. The intangible aspects can be described as qualitative, often invisible and inner cultural aspects. For example, information, understanding, misunderstanding, aesthetic and emotive considerations are all intangible culturally dependent phenomena that have a significant impact on the sustainability processes. Such aspects are not easy to measure or compare, and dealing with them can easily get confusing and time-intensive, which are some of the main arguments for omitting cultural aspects or including them only to a limited extent in the mainstream development discussions (Tamm 2017). This also excludes much of what is crucial and meaningful for people when envisioning the future along with the possibility to question the ability of current systems to foster sustainability beyond mitigating some of the most devastating impacts. The reductionist perception of humans as consumers and their personal contribution as green consumption is not sufficient to motivate people in the long run.

One further argument for not including the intangible aspects has to do with the need to protect the individual freedom: as long as people do not harm others, the private sphere should not be regulated and they should have the right to do as they please. Even if the intangible aspects influencing development are not explicitly addressed and included, it is impossible for humans to act outside of culture, as normative qualitative aspects are an unavoidable part of human lives. The reluctance to include cultural, invisible and inner aspects also reflects the interest of protecting the current system from change. Thus, by leaving the intangible value-related aspects out of political discussions and decision-making, the existing value orientation is perpetuated as it is easier to continue in the old way.

As aspects like values and thoughts, emotions and memories, judgements and prejudices play a significant role in fostering or hemming sustainable development-related processes, there should be more awareness of their impact. Brian Goodwin has called such subjective knowledge "contextual knowledge" (Brockman 1997) and argued that both "objective" as well as "subjective" ways of knowing are relevant factors of human development. Whereas the representatives of the disconnection metanarrative are mostly concerned with knowledge concerning the outer world, the representatives of reconnection metanarrative stress the significance of researching also the inner world. In some disciplines, much value is placed on subjective knowledge, for instance in anthropology, where it is considered a legitimate way of knowing, intrinsic to human societies, regardless of the fact that it cannot be evaluated with the measuring sticks of modern science (Motz 1998: 340).

The role of individuals in making a difference

The desire to change the world for better is not new. Already 2,000 years ago Cicero commented on the human desire to create a better world within the existing world of nature, shaping it according to human needs: "In fine, by means of our own hands, we essay to create as it were a second world within the world of nature" (Goggin 2009: 1). Whereas the reconnection approach encourages acting within the given natural framework and fitting our civilisations to its limits, the disconnection approach encourages trying to adjust nature to our needs and wishes.

Which is the role of the individuals in making a difference according to these metanarratives? Why do people in contemporary societies use their change-making potential in such a limited manner, although there are many ways to make a difference?

One reason for the passivity is that in the face of excessive ecological destruction, social suffering and economic injustice, people often feel overwhelmed by these big-scale processes and remain passive. Practitioner's experience has shown that when people start to solve big-scale problems, they tend to burn out rather fast without a solid basis and a good team (Tamm 2017). The reconnection approach with its emphasis on downscaling suggests starting small. This does not necessarily mean low expectations or impact, but it means choosing a way that does not overwhelm.

Further, the ease of fulfilling short-term desires and goals seems to have made us lose sight of long-term processes and goals. Life in comfort seems to be taken for granted. However, the sustainability threats can easily cause the comfortable petroculture-based world to fall into pieces. Nevertheless, the potential of losing profit and power positions in the short run by making unpopular decisions still outweighs tackling the seemingly abstract long-term threats.

The third reason can be described as the "duplicity syndrome". There is a cognitive gap in sustainable development issues between the urgent rhetoric and slow pace of actions in change-making on the personal and societal levels. Referring to the communist regime characterised by censorship and banned freedom of speech, the Estonian sustainable development strategy for example describes the duplicity syndrome as a type of cognitive gap whereby people act "as one should" in public, whereas their talk and deeds in private life differ from that ideal (Government of the Republic of Estonia 2005: 42). This syndrome is certainly more obvious in repressive regimes, but principally, it is also present in our current daily lives in contemporary democratic societies. The disconnection proponents do not consider this an issue, while the reconnection proponents attempt to overcome this gap by walking their talk.

The fourth reason concerns participation. The question whether it is possible to bring contemporary democratic capitalist systems in line with the requirements posed by the strong sustainability agenda of the reconnection metanarrative has been discussed since the 1970s by grassroots groups and political scientists (Doherty, de Gues 1996). Giddens (1998) has suggested a "third way" that involves adopting the politics of self-actualisation pushed by new social movements instead of the politics of inequality run by political parties. However, much of the population tends to be passive instead of participating in pushing for this "politics of self-actualisation". When comparing the different degrees of involvement that these approaches allow to individuals, substantial differences emerge. In the reconnection approach, the intensity of participation varies from empowerment and collaboration to co-creation and joint decision-making. The disconnection approach tends to prefer not sharing control and forms of partici-pation with top-down decisions, favouring information exchange and consultancy. This seemingly gives participants a voice and calms them down, but on the long run, it frustrates and demotivates participants, resulting in lack of ownership, because people feel heard but not listened to (Tamm 2017).

Depth of change

Representatives of both metanarratives agree on the rhetorical level that for reducing serious negative impacts, changes in the way people live, produce and dispose are necessary. Opinions on the depth and scope of change vary considerably, however, and depend on which sustainable living agenda we are talking about. The weak sustainability approach represented by the disconnection metanarrative with its focus on raising competitiveness and fostering green growth is compatible with the current systems and only needs some reforms to adjust to it. The strong sustainability approach of the reconnection metanarrative does not meet eye-to-eye with the current political, economic, social systems and ways of dealing with nature, and its realisation without a systems' change would not be realistic.

The time of aggressive confrontation, which saw environmental and peace activists commit fierce acts of civil disobedience, is largely over. The proponents of the reconnecting approach have a relatively pragmatic opinion of their own ability to bring about change, agreeing that while their actions are not enough, it is better than simply sitting back, feeling discontent, disconnected and overpowered. Changing the outer world is not considered sufficient to solve the problems, because the causes of certain processes are in the inner world. An example of this attitude that solutions have to start from the inside is the way climate change is not seen as something which must be fought against so much with technological means, but more a challenge to be dealt with by inner climate change, meaning primarily awareness change.

The well-known quotes by Margaret Mead and Karl Marx about impacting societal processes relate to this discussion. Mead is optimistic about the power of groups of people to make a difference: "Never doubt that a small group of thoughtful, committed citizens can change the world. Indeed, it is the only thing that ever has" (Lutkehaus 2008: 261). Marx, on the other hand, argues that human agency is restricted with predetermined conditions: "Men make their own history, but they do not make it just as they please; they do not make it under the circum-stances chosen by themselves, but under the circumstances directly encountered, given and transmitted from the past" (Marx *et al.* 1978: 595). Interestingly, both are right. Metanarratives are legitimising stories about the natural conditions, economic and socio-cultural systems that our ancestors inherit us. As such, they are part of the predetermined frameworks limiting our ability to feel, think and act freely. In case of the unreflexive course of things, people automatically con-tinue with respective preconceived mindsets and behaviours. However, when a group of people becomes aware of the situation by reflecting on it and have decided to make a difference, they have a good chance of breaking free from the constraints of the metanarratives and finding new, innovative solutions.

Solutions: creating new narratives or building reflexive capacity?

It is argued that the disconnection development direction has become too dominant, undermining a healthy diversity and producing problems. This chapter argues that the dominating disconnected approach is not sufficient for understanding and making changes happen, because achieving sustainable development is a complex interconnected long-term issue that cannot be grasped sectorally. Which is the best way forward? Below, two options for dealing with the crisis are discussed: creating a new narrative for balancing the development directions and building reflexive capacity for transcending the metanarratives.

The role of interpretative freedom

Linking back to the discussion of the role of narrativity in human meaning-making (semiosis) at the beginning of this chapter, I argue that one of the reasons for the current sustainability crisis is the unreflexive use of the species-specific ability for abstraction. The growth of the abstract human part of reality based on language and culture, which has enabled the growth of interpretative freedom, has also enabled the current situation where people mistake the unlimited growth on the abstract level for no limits to material growth in the physical world. The key to understanding human meaning-making lies in the ability to realise that the meanings we assign objects are separable from them, individually and culturally dependent, often based on convention. A reflexive person who is able to grasp this arbitrary nature can recognise and exit pre-set meaning structures and as such, the limits of a metanarrative. Indeed, Deely has argued that the meaning-making freedom humanity enjoys arises from a specific kind of knowledge – the conscious observing of the meaning-making process and the ability to reflect upon it (Deely 2005b). Such a reflexive person, whom we might call *homo semioticus*, is aware of the meaning-making process and acknowledges that reflecting upon it depends on a wider context (Deely 2005b: 227–228).

Creating a new narrative or building reflexive capacity?

Often, creating a new narrative, a new culture or a new paradigm is suggested as a way of exiting the crisis. This is considered one possible solution that would help to balance the currently dominating quantitative development approach by integrating qualitative aspects into it, making it more interrelated and humane. From the perspective of surviving the socio-ecological crisis, developing a more interrelated and cooperative approach with nature and each other appears more reasonable than continuing with the disconnected stance (Tamm 2013). Attempts to create a new narrative or a new culture are likely to result in new forms within existing strands of thought, e.g. on the lines of "limits to growth". The downside of this idea is the realisation: how should millions of people come to abandon their existing narratives? Imposing the new narrative does not suit liberal democracy. If it were done in a compulsory way, it would be akin to ecofascism. The only liberal way to achieve this would be by supporting reflexive capacity of citizens in a substantial societal dialogue process for rehumanising the way sustainable development is thought about and practiced. However, it would probably not bring about the great transformation that the people suggesting this solution are hoping for, as there will always be people who follow other narratives and belong to other (sub)cultures.

The alternative option is to support developing the ability to become aware of metanarratives and their limits; not for people to turn to another metanarrative, but in order to build capacity for transcending its limits and finding new ways for dealing with pressing problems. This can be done by fostering a reflexive turn in the society beginning on the individual level. Becoming more aware of the surrounding situation in its diversity and broadening the scope of conscious actions offers freedom from the thought and behavioural patterns. Becoming aware of the benefits and limits of the metanarratives enables freeing oneself from their monopoly. Developing the skill of being reflexive enables seeing beyond the metanarrative a person currently follows and understand that another person might follow a different one. This might help to find common ground and facilitate cooperation on finding practical solutions to shared problems in a new, solution-oriented way. In order to overcome the gap that the metanarratives create in the heads and hearts of the people, the differences need to be acknowledged and studied. It is indeed relevant to become aware and able to transcend the limits of a given metanarrative in order to look more realistically at the given situation. More often than not, choosing the best development path depends on the given situation, and the metanarratives with their ideological and legitimising character tend to make the perception biased.

So instead of suggesting that everyone needs to adopt a new, less harmful and wasteful narrative or a new culture, a qualitative leap towards open-minded reflexive knowledge society is suggested as a solution by developing reflexive awareness and the sense of responsibility and ownership via lifelong learning. Lifelong learning that helps to increase awareness of the interconnectedness of life, openness for not necessarily controlling or knowing, but learning by experimenting are further factors supporting this alternative way of living.

In the face of the current urgency, the "one heart at a time" pace of change, seems too slow. However, it ensures long-lasting change, as instead of outer pressure, it fosters self-motivated long-term commitment for making a difference. Such a reflexive turn starting from the individual level has the potential to gradually facilitate mesolevel (community level) and macro-level (national, global) sustainability transition.

In a way – unavoidably – this also suggests a new narrative of reflexivity. However, instead of suggesting following certain pre-set ideas and practices, it emphasises the way we as humans relate to the world and our ability to reflect on different options. In comparison to *homo narrans*, who is driven by a certain meta-narrative, *homo semioticus* is much more aware of alternative options. For *homo semioticus*, the development of reflexive awareness and meaning-making freedom that enable finding innovative solutions are central. Such an awareness change could be described as a silent revolution.

Conclusions

Living according to an overarching legitimising story of reality, as exemplified by the reconnection and disconnection metanarratives, means interpreting sustainable development processes in a certain manner, often unaware of using a certain framework. Both of these metanarratives are part of the daily world-making, informing the emotions, thoughts, words and actions of certain groups of people and producing consequences which are considered sustainable or unsustainable from different perspectives. Nevertheless, each approach has a certain impact, which makes it possible to estimate their value. On the other hand, the results of this evaluation depend on the criteria of the evaluator. This means that "sustainable development for whom?" should remain among the central questions when discussing sustainability issues.

This situation can perhaps be compared to the metaphor of blind people describing an elephant – what can seem as absolute truth from one standpoint, using one set of criteria, seems relative or even false from other points of view. It is in cooperation that the whole picture of an elephant can be put together, but this requires much tolerance, patience and reflexivity for not jumping into conclusions.

The analysis of the disconnection and reconnection metanarratives demonstrates how different the intent to form a better, more sustainable life can be across individuals and societal groups representing different metanarratives, ranging from disconnecting, upscaling and focus on tangible, quantitative aspects to reconnecting, downscaling and focus on intangible, qualitative aspects as ways towards sustainable development. This diversity clearly shows the relevance of delving deeper, beyond the seeming rhetoric consensus that sustainable development is needed.

Sustainable development has been a macro-level concept since the outset; the micro-level has mostly been left out of the discussions or tackled merely in a limited way. However, finding macro-scale solutions to sustainability issues is often problematic as the plans tend to remain too ambiguous. Downscaling, reconnecting and considering the intangible aspects would help to bring sustainability closer to people, making it more understandable and relevant.

Without understanding the relevance of intangible, qualitative aspects influencing personal choices as well as societal developments, it is difficult to comprehend that the way things are believed and perceived to be is not the only way, but only one way among others. Indeed, a qualitative analysis of micro-level processes starting from individuals and their personal sustainability is considered instrumental for facilitating larger scale sustainability transitions and deserves much more academic and empirical attention. Becoming aware of the core meaning structures informing different metanarratives makes looking beyond these habitual frameworks possible and increases the probability of developing innovative solutions benefitting different stakeholder groups.

In terms of dealing with the current imbalanced situation, two options were discussed: developing a new narrative and fostering a reflexive turn to transcend the narrative. Developing a new inspiring and empowering narrative as a solution for exiting the crisis could happen when attempting to balance the dominating disconnection metanarrative by bringing in some aspects from the reconnection narrative, resulting in a new, synthesised narrative. This would help to re-humanise the sustainability perception that has become too abstract and overwhelmingly global, and foster a sense of positive responsibility and ownership among people and communities. However, achieving a switch to this new metanarrative among the population does not seem realistic. The new narrative would rather be adopted only by some groups and this would not bring about a dramatic change of perspectives that the authors of this solution are hoping for.

Instead, fostering a reflexive turn in the society beginning on the individual level is suggested. Becoming more aware of the inner and outer situation and broadening the scope of conscious actions to more aspects of life is suggested as the key to personal and, consequently, communal and macro-level sustainable development. Reflexivity is needed to overcome the habitual patterns people automatically follow in order to become aware of further options and alternatives. In short, it is suggested that becoming more aware of the habitual mental and emotional patterns common to metanarratives helps to build a reflexive basis necessary for facilitating transformations towards a much more broad-based personal and societal sustainability.

Cultivating reflexivity and raising awareness of alternatives are suggested as ways for overcoming ignorance and prejudice and fostering mutual understanding. A better understanding of the differences between the groups can stimulate a more symmetric communication for moving towards a better cooperation among stakeholders interested in bringing about change. Qualitative growth in reflexivity and awareness are inner processes that happen on the individual level, one heart and head at a time. As a lifelong learning process, this change might be relatively slow, but it will be self-motivated, not depending on the outer pressure.

Diversity is healthy in nature and also helps to ensure the resilience of human cultures and societies. So instead of trying to establish a new dominating metanarrative, growing in reflexive awareness is the preferred solution. The difference lays in our level of awareness of the role metanarratives play in our lives and accordingly, we have more or less interpretative and creative freedom.

Notes

1   The underlying research of the author consisted of two parts: an empirical case study analysis of sixteen cases to study the sustainable development-related rhetoric and practices on the civil society and governance level in the period between 2000 and 2015

in the European Union (EU), and a theoretical analysis contextualising the results in existing international research.
2   Author's translation from Estonian.
3   The author's research project "Metanarratives of Change: Analysis of Civil Society and Governance Approaches to Sustainable Development in Europe. Exploring the Relevance of Culture for Sustainability" (2017) informing this chapter used constructivist grounded theory methodology to explicate and explore some civil society and governance approaches to sustainable development issues in contemporary Europe. The sample included the EU, Estonia, Germany and Portugal representing the governance sector, and the Global Ecovillage Network, the Transition network and the Let's Do It network, local initiatives from all the participating countries, plus the international networks themselves, from the civil society sector.
4   This dichotomy includes the qualities of visible and invisible, inner and outer, qualitative and quantitative, meaningful and random.

References

Beder, S. (1996): *The Nature of Sustainable Development.* Newham, Australia: Scribe Publications.

Berry, T. (1998): *The Dream of the Earth.* The Capital Institute report *Economics, Finance, Governance, and Ethics for the Anthropocene.* Retrieved October 2016: www.capital institute.org/sites/capitalinstitute.org/files/docs/Economics, Finance, Governance, and Ethics for the Anthropocene.pdf.

Brockman, J. (1997, 29 April): *A New Science Of Qualities. An Interview with Brian Goodwin.* Retrieved May 2014: www.edge.org/3rd_culture/goodwin/goodwin_p2.html.

Brown, B. (2010): *The Gifts of Imperfection. Let Go of Who You Think You're Supposed To Be and Embrace Who You Are.* Center City, MN: Hazelden.

Brown, B. (2012): *Daring Greatly. How the Courage To Be Vulnerable Transforms the Way We Live, Love, Parent, and Lead.* New York: Gotham Books.

Capra, F. (1996): *The Web of Life: A New Scientific Understanding of Living systems.* New York: Anchor Books.

Dauvergne, P. (2009): *The A to Z of Environmentalism.* Lanham, MD: Scarecrow Press.

Deely, J. (1993): *The Human Use of Signs, or, Elements of Anthroposemiosis.* Savage, MD: Rowman & Littlefield Publishers.

Deely, J. (2005a): *Defining the Semiotic Animal. A Postmodern Definition of "Human Being" to Supersede the Modern Definition of "Res Cogitans".* Sofia, Bulgaria: New Bulgarian University.

Deely, J. (2005b): *Basics of Semiotics.* Tartu, Estonia: University of Tartu (Tartu Semiotics Library, 4).

Devall, B. (2001): The Deep, Long-Range Ecology Movement: 1960–2000 – A Review. In *Ethics and the Environment* Vol. 6, No. 1, pp. 18–41.

Diamond, J. (2005): *Collapse: How Societies Choose to Fail or Succeed.* New York: Viking Press.

Doherty, B.; de Geus, M. (Eds) (1996): *Democracy and Green Political Thought. Sustainability, Rights and Citizenship.* London: Routledge.

Ehrlich, P; Ehrlich, A. (1975): *The Population Bomb.* Mattituck, NY: Amereon.

Faber, N.; Jorna, R.; van Engelend, J. (2005): The Sustainability of "Sustainability" – A Study into the Conceptual Foundations of the Notion "Sustainability". In *Journal of Environmental Assessment Policy & Management* Vol. 7, No. 1, pp. 1–33.

Garrett, H. (1968): The Tragedy of the Commons. In *Science* Vol. 162, No. 3859, pp. 1243–1248.

Geertz, C. (1973): Thick Description: Toward an Interpretive Theory of Culture. In *The Interpretation of Cultures: Selected Essays*, pp. 3–30. New York: Basic Books.

Giddens, A. (1990): *The Consequences of Modernity*. Redwood City, CA: Stanford University Press.

Giddens, A. (1991): *Modernity and Self-Identity: Self and Society in the Late Modern Age.* Redwood City, CA: Stanford University Press.

Giddens, A. (1998): *The Third Way: The Renewal of Social Democracy*. Cambridge: Polity Press.

Giddens, A. (2000): *Runaway World: How Globalization is Reshaping Our Lives*. New York: Routledge.

Goggin, N.P. (Ed.) (2009): *Rhetorics, Literacies, and Narratives of Sustainability*. London: Routledge.

Goodwin, B. (1995): Neo-Darwinism Has Failed as an Evolutionary Theory. In *The Times Higher Education Supplement*, 19 May.

Government of the Republic of Estonia (2005): *Estonian National Strategy on Sustainable Development "Sustainable Estonia 21" (SE21)*. Retrieved 20 March 2014: https://riigikantselei.ee/sites/default/files/content-editors/Failid/estonia_sds_2005.pdf.

Gutting, G. (2005): *The Cambridge Companion to Foucault*. Cambridge; New York: Cambridge University Press.

Halpin, D. (2003): *Hope and Education: The Role of the Utopian Imagination*. London, New York: Routledge.

Huber, J. (2000): Towards Industrial Ecology: Sustainable Development as a Concept of Ecological Modernization. In *Journal of Environmental Policy & Planning*, Vol. 2, No. 4, pp. 269–285.

Jäger, J. (2009): The Governance of Science for Sustainability. In W.N. Adger, A. Jordan (Eds) *Governing Sustainability*. Cambridge: Cambridge University Press.

Kaplinski, J. (2003): Mitte keskkond, vaid LOODUS. In *Looduskaitsealaseid töid* VII, p. 9. Tartu: Tartu Üliõpilaste Looduskaitsering. Retrieved December 2016: www.elks.ee/index.php?id=1088.

Khalili, N.R. (2011): *Practical Sustainability: From Grounded Theory to Emerging Strategies*. New York: Palgrave Macmillan.

Leopold, A. (1992): *Am Anfang war die Erde. Plädoyer zur Umwelt-Ethik*. Munich, Germany: Knesebeck.

Liftin, K. (2003): Towards an Integral Perspective on World Politics: Secularism, Sovereignty and the Challenge of Global Ecology. In *Millennium: Journal of International Studies*, Vol. 32, No. 1, pp. 29–56.

Lyotard, J.-F. (1979): Introduction: The Postmodern Condition: A Report on Knowledge. Retrieved May 2016: www.idehist.uu.se/distans/ilmh/pm/lyotard-introd.htm.

Lutkehaus, N.C. (2008): *Margaret Mead: The Making of an American Icon*. Princeton, NJ: Princeton University Press.

MacIntyre, A. (1984): *After Virtue: A Study in Moral Theory*. Notre Dame, IN: University of Notre Dame Press.

Macy, J.; Johnstone C. (2012): The Great Turning. In M. Harland, W. Keepin (Eds) *Worldview Key: The Song of the Earth. A Synthesis of the Scientific and Spiritual Worldviews*, pp. 93–98. East Meon, UK: Permanent Publications

Malthus, T. (1826): *An Essay on the Principle of Population; or, a View of Its Past and Present Effects on Human Happiness*. London: John Murray. Volume 1. Retrieved May

2017: http://darwin-online.org.uk/content/frameset?pageseq=1&itemID=A545.1&view
type=text.

Marx, K.; Engels, F.; Tucker, R.C (Eds) (1978): *The Marx-Engels Reader*. New York,
London: W.W. Norton & Company.

Meadows, D.H.; Meadows D.L.; Randers J.; Behrens III, W.W. (1972): *The Limits to
Growth*. New York: Universe Books.

Merchant, C. (1992): *Radical Ecology: The Search for a Livable World*. New York:
Routledge.

Merchant, C. (1995): Reinventing Eden: Western Culture as a Recovery Narrative. In
W. Cronon (Ed.) *Uncommon Ground: Toward Reinventing Nature*, pp. 132–159. New
York: W.W. Norton & Company.

Mestrovic, S. (1998): *Anthony Giddens: The Last Modernist*. New York: Routledge.

Motz, M. (1998): The Practice of Belief. In *The Journal of American Folklore*. Vol. 111,
No. 441, pp. 339–355.

Naess, A. (1973): The Shallow and the Deep, Long Range Ecology Movements. In *Inquiry*,
Oslo, No. 16. Retrieved April 2016: www.ecology.ethz.ch/education/Readings_stuff/
Naess_1973.pdf.

Prugh, T.; Assadourian, E. (2003): What is Sustainability Anyway? In *World Watch
Magazine* 16 (No. 5). Retrieved November 2016: www.worldwatch.org/epublish/1/95.

Sachs, W. (1997). Sustainable Development. In M. Redclift, G. Woodgate (Eds) *International Handbook of Environmental Sociology*, pp. 71–82. Cheltenham, UK: Edward
Elgar.

Sahtouris, E. (2000): *Earthdance: Living Systems in Evolution*. San Jose, CA: University Press.

Schoch, R. (2002): A Conversation with Carolyn Merchant. In *California Monthly* Vol.
112, No. 6, pp. 26–30.

Sebaldt, M. (2002): *Sustainable Development – Utopie oder realistische Vision? Karriere
und Zukunft einer entwicklungspolitischen Strategie*. Hamburg: Kovac.

Spitzer, L. (1942): Milieu and Ambiance: An Essay in Historical Semantics. In *Philosophy
and Phenomenological Research* Vol. 3, No. 2, pp. 169–218.

Tamm, K. (2013): Reflections on Grassroots and Governance Approaches to Sustainable
Development in Current Europe. In Meltzer, G. (Ed.): *Proceedings of the 11th
International Communal Studies Association Conference "Communal Pathways to
Sustainable Living"*, pp. 201–213. Findhorn, UK.

Tamm, K. (2017): "Metanarratives of Change: Analysis of Civil Society and Governance
Approaches to Sustainable Development in Europe. Exploring the Relevance of Culture
for Sustainability". In print-preparation.

Victorri, B. (2007): Homo Narrans: The Role of Narration in the Emergence of Human
Language. In HAL, a Multi-disciplinary Open Access Archive for the Deposit and
Dissemination of Scientific Research Documents. Retrieved June 2016: https://halshs.
archives-ouvertes.fr/halshs-00153724.

White, H. (1980): The Value of Narrativity in the Representation of Narrativity. In *Critical
Inquiry*, No. 1, Autumn, pp. 5–27.

White, Jr. L. (2008): Meie ökoloogilise kriisi ajaloolised juured. In. R. Keskpaik, K. Keerus,
A. Vaher (Eds) *Keskkonnaeetika võtmetekste*, pp. 36–50.

Wilde, Oscar (1891): *The Soul of Man under Socialism*. Retrieved August 2017: http://
libcom.org/library/soul-of-man-under-socialism-oscar-wilde.

World Commission on Environment and Development (WCED) (1987): *Our Common
Future*. Oxford: Oxford University Press.

11 Sustainability without the I-sense is nonsense

Inner 'technologies' for a viable future and the inner dimension of sustainability

Shelley Sacks

Introduction

This chapter presents a *social sculpture-connective practice* methodology that depends on the I-sense[1] in the context of the movement towards personal sustainability or sustainability in transition explored in this book.

The concept of "technology" is used here to signify systematic engagement in the Aristotelian sense and in special reference to the new concept "inner technologies" discussed in this chapter. It is not used with the connotation of dominating over nature or humans, but rather in line with Aristotle, for whom technê was the mode of bringing something into existence, which has its efficient cause in the maker and not in itself.[2]

The term social sculpture ("Soziale Plastik" in German) was developed in the 1970s by Joseph Beuys, German interdisciplinary artist, to highlight our role as artists of our own lives and of the social sphere. Beuys argued that we do not need to feed an outmoded social-economic system and create the great suffering of nature that causes all beings to suffer (Beuys, Mennekes 1996). The *I-sense* is an important concept in the field of contemporary social sculpture. As one of the social senses in Rudolf Steiner's "12 Senses" it enables the encounter both with oneself and with the being of another (Steiner 2009).

Social sculpture as an experiential-knowing methodology highlights 1) the nature of the imaginal process in our everyday thought, 2) the inner atelier or rent-free inner workspace[3] in which this imaginal work[4] takes place, and 3) the role of imaginal work in enabling the encounter with myself, the other and the world.

In so doing this chapter also seeks to open up awareness of personal sustainability and the largely ignored inner dimension of sustainability – a frame predominantly used in this chapter. This chapter argues that both these dimensions of sustainability are central for raising awareness of the relevance of inner technologies alongside the outer technologies and for developing new imaginaries for transitioning from the dualistic mindsets of the anthropocene era to the ecological age. Thomas Berry described this ecological age as "the ecosoic era", which "seeks ultimately to bring the human activities on the Earth into alignment with the other forces functioning throughout the planet so that a creative balance will be achieved" (Berry, Swimme 1992: 261).

The role and responsibility of the human being

This recognition of both *personal sustainability* and the *inner dimension of sustainability* in the sustainability discourse has several, important implications. It foregrounds the role and responsibility of the human being in sustainable development, and as a being in-the-state-of-becoming, which, in turn, creates an additional arena in the field of sustainability. This includes an understanding of the connection between inner and outer human action: of the I-sense. This activating of the inner field, with the kind of strategies of disruption and alienation that Berthold Brecht speaks of (Brecht 1961), enables forms of *internal mobilisation*, which in turn gives a particular tone and meaning to our perception of human agency. For, although there is much evidence that other life forms have agency, it is only human beings that can take responsibility for the human value systems and habits of mind[5] informing human actions of the past, present and future. Accepting and recognising this responsibility for how we think, perceive and relate to the world, illuminates the need for a dimension of sustainable development that engages actively with the world "in here" – our mindsets,[6] values and attitudes – as much as with the world "out there". If human beings are to face the sustainability challenges of living more carefully, consciously and cooperatively with each other and all life forms, in a fragile biosphere, understanding these personal and inner dimensions of sustainability is essential.

Working with these sustainability dimensions also means learning to work with the *invisible materials*[7] of our values, attitudes, perceptions and ways of thinking, in order to reconfigure our relationship to the world, and to develop a mindset based on interdependence as the only sound basis for a viable future. This perspective highlights the role of consciousness, imagination and aesthetic, enlivened thinking in which the human being and the inter-connective I-sense are central. This, however, is quite different from hierarchical anthropocentrism. Rather it is about experiencing with this enlivened I-sense and recognising, in all humility, that how we think and act *is* our responsibility. This focus on creative consciousness as a primary *means of production* – of self-production and societal production – is based on a phenomenological reflective practice. This inner creative practice that depends on "*imaginal* thinking" enables the distillation of experience through "connective distance" (Sacks, Zumdick 2013: 8) and underpins the process of "making sense". It is this capacity to see what we see including what we feel and think, that creates the conditions for becoming free, self-determining beings. Such experiential perception enables us to confront our values, attitudes and habits of thought, and potentially therefore to make choices informed by holistic thinking and a perception of interdependence. For this we need to develop our capacities of perception and understanding, which will enhance our subtle potential and our appreciation of connective thinking and promote inner technologies as an essential aspect of working towards a viable future.

What is being sustained and from whose perspective?

One of the weaknesses of the concepts of "sustainability" and "sustainable development" is reflected in the ease with which these terms have been co-opted. For although both terms can signify radical changes in lifestyle, non-destructive technologies, and, ways of approaching situations whose goal is a material, economic and socially viable future, in the current system of growth economics, they can have a limiting view of what "sustaining" means, what is being sustained and whose interests this is in.

Even if "sustainable" was originally intended to mean development that is *viable in an ongoing way* that protects and sustains the biosphere for all life forms, sustainability has in many instances, local and global, been confused with a particular growth agenda to the point where its priority is to increase corporate dividends, with environmental benefits as a secondary factor. These gains in the name of sustainability are often made possible by the green washing of destructive practices and intentions, and through complex forms of mitigation. One only has to look at the carbon credits and biofuel industries. The term sustainability has in fact got so stretched that an ecologically suspect, exploitative business could be deemed "sustainable" if its profitmaking trajectory is good, and it has growing markets.

"Sustainable development" is an even more problematic term. The distorted interpretations of sustainability are compounded by notions of *development* deriving from the capitalist extractive agenda, from a western idea of what "developed" means, and from Gross National Product as a primary measure of wealth and progress. In this agenda sustainable development could mean that members of a subsistence economy become stakeholders in a corporate deal to ensure a more sustainable yield, without being in a position to consider the long-term effects to their lifestyle and the land. And this can happen even when an environmental impact study has been done but has overlooked the human issues. One example of this is in central Africa, where the declaration of eco-conservation areas, 'job creation' eco-lodges and game parks, have resulted in hundreds of thousands of people being displaced from the rainforest, and almost forced into becoming poachers. "Participatory mapping" approaches[8] in the Congo River basin engage rainforest communities in imaginal work towards future scenarios, which begins to link inner and outer forms of sustainability.

Despite such issues with "sustainability" and "sustainable development", their widespread currency makes it strategic to use them to keep expanding the sustainability discourse and reach the world of the corporations, science and policy making in which they now hold sway. Although not resolving issues with "sustainability" or "development" the terms "personal sustainability" and the "inner dimension of sustainability", begin to redress something of what is missing.

In the field of contemporary social sculpture and connective practice I nevertheless find it more appropriate to think in terms of a just and ecologically *viable* future for all life forms. The German word "zukunftsfähig" – sometimes used to replace "sustainable development" and "sustainability" – is not open to the same kind of distortions. This is partly because in the word "zukunftsfähig", "viable" and "future" are interconnected. In addition, the term "viable" is clearly a value judgment that requires criteria and discussion. It does not pass for neutral as easily as "sustainable development".

Taking responsibility and shifting responsibility

The other frame that is legitimately questioned is the "anthropocene era" (Vansintjan 2015). Amid much controversy, scientific bodies nevertheless agreed in 2016, that a new descriptor was needed to differentiate between the Holocene age and the recent period in which human actions have caused far-reaching changes to the earth and its biosphere (Carrington 2016). What they did not adequately consider was that these anthropogenic changes result from the actions of a minority of cultures and countries. To overcome this distortion it has been suggested that this period of extreme human impact might more appropriately be termed the "capitalocene" (Kunkel 2017).

On the other hand, the "anthropocene" does provide a larger frame for the anthropogenic destruction in the countless ill-considered human interactions with the world and their often, unintended consequences. Many who use it as a signifier, seek to develop integrative systems of living, including production and consumption, which reduce further destruction of the climate, the forests, the rivers, the oceans, the soil and the myriad creatures that enliven this world. But sustainability as a modus operandi – despite the 1990's more "integrative, multidimensional approach to sustainability" (Kopfmüller 2011 as cited by Banse, Parodi 2012) – has concerned itself largely with the environment 'out there', even if it now includes the social and cultural dimensions (Parodi 2015). Sustainability, one could say, has not engaged sufficiently with the forms of thinking that have created this exploitative juggernaut; or with the dominant mindset, whose self-interest and alienating attitudes shape how we relate to persons, cultures and the other-than-human world. By paying insufficient attention to *the inner dimension of sustainability* in the transition from the anthropocene to a more humane and ecologically viable world, sustainable development – even when it includes the economic, social and cultural dimensions alongside the environmental – threatens to eclipse the human being: the very source of its transformative agenda.

Personal and inner dimensions of sustainability

Although personal sustainability, with its focus on values and mindsets, is significant in addressing this partial eclipse of human agency, the term, if used alone, can suggest that its concern is primarily with individuals. It therefore seems more appropriate for me to use "inner dimension of sustainability" for framing integrative social sculpture methodologies, which seek to enable connective action based on both individual transformation and through empathic engagement and exchange between individuals, groups and cultures.

Imagination also serves – individually and collectively – to connect us emotionally, aesthetically and morally with what otherwise can remain conceptual understandings. By enabling new personal and collective imaginaries to arise, which mobilise us internally, *responsibility* instead of being an externally driven, moral imperative becomes an internally motivated *ability-to-respond.*[9] By reclaiming the *aesthetic* as that which enlivens our being, in contrast to the *anesthetic* or numbness, we can begin to see the connection between the enlivening aesthetic process and the *ability-to-respond* (Sacks 1998, 2011, 2017; Kurt, Sacks 2013). The way such connective practices enable the enlivening of both individual and social processes shows why "inner dimension of sustainability" is more appropriate than "personal sustainability".

Until fairly recently however, both *personal sustainability* and *the inner dimension of sustainability* have largely been overlooked, at least in practice. Even the *Sustainable Development Goals* for 2015–2030 (United Nations 2015), which give substantial consideration to the economic, social and cultural dimensions of sustainability, largely bypass its *inner* dimension. This eclipse of the inner dimension of external transformation and action begins way back in western culture in the division between *technê* (skill) and *epistêmê* (knowledge), as well as *technê* (outer craft) and *psyche* (inner field).

Eclipse of the inner dimension

"Technê" is a concept from ancient Greek philosophy from which our "technosphere" (Puech 2016) derives. Although related primarily to art, skill and craft, and seen mostly as a lower form of knowledge, philosophers like Aristotle included in technê, the arts of speaking, discussion and thinking,[10] while the Stoics regarded "virtue" to be a kind of technê to do with the art of life (Parry 2014). Over the centuries the differences between technê (skill) and *epistêmê* (knowledge), between practice and theory, widened into a seemingly unbridgeable chasm. By the time of the Enlightenment the separation was complete. Doing and thinking, subject and object, inner and outer fields were binaries. Even though these oppositions were theoretically overcome in Einstein's unified field thinking, and then in quantum physics, the legacy of this ancient western division is still visible. It manifests in the separation between literalness and the poetic, objective *fact* and subjective *fiction*, and in the emphasis on tools, prosthetics, devices and data for solving all manner of problems and enhancing human agency. A key problem with this is that the source of many eco-social problems – the consciousness and mindsets of individuals, groups and cultures – is not adequately engaged with by focusing on solving the external problems.

The introduction of the "noosphere" by Teilhard de Chardin and Vladimir Vernadsky in 1925 (Fuchs-Kittowski, Krüger 1997) aimed to complement their notion of the "biosphere" and offered a counterpoint to the growing "technosphere".

Noosphere[11] was the missing sphere of consciousness. The noosphere refers to the mental envelope or sphere of thought they saw as encompassing the earth. Since then many western philosophers and scientists – among them David Bohm, David Peat, Rupert Sheldrake, Jon Kabatt Zinn, Francisco Varela and Arthur Zajonc, who have also engaged with Eastern and Indigenous Knowledge traditions – have tackled this subtle field. Through their work they have shown that what seems insubstantial interacts with the visible world and has consequences. This noosphere is the arena of "collective intelligence"[12] and "subtle activism" (Nicol 2015) in which forms of meditation, mindfulness, prayer and other subtle processes are practiced to contribute to shifts in consciousness. In the past few decades, proposals have been put forward that consider the Internet (Nicol 2015: 166) to be part of this sphere of collective intelligence enveloping the planet.

But even if we can cause shifts in consciousness in this noosphere, this is somewhat different from the imaginal work done with the connective practice methodology as an individual in a group, which enables a *direct experience of agency* and with it new creative strategies for developing an integrative relationship to ourselves, to each other and to the planet. This has certain parallels with Thich Nhat Hanh's methods (Hanh 2003), Trungpa's "meditation in action" (Trungpa 1970) and the Dalai Lama's emphasis through the Mind & Life Institute[13] on the need to bring forms of contemplative thinking from the spiritual traditions into the secular field.

Examples of connective practice methodology: imaginal work in inner atelier and the development of the Earth Forum

James Hillman, Paul Klee and Joseph Beuys all use the term "imaginal thought" ("bildhaftes Denken" in German). Imaginal work is my term for the processes that involve imaginal thought. The imaginal work in the inner atelier originated in my childhood when I realised I could gather, hold and convey perceptions, feelings and thoughts from my inner space to the space of another, and in doing so I could affect the perceptions, feelings and thoughts of another (Kurt, Sacks 2013). My contact with Beuys years later confirmed how this intuitive and imaginal thinking can be understood as a form of inner sculpting that is central to Beuys' 'expanded conception of art'. This inner sculpting gives rise to external forms that are not confined to the art-world. Beuys regularly emphasised that it is the context and the need that determines the type and appropriateness of the form (Beuys 2004). Examples of the external forms resulting from inner sculpting in the inner atelier include dialogue processes, participatory actions, educational forms, direct action practices and socio-economic forms like unconditional basic income. Beuys clarified the term "social sculpture" by emphasising both the inner sculpting process and "the invisible materials of thought, speech and discussion" (Beuys in Tisdall 1979). Over the years, I have widened these invisible materials to include also questions, attitudes, values, habits of mind and forms of experiential knowing. This makes it easier to see the relationship between the inner and outer field: how attitudes become form and questions lead to responses and actions.

The imaginal practice and the development of the Earth Forum methodology

The imaginal practice in the inner atelier is one example of what the inner dimension of sustainability can involve. It is also a set of understandings and creative strategies,[14] integral to several social sculpture instruments of consciousness.

One of the stand-alone, scalable and more widely known of these social sculpture instruments of consciousness is Earth Forum.[15] In the Earth Forum methodology the participants are introduced to their inner ateliers and an imaginal thought practice. In this inner atelier each person explores the inner images that arise from their experiential walk on the planet in Phase 1 of the Earth Forum process. Re-entering these images enables participants to experience how they think, how they see and how they could change the lenses with which they see, what is emerging in them and in the group, and what possibilities exist for inner and outer connective action. This enhances ones sense of agency for personal, social and system change. Through such instruments of consciousness the aesthetic, enlivening process can be understood as a connective process that enhances our ability-to-respond by mobilising us internally in both inner and outer field of action. This ability-to-respond is a term I developed to signify the ethical and moral responsiveness that can be activated through connective strategies and is completely different to responsibility as duty and a moral imperative that comes from the outside.

The following narrative sections introduce core elements of the inner atelier practice through describing a few key situations of its evolution into the Earth Forum *methodology*. This will introduce the special character of the practice, and provide a sense of the potential in such practices and strategies as instruments of consciousness.

Situation 1: conflicting visions of sustainability around the table

The roots of Earth Forum lie in a frustrating situation from 1999 to 2002, which was triggered by a generous donation I received to do something innovative in the field of sustainability. Although there were no strings attached, I wanted the donor to also participate in the exploratory process. We decided to involve people we each respected for their involvement in the field of sustainability. After 18 months of regular meetings, events and experiments, I realised why we were struggling to develop a way forward. Despite using the same phrase "sustainability", each of the eight people at the table had different perspectives, priorities and even values – each person's take on sustainability valued a somewhat different future. Instead of giving up, I realised that these different takes on a sustainable future were in fact a microcosm of the macro situation. If we could not find a way to work with our conflicting worldviews and different sustainable development perspectives, then how could we hope others might succeed? We agreed to articulate the worldviews at the table and try to live into our different pictures.

This process although productive was never completed, due to differences in priorities and modes of engagement. At that point I had not yet developed the appropriate creative strategies to adequately engage people in this inner image-making process.

Situation 2: conflicting visions of the future in a South African village

A few months later in 2002, arising out of my involvement in the World Summit for Sustainable Development in Johannesburg,[16] I got a request to come to a village deep in the bush, near the north-western boundary of South Africa. I was told there was a conflict about a 'sustainable development' proposal. Although it was not entirely clear why I was being invited, I agreed to go and listen. I discovered that the conflict had arisen because a car manufacturer wanted to create a 'sustainable development' project in the area where the traditional healers gathered their plants. The new young and politically progressive mayor who had recently moved in from one of the big cities had welcomed this because it would boost employment. She had set aside new land, double the size, where the healers could plant their sacred medicines. She thought they could even produce more to sell in the town. The healers were shocked and had refused: sacred plants were found and gathered, not planted. Furthermore, the elders were concerned that the project might poison the river.

Upon arrival in the mayor's hot concrete office I was introduced to six men, ranging in age from 25 to 80, representing different interest groups involved in the conflict. There were the local church leader, the youth leader, a representative of the traditional healers, a young representative from the car company and two elders from the village committee. All looked rather stern and bothered. It emerged that the mayor had invited me at the suggestion of her friends, but as she was not that popular I was in a rather awkward situation. And, to make it worse, she had introduced me as coming to help solve their problems! To ease the initial setting of mistrust I re-introduced myself as an artist who explored things together with people and that I was there, not to solve problems, but to hear about the situation if they wanted to share it. So this was the setting. Mistrust, deadlock *and* different worldviews!

In response to their questions about me, I described the Exchange Values project and its social sculpture process with small producers in the Caribbean and consumers in Europe and how we had worked exploring inner pictures of the external situation. The church leader said this sounded very interesting and asked why I did not do the same with them. Suddenly what had been a 3-month long social sculpture process with banana farmers in the Caribbean was about to become an unprepared 2-hour imaginal process in this village.

Before asking everyone to close their eyes, I introduced the rent-free inner atelier/workspace that we each carry with us: the space in which we can see our memories and our dreams, and even experience past feelings. I asked everyone to make a picture in this inner space of the contested area by the river: to hold it, look at it very carefully, and also try to see the things that were not directly there, like the village upstream and the village downstream, and the seasons. After 10 minutes with everyone absorbed in their inner space I asked them to re-enter their picture, trying to imagine the car factory as well and see how the picture changed and how they felt about it. Next I asked them to imagine how they hoped this area would look in 100 years. After a few more minutes in their inner space, everyone was invited to share their experience in the setting of active listening. This meant listening carefully to each other's pictures, without discussion, simply trying to see the different pictures in our own inner space, without liking or disliking what the person was describing. At this point the company representative left. The process of sharing the inner pictures was intense and significant. I realised that people were not only hearing each individual person's picture, but also experiencing all the pictures together. The pictures hung in the atmosphere, speaking volumes, not only about the outer situation, but also carrying people's fears, hopes, dilemmas and feelings. Despite the difficulties embodied in some of the pictures, there was also more energy in the room. Everyone seemed intrigued about the inner space and energised by what we had just done. The participants felt that this was a real outcome – to see each person's picture and the pictures altogether – and that they could now continue to explore with some respect for each other's views, what progress and sustainability might mean for this village and the surrounding area. For me it confirmed the huge difference between trying to resolve things by debating and arguing, in contrast to engaging with a situation in a mode that enables collective imaginal engagement. Unsurprisingly the car company dropped the project. The gain was however, that key people in the village had experienced a process that enabled them to work with differences, and engendered some enthusiasm for thinking together about the future.

Having been involved in cultural activism and alternative development in South Africa in the 1980s, and working with Paulo Freire's methodology (Freire 2013), I recognised that what had taken place was an example of real capacity building, and a confirmation that people could experience this kind of imaginal work with invisible materials as an outcome. Analysing this largely unplanned session I realised there was a whole set of interconnected strategies that could enable people to engage with their own and each other's attitudes, worldviews and perceptions of sustainable development.

Situation 3: a process to engage people with the climate crisis

In 2010 I was invited to develop a practice for communities and citizens in South Africa, in the run up to the 2011 Climate Summit. Convinced by then of the mobilising, connective value of the inner atelier/workspace process, I proposed a new version of this process titled Earth Forum, aiming to enable people to relate to the climate crisis individually and as communities, and with the potential to be scaled out to an unlimited number of people.

Since the first explorations with the inner atelier/workspace process in 1996 with the farmers in the Caribbean and in 2002 in the South African village the method had developed significantly. In 2007 and 2011 in Switzerland – in the Goetheanum cultural centre near Basel and the Voegele Kulturzentrum, Zurich – I had experimented with this process working with citizens and producer-consumer groups in the Exchange Values project. These two opportunities to engage in a very different context with many hundreds of people over extended periods of 4 to 5 months helped me to refine the imaginal work practice. It had also enabled a much closer look at the transformative potential of this expanded aesthetic process and the opportunity to reflect on the aesthetic as enlivened being and its relationship to the ability-to-respond.

Working with organisations and groups of 20–30 individuals during this 3-hour process, I introduced people to their inner atelier/workspace. The imaginal work and active listening process was now focused on issues in the global economy, relating them to oneself as a producer and consumer, and exploring different dimensions of one's agency. The process was initiated by three questions: *In what sense am I an artist? What do I produce? What helps or hinders this?* These questions enabled the participants to uncover their own conceptions of work and productivity, and connect imaginatively to their position in the global economy. To enable this I encouraged people to see images of their daily life and actions in their inner workspace, instead of trying to *think about* the questions. Then, avoiding judging what had emerged, to see it all carefully, with generous eyes, and from as many different angles as possible. This process of letting images come, re-entering and mining them for new perspectives, and of gathering substance through the active listening to each person's discoveries enabled collective insights to emerge that went beyond the individual contributions. What had been gathered was often more than the sum of the parts. It was as if a kind of 'social substance' had been generated. It was also clear that the whole process inspired a great many participants, enabling a new sense of agency that encouraged and surprised them.

Over the months it also became clear that several people wanted to try and guide the process, which led me to develop an informal manual.[17] Participating in a process that someone else was guiding, I noticed certain things that greatly diluted the focus. One of these had to do with the role of facilitator who is outside of the process. Instead of 'facilitator', I experimented with 'responsible participant' who was fully engaged and on an equal level. It changed the character of the process significantly. It meant that no one was outside of the process. This echoed a phrase that we use to speak about social sculpture: "There is only one field of transformation, and no one is outside". With each new element added, and more people wanting to guide the process, it became clear that in addition to a manual some kind of training was needed.

Based on the insights and success of the imaginal practice in the Exchange Values project I decided to design a similar but completely mobile process that would create an aesthetic arena without a complex installation. The Earth Forum was the outcome: an arena in which people can encounter themselves, one another, and their relationship to the planet.

Earth Forum: *its components and principles*

Earth Forum was developed for the 2011 Climate Summit in South Africa as an 'instrument of consciousness' that creates an arena for working imaginatively together on the personal and collective past, present and future.[18] Its in-depth, accessible capacity-building process gives people a real sense of being artists sculpting with 'invisible materials' and creates the conditions for an emergent social process and exploring new social processes and imaginaries. Designed for six to twelve participants as individuals or members of organisations, it can be adapted to need and used in different contexts and situations. The minimum duration is around 3 hours, while to come to specific actions and ways forward, it is best as a full, 2-day process. A round oiled cloth, placed on the ground is part of the 'instrument', and has a number of significant functions. As a portable arena, it creates a place to gather and to hold the traces of the "planet" brought to the cloth by each participant, after their short "walk on the planet". Being infused with plant oil lifts it from the everyday, incorporating the Brechtian strategy of "making strange" (Brecht 1961). This oiled cloth on the ground, no longer simply a cloth, now takes people out of literalness into an imaginal, perceptive mode of *making* sense. It is a strategy used in many social sculpture practices – that enables the instances of the everyday to open up and become spaces for meaning and transformation. Perhaps the power of the oiled cloth has something to do with the mystery embodied in the oil: in the transformation of sunlight through the plant into oil that is central to the life sustaining process.

The Earth Forum process consists of four phases and two capacities that run through all phases: the *capacity for imaginal thought* and the capacity for active listening. *Phase 1* involves going for a short 10-minute "walk on the planet". This takes place after a guided process in the inner atelier/workspace, in which participants experience their capacity for imaginal thought: for seeing images of the past, present and future as well as being able to re-enter them. This provides the basis for seeing what one sees and how one sees. Without any explanation participants experience directly the taken for granted but profound epistemological process of 'making sense'. Most participants are quite astonished by this process. This inner space process has several other valuable attributes. Since everyone has this space and is able to call up images from the past, i.e. have memories, a certain equality of human capacity is starkly apparent. The second advantage is the tone of awe and respect for the absolutely ordinary process of perception that most people have never thought about before. So, again without talking about respect for the gifts and capacities every participant has been given, like the rent-free space, the wonder and respect is engendered through the doing.

After their short "walk on the planet", and before sharing their experiences, participants are introduced to the second *capacity for active listening*. They experience how this disciplined, phenomenological process of "staying with what is", enables one to enter one's own perceptions and thoughts, as well as another's. *Phase 2* begins after participants have each shared something, often an object or some soil, that reflects their short journey on the planet. The 'gesture' of the whole process is also significant. Having 'gone out' in *Phase 1* onto the planet and the

Table 11.1 The four phases of Earth Forum and its capacity-building processes

4 Phases of Earth Forum	Pre Phase 1 Introducing the Earth Forum and the UOT: Lab	Phase 1 "Going out to come in" using the inner atelier for a 10-minute "walk on the planet"	Phase 2 "Going out into the future to come back to action": exploring "how I would like to see the future"	Phase 3 Returning to the present field of inner and outer action: connecting the future images with the present	Phase 4 Making 'social honey': from 'I' and 'you' to 'we'
Capacity 1 in each of the phases: The Space of Imagination		Introducing the Space of Imagination; Employing the space of imagination in the "walk on the planet"	Using the space of imagination process to explore "how I would like to see the future"	Using the space of imagination process to see what exists in inner and outer field and what is moving in that direction	Using the space of imagination process to re-enter previous three phases to distil insights and explore ways forward
Capacity 2 in each of the phases: Active Listening		Participants share experiences after walk: and employ "Active Listening"	Participants share responses and perceptions employing "Active Listening"	Participants share responses and perceptions employing "Active Listening"	Participants share responses and perceptions employing "Active Listening"

world of experience, to then 'come in' to oneself and each other, *Phase 2* takes one 'out into the future'. The invitation here is to use the inner space to explore how one would like the world to look in 5, 50 or 500 years. After sharing something of their experiences, *Phase 3* begins with a process of 'coming in' back to the present. Now each participant gathers images and perceptions of their daily life to reflect on in relation to their *Phase 2* images of a desired future. It is made clear that seeing what one is doing in the present could involve a spectrum of actions: personal, collective, outer and inner. This frees people to discover much more about their current 'actions' and creates a new multidimensional awareness of agency. The substance gathered in these three phases is then re-entered and explored in *Phase 4*. Having heard not only ones own but all the experiences together, we are invited to try and perceive, as Goethe did in looking at the plant, the whole that is more than the sum of the parts, and the invisible potential that is waiting to be recognised and come to life.

The image offered at this point, to inspire the process of emergent understandings is one of 'making social honey'. Just as bees bring all their individual streams of nectar back to the hive, but together must work to transform it into honey, so too do we have to work intensively together to transform our individual perceptions into social substance and imaginaries of a viable future.

Through re-entering their experience gathered throughout the Earth Forum, again in *Phase 4*, enables an experience of *thinking together*[19] as well as creative processes of evaluation that enhance and value our individual and collective experience. It is also meaningful in bringing together stakeholders from a shared context or geographic area with very different 'takes' on what progress or sustainable development might mean. Surprisingly it also works well with groups of disparate individuals. In Berlin in 2012, 110 individuals participated in Earth Forums over a week. Although most were strangers at the start, many of them went on to work as groups and scaling out the Earth Forum process. The organisers said that through the Earth Forum "a small movement" had come into being. In and around the German city of Kassel, Earth Forum has been used extensively since 2012, in all these different ways: for deepening and clarifying personal and inter-organisational agendas; as a process of strengthening collective and individual will; for connecting individuals and for opening up new shared vision.

Like many other socially engaged art practices Earth Forum creates opportunities for insights through participation in processes that have a strong experiential-sensuous component and activate the imagination. But being a social sculpture process Earth Forum is also about enabling a direct experience of our inner means of production: the inner technologies and capacities for making sense and imagining a viable future. Earth Forum in this sense is an experience of "theory of knowledge" in practice, an epistemic process and a process of self-awareness. In illuminating that we can 'see *what* we see' as well as '*how* we see', this "Erkenntnispraxis" or "practice of knowledge", makes tangible that we can also *rethink what we think*! In this sense it is a practice-based version of 'the philosophy of inner freedom', which, drawing on the 'social senses' work of Joseph Beuys and Rudolf Steiner, foregrounds the I-sense in transformative process.

It is this that connects the outer dimension of sustainability with the inner. Other elements and strategies in this much used and valued[20] instrument of consciousness, help to scale out the process. They are detailed in the Earth Forum handbook used in training new 'responsible participants'.

In conclusion

Inner technologies and the field of freedom

Although recent developments in technology, in particular artificial intelligence, have called into question the all-knowing human agent, the extent of our human responsibility for how things are in the world should not be overlooked. The more the agency of external technology grows, the more we have to face the consequences of this and the extent to which we are allowing this to shape the world (Grunwald 2013). Unless we engage with this and the questions it poses, humanity runs the risk of losing both the freedom to imagine and working towards a viable future, and the responsibility that is the other side of this freedom.

Trying to move beyond anthropogenic destructiveness towards an ecological era should not be conflated with devaluing of the human being, the diminishing of human agency and privileging outer technologies to save us. Inner technologies, that enhance the connective-reflective dialogue with oneself and with the world and increase the human ability-to-respond, are also an essential aspect of the work towards a viable future.

Imaginal work in the inner atelier, as used in the Earth Forum method, is one of these inner technologies. The inner atelier is the space from which the radical social artist in everyone can take a hard look at what is going on and then by *re-entering* this, reflect on its implications. It is also the sphere in which the inner space is activated and new social imaginaries can arise and be explored. To balance the disproportionate emphasis on enhancing human beings from the outside I argue that it is time to take the inner space and the inner field seriously: to explore the cognitive-imaginal capacities of the human being as profound inner technologies and integrate *technê* and *epistêmê*, and *technê* and *psyche*.

One of our key interfaces with the world is imagination: the imagination that encounters, the imagination that enables us to re-enter sensuous experience and information to 'make sense'. It is this understanding of imagination as an integrative process that is central to connective thought. This imaginal reflective-connective capacity derives from and enhances the I-sense and has the potential of becoming a new kind of differentiated yet interdependent "we": thinking and imagining together in ways that might allow a viable future to emerge.

Sustainability without the I-sense is nonsense

The shorthand language used in certain leadership for sustainability programmes (Scharmer, Kaufer 2013) that describe the way forward as "eco-centric not ego-centric" might unintentionally encourage a devaluation of the role of individual consciousness and agency. On the other hand, foregrounding the I-sense might seem to reinforce the anthropocentric worldview that privileges human desires above the needs and rights of other beings. However, if one understands the I-sense as the sense with which we are able to recognise the being and integrity of all life forms, this will help us to recognise its value as sense through which the other-than-human-world as well as fellow human beings can be appreciated and properly respected. Without strengthening the capacities of the inner human being to enable shifts in how we see, feel and think about interdependence and inter-relatedness, discussed in this book as the personal and inner dimension of sustainability, we cannot hope to shape a viable, eco-social future. Building these capacities for connective imagination through instruments of consciousness such as the Earth Forum and the inner atelier practice needs to be understood as a global civic project. Only this kind of consciousness work that parallels the work in the outer field can enable the 'paradigm shift in practice' and transformation towards a more viable future.

Notes

1 The phrase "Sustainability without the I-Sense is nonsense" is part of the social sculpture process that I developed in 2011, for the Über Lebenskunst Festival, Haus der Kulturen der Welt, Berlin.
2 Along the same lines The "Dictionary of Philosophy" (Runes 1964) defines technê as the set of principles, or rational method, involved in the production of an object or the accomplishment of an end; the knowledge of such principles or method; art. Techne resembles episteme in implying knowledge of principles, but differs in that its aim is making or doing, not disinterested understanding.
3 I developed this term for the Earth Forum process in 2010, it is discussed in detail in Sacks *et al.* 2013.
4 James Hillman, Paul Klee and Joseph Beuys all use the term "imaginal thought" ("bildhaftes Denken" in German). "Imaginal work" is my term for the processes that involve imaginal thought.
5 "Habit of mind" and "mindset" in this text and in the field of contemporary social sculpture, refers not only to ideas, forms of reasoning and intellectual frameworks, but includes longings, attitudes, feelings and perceptions – which also contribute to prejudices, habits of perception and habits of responding. This is the significance of Beuys' and others' notion of *imaginal thought*. It enables us to get to the habit level described in many forms of phenomenological reframing, therapy and mindfulness work, and to begin to experience – at least on a personal level – what I now describe as "paradigm shift" in practice.
6 As the work in "the inner atelier" and the "Earth Forum process" described in this text highlight, the field of mind includes the imagination and "imaginal work". The notion of "imaginal thought" ["bildhaftes Denken"] refers to a phenomenological mode of perception, which is central in the interdisciplinary pedagogies of Kandinsky, Paul Klee and Joseph Beuys. In Beuys this is intimately connected to his theory of Social Sculpture, referring to forms of aesthetic and intuitive thinking, inspired by Goethe's explorations concerning the intuitive mode of thinking (Bortoft 1996), and Schiller's understanding of aesthetic thought. Matthias Bunge's *Zwischen Intuition und Ratio: Pole Des Bildnerischen Denkens bei Kandinsky, Klee und Beuys* (1996) describes this field of aesthetic thought or mind which foregrounds non-intellectual thought that includes feelings and perceptions. The methodologies of the Social Sculpture Research

Unit incorporate and relate the work of psychologist James Hillman on "imaginal thought" to the "plastik theorie" of Joseph Beuys. "Mindset" is therefore used here to include non-intellectual, embodied awareness such as feelings and perceptions. These root methodologies are referred to on the Social Sculpture Research Unit website (www.social-sculpture.org/category/our-focus/our-methodologies), in ATLAS of the Poetic Continent (Sacks, Zumdick 2013) and in my keynote paper for a conference on socially engaged practice and the field of transformation (Sacks 2017).

7 "Invisible materials" is a phrase Beuys used regularly, describing the invisible materials of social sculpture as speech, discussion and thought (Tisdall 1979). Over the years I have added attitudes, questions, values, habits of thought.

8 George Thierry Hanja of the Rainforest Foundation who has been using such methods for almost a decade, is now beginning to link this work to the field of social sculpture.

9 Redefining responsibility as "an ability-to-respond" in my unpublished presentation for the UNESCO *Summit on Culture and Development* in Stockholm 1998 was a breakthrough in my work that enabled me to connect it to the way I was rethinking "aesthetic" as the opposite of numbness.

10 It is interesting that Beuys, who read Aristotle quite closely, used the same three terms (discussion, speaking and thinking) to refer to the invisible materials of social sculpture.

11 Related to the Greek "nous" for mind – from which we derive "noumena", the invisible forms of the inner sphere, and "phenomena", the perceptible forms of the outer world.

12 Ken Wilber's concept is discussed in Gunnlaugson and Moze 2012.

13 The Mind & Life Institute (www.mindandlife.org) was formed by Tenzin Gyatso, the 14th Dalai Lama, Adam Engle, a lawyer and entrepreneur; and Francisco Varela, a neuroscientist in 1987. Arthur Zajonc, professor of physics at Amherst College, Buddhist and anthroposophic meditation practitioner was President of the Mind-Life Institute form 2012 and Director of the Centre for Contemplative Mind in Society (www.contemplativemind.org).

14 This set of strategies has been developed by the author over the past three decades since Beuys' death and underpins both the Masters and Doctoral Programmes in Social Sculpture and Connective Practice at Oxford Brookes University, UK (www.social-sculpture.org) as well as the work via the University of the Trees: Lab for New Knowledge and an Eco-Social Future (www.universityofthetrees.org) with organisations beyond the academic institutions.

15 Earth Forum is part of the University of the Trees: Lab for New Knowledge and an Eco-Social Future (a mobile university that develops, researches and co-creates interdisciplinary practices with special reference to the inner dimension of sustainability. It works with individuals, communities and organisations. Begun in 2000 as a social sculpture in Ireland, in April 2017 it became a registered social enterprise. Its instruments of consciousness include enquiry labs, methodologies and practices designed to facilitate new ways of thinking together, agendas for transformation and developing new forms of creative action in response to the huge challenges facing us all. Earth Forum aims to enliven ways of thinking and doing, which enable positive [r]evolutionary change (see also www.social-sculpture.org).

16 I was working there on my *Exchange Values* producers-consumers project (www.exchange-values.org).

17 In dialogue with Social Sculpture Research Unit collaborators Prof. Alex Arteaga, James Reed and Nicolas Stronczyk.

18 Since the Climate Summit thousands of people have taken part in the Earth Forum process in collaboration with many initiatives including Citizen's Art Days, Berlin; the Ueberlebenskunst programme at the Haus der Kulturen der Welt; the Art and Social Practice Group, Mumbai, CSR workshops and the Pune Biennale, India; Boell Stiftung, Berlin workshops and conferences; Green Party congress, Duesseldorf; Creative

Challenge, London; the Earth Conference in Ireland; and the Making a Difference-Asia event in Hong Kong for hundreds of young change-makers.
19 "Thinking" is here used in the expanded sense in which Paul Klee, Kandinsky, Schiller, Goethe, Hillman and Beuys use it – which depends on phenomenological close noticing . . . a process in which perceptions, awareness and feelings are integral.
20 "Reflexionfeld", "Journaling for Change" and "Dialogue with Oneself: Dialogue with the World" are examples of specifically designed social sculpture processes of evaluation that enable participants to re-enter and distil the value of their experience, while enabling us to sense the powerful impact that instruments of consciousness like Earth Forum have on individual lives, organisations and social processes.

References

Banse, G.; Parodi, O. (2012): Sustainability and Culture: An Expanded View. In *Periodica Oeconomica*, pp. 17–27. Special Issue on the Regional Aspects of sustainability, www.gti.ektf.hu/PO2012.html, accessed 15 September 2017.
Berry, T.; Swimme, B. (1992): *The Universe Story*. San Francisco, CA: Harper.
Beuys, J. (2004): *What is Art? Conversation with Joseph Beuys* (Ed. V. Harlan; Trans. S. Sacks). Forest Row, UK: Clairview Books.
Beuys, J.; Mennekes, F. (1996): Joseph Beuys: Christus "Denken" – "Thinking" Christ. Stuttgart, Germany: Verl. Kath. Bibelwerk.
Bortoft, H. (1996): *The Wholeness of Nature: Goethe's Way of Science*. Edinburgh, UK: Floris Books.
Brecht, B. (1961): On Chinese Acting. In *The Tulane Drama Review*, Vol. 6, No. 1, pp. 130–136.
Brown, M.; Macy, J. (2004): Teaching Sustainability: Whole Systems Learning. In C. Galea (Ed.) *Teaching Business Sustainability: From Theory to Practice*, pp. 218–228. Saltaire, UK: Greenleaf.
Bunge, M. (1996): *Zwischen Intuition und Ratio*. Wiesbaden, Germany: Franz Steiner Verlag.
Carrington, D. (2016): The Anthropocene Epoch: Scientists Declare Dawn of Human-Influenced Age. *The Guardian*, 29 August. www.theguardian.com/environment/2016/aug/29/declare-anthropocene-epoch-experts-urge-geological-congress-human-impact-earth, accessed 15 September 2017.
Freire, P. (2013): *Education for Critical Consciousness*. London: Bloomsbury Academic.
Fuchs-Kittowski, K.; Krüger, P. (1997): The Noosphere Vision of Pierre Teilhard de Chardin and Vladimir I. Vernadsky in the Perspective of Information and of World-wide Communication. In *World Futures*, Vol. 50, No. 1–4, pp. 757–784.
Grunwald, A. (ed.) (2013): *Handbuch Technikethik*. Stuttgart, Weimar, Germany: Metzler.
Gunnlaugson, O.; Moze, M. B. G. (2012): Surrendering into Witnessing: A Foundational Practice for Building Collective Intelligence Capacity in Groups. In *Journal of Integral Theory and Practice*, Vol. 7, No. 3, pp. 105–115.
Hanh, T. N (2003): *Joyfully Together: The Art of Building a Harmonious Community*. Berkeley, CA: Parallax Press.
Kunkel, B. (2017): The Capitalocene. In *London Review of Books*, Vol. 39, No. 5, pp. 22–28.
Kurt, H.; Sacks, S. (2013): *Die rote Blume: Ästhetische Praxis in Zeiten des Wandels*. Klein Jasedow, Germany: Think-Oya imprint of Drachen Books.
Nicol, D. (2015): *Subtle Activism: The Inner Dimension of Social and Planetary Transformation*. Albany, NY: State University of New York Press.

Parodi, O. (2015): The Missing Aspect of Culture in Sustainability Concepts. In J. C. Enders, M. Remig (Eds) *Theories of Sustainable Development*, pp. 169–187. London, New York: Routledge (Routledge Studies in Sustainable Development).

Parry, R. (2014): Episteme and Techne. In E. N. Zalta (Ed.) *The Stanford Encyclopedia of Philosophy*. Retrieved 14 March 2017, from https://plato.stanford.edu/archives/fall 2014/entries/episteme-techne.

Puech, M. (2016): *The Ethics of Ordinary Technology*. Oxford: Routledge.

Runes, D. (1964): *Dictionary of Philosophy*. London: Peter Owen Publishers.

Sacks, S. (1998): Warmth Work: An Expanded Conception of Art for the 21st Century, Stockholm: UNESCO Summit for Culture and Development [unpublished presentation, 31 March 1998], as part of 'The World Beyond 2000: Shaping Histories – Imagining Futures'.

Sacks, S. (2011): Social Sculpture and New Organs of Perception: New practices and New Pedagogy for a Humane and Ecologically Viable Future. In M. C. Lerm-Hayes and V. W. Beuysian (Eds) *Legacies in Ireland*, pp. 80–97. Münster, Germany: LIT Verlag.

Sacks, S. (2017): *Contemporary Social Sculpture and the Field of Transformation*. Oberhausen, Germany: Athena.

Sacks, S.; Kirchgaesser, A.; Stefan, M. (2013): *Earth Forum Handbook*. Oxford: University of the Trees. [available only for trained practitioners].

Sacks, S.; Zumdick, W. (2013): *Atlas of the Poetic Continent: Pathways to Ecological Citizenship*. Forest Row, UK: Temple Lodge Publications.

Scharmer, C. O.; Kaufer, K. (2013): *Leading from the Emerging Future: From Ego-System to Eco-System Economics*. Oakland, CA: Berrett-Koehler.

Steiner, R. (2009): *Die zwölf Sinne des Menschen in ihrer Beziehung zu Imagination, Inspiration, Intuition*. Dornach, Germany: Rudolf Steiner Verlag.

Tisdall, C. (1979): *Joseph Beuys*. New York: Solomon R. Guggenheim Museum/Thames and Hudson.

Trungpa, C. (1970): *Meditation in Action*. Boston, MA: Shambala.

United Nations Department of Public Information (2015): https://sustainabledevelopment.un.org/?menu=1300, accessed 15 September 2017.

Vansintjan, A. (2015): The Anthropocene Debate: Why is Such a Useful Concept Starting to Fall Apart? In: *Resilience*. www.resilience.org/stories/2015-06-26/the-anthropocene-debate-why-is-such-a-useful-concept-starting-to-fall-apart/, accessed 15 September 2017.

12   Personal sustainability – conclusions and perspectives

Oliver Parodi, Sabin Wendhack and Kaidi Tamm

Now, after all the different approaches to personal sustainability have been presented throughout the book we want to round up the broad spectrum of ideas by condensing some characteristic features from the steps we took into this new field of research. First, we want to draw some general conclusions concerning the endeavour of this book. This is followed by a differentiation of usage of the search term "personal sustainability". The potential of research in the proposed field and some significant and valuable findings from the book are addressed in this chapter "Highlights". However, the approach we want to promote does imply certain limits and dangers. We want to address the most important ones in this chapter. Finally, we will summarise the perspectives offered by an approach of personal sustainability research, as well as those offered by personal sustainability itself and that way complete our preliminary map of personal sustainability.

Conclusions

First of all, looking back at all the chapters of the book we can sum up that a lot of personal, human, inner, mental, etc. aspects are mentioned which are – following the authors – closely connected to and relevant for sustainable development. In consequence, we can draw a first triple conclusion:

1   "Personal sustainability" works as a search term. Various aspects from very different contexts and perspectives have been brought together.
2   Personal sustainability is closely related to and relevant for sustainable development. Many links have been drawn between an 'outer' sustainable development and inner, personal aspects.
3   The research field "personal sustainability" is wide, including a variety of topics and (scientific) perspectives. With this book we can give a brief idea of the field but cannot deliver a consistent theory of personal sustainability.

However, many issues concerning personal sustainability remain and need further research, dialogue and discussion. Instead of giving a vague definition of the concept of personal sustainability, we want to clarify the different ways of usage and meanings of the term "personal sustainability" that have become visible throughout the book – as conceptual contribution and element for theory development.

Different use of the term "personal sustainability"

From an epistemic point of view the term "personal sustainability" points to categorically different subjects throughout the chapters of the book. What is addressed employing "personal sustainability" varies widely. That is not surprising and rather natural when opening a very new and broad field of topics and entering it from various starting points with different perspectives. Hopefully, a broad discourse about personal sustainability will start and clarify the usage of the term. We want to contribute to this discourse with the following distinctions and suggestions.

Personal sustainability as a field or collection of subjects

The initial idea for this book was to bring together all kinds of human, inner and personal aspects, to show that it is fruitful to consider them in the context of sustainable development and that they are related to each other. We showed that there is a huge field of topics of such kind related to sustainable development and that these topics are not really perceived and processed so far. We can conclude that using "personal sustainability" as a term pointing to a variety of things (in the above mentioned manner) works and is useful. The relevance of the research field has been shown, however, the issues remain isolated up to now and therefore, "personal sustainability" refers to an incoherent collection of subjects up to now.

Personal sustainability as a specific subject

Most of the authors have used the term not for a collection of aspects or entities but to address a specific part of sustainable development or human living. Helena Lass for example designates with "personal sustainability" a state of human health and wellbeing, Marcel Hunecke refers to capacities for wellbeing, Reiner Manstetten addresses personal aspects as a condition for a(n outer) sustainable development, and so on. This situation, pointing at different meanings with the same term, implies the danger of misunderstanding as well as that of reducing the understanding to one specific topic from one specific perspective. That way there is no added value provided by the term. In consequence, we suggest to clarify the interconnections of topics and perspectives in the future, in order to pave the way to a kind of theory of personal sustainability. With our suggestion to distinguish between personal sustainability as a condition, part or goal of sustainable development (see Chapter 1, "What is meant by sustainable development"), we want to contribute to this process. However, at this point we do not want to restrict the usage to one specific subject so far.

Personal sustainability as a perspective and endeavour of perception

A distinction that is often not made (in our times dominated by science) is the differentiation between the subject of research and the perspective on it.[1] This distinction has to be made clear for future debates: personal sustainability in our understanding is not meant as a perspective, as a way of looking at the world, and in consequence "personal sustainability" is not the name for a scientific research endeavour or discipline, but addresses the above mentioned field of subjects. To talk about the perspective and the way of getting new insights into this field, should be clearly named as "personal sustainability *research*" or similar. However, "research" in this case would not imply an exclusively scientific understanding but includes also non-scientific, individual insights e.g. by carrying out self-reflexive inner research (see below).

Personal sustainability as an inter- or transdiscipline

"Personal sustainability" is no scientific perspective or discipline. However, there are various perspectives and disciplines looking at aspects from the field of personal sustainability. Thus, "personal sustainability *research*" is supposed and characterised as a multi-, inter- and transdisciplinary endeavour. In a distant future there might be a(n) (inter-)discipline dealing with personal sustainability, perhaps called "personal sustainability science" or "personal sustainability research", that would have to include different approaches from various disciplines such as psychology, anthropology, philosophy, cultural studies, human ecology, etc. Concerning this, we want to stress that for us looking at personal sustainability should not end at the borders and limits of the (established) sciences but include inner experiences, personal (and subjective bodily) perspectives and approaches, as intended within this book. In consequence, we think that a research that is adequately dealing with personal sustainability must be transdisciplinary (including science).

Personal sustainability as a theory

There is no theory of personal sustainability yet. We are working on it and want to contribute to the discourse in order to achieve a theory, as consistent as it may be possible and adequate in the future. However, such a theory should not be a scientific one reached by thinking and cognition only. We want to include personal, inner experiences and (practical) knowledge that is not derived from science. So when using the term "theory of personal sustainability" for us it is meant in a broader sense referring to the original understanding of "theory" (coming from the Greek terms "theorein" and "theoria": "view, conception, inspection, insight"). This implies to overcome categorical gaps (see below and Chapter 1 "The term and history of 'personal sustainability'") and will be a major challenge.

Personal sustainability as a guiding principle and programme

Like sustainable development is meant as a theory that comprises values and objectives, as well as a programme to change the situation, personal sustainability is – at least potentially – a guiding principle and programme, too. For us personal sustainability should be seen as part of sustainable development or as its other (inner, personal) and so far unattended half. As such it is the part of the programme of sustainable development that is not verbalised so far. By now no aims of personal sustainability have been clearly stated neither has a portfolio of 'personal *sustainable development goals*' been adopted by the United Nations. However, this might be a good idea and worth to develop, even if it would be a delicate and perhaps dangerous endeavour (see this chapter "Concerns").

Personal sustainability as a practice

"Personal sustainability" could also describe a practice, even if there is no such thing as a manual so far. In the same way as sustainable development is meant as a real development, wherefore a huge bundle of actions are necessary (and some are practiced already), it could be imagined that personal sustainability was lived, practiced and realised. Some of the authors regard personal sustainability as a kind of practice, such as Michael Niehaus, Ingvar Villido, Stella Veciana or Shelley Sacks (and co-authors), who are describing specific ways of doing things as (part of) practicing personal sustainability.

Personal sustainability as a way of life

Until now there is no personal sustainability as a specific lifestyle or way of life. However, being personally sustainable would mean an entirely new way of life, existing and being human, as Oliver Parodi hinted at. As soon as sustainable development will be incorporated in our everyday life in the (hopefully not too distant) future, as soon as acting according to and practicing sustainable development becomes common, personal sustainability could become the habitual way of life embedded in a culture of sustainability.

Highlights

Even if the chapters of this book offer a wide range of topics connected to personal sustainability and a common research area only shines through up to now, there are some very interesting findings that become clear throughout the contributions. In the following we want to present those we considered most noteworthy and promising.

Bridging fundamental gaps for a holistic (understanding of) sustainable development

Dealing with personal sustainability as a transdisciplinary endeavour – if taken seriously – you come across categorical gaps (for example such as between science and Eastern philosophy or theory and practice, as mentioned in the Introduction and explained later in this chapter). Like deep gorges they seem too wide and dangerous to bridge over. However, approaching personal sustainability, right here the most interesting and precious insights might be found.

Indeed it would be possible to stop in front of these gorges and formulate a theory of personal sustainability without bridging these gaps. For us, that would not be reaching far enough and as mentioned in some of the chapters as well (see for example Tamm, Parodi, Sacks) it would be not sufficient to realise a sustainable future. Following Albert Einstein: "We can't solve problems by using the same kind of thinking we used when we created them", we have to think and act in a different mode. If science – besides being part of the solution – also is part of the problem of our unsustainable state of the world, striving for sustainability we have to go beyond sciences – not to abandon but to complement them.

Accordingly, research and development in the fields of personal sustainability, bridging the gorges, could and should partly be a radically new endeavour. A systematic elaboration of the gaps, gorges and contradictions that have to be over-come in the field of personal sustainability would mean an epistemological and historico-cultural investigation, reflecting upon the history of ideas over the last 2,000 or even 5,000 years. We would strongly suspect that many existing funda-mental gaps between worldviews of different cultures or (political) ideologies all over the world will mirror in the field of personal sustainability.

Not with the objective of a systematic approach but to provide an impression of the scope of these gaps and the (sometimes contradictory) poles that are to bridge we want to mention some of them: against the background of sustainable development, within personal sustainability research, we have to establish links between the outer and the inner world, between scientific and non-scientific approaches, between inter-subjective, highly collective clarified knowledge and (sometimes very powerful) subjective, personal and individual experiences, between technology and spirituality as well as between truth and love.

The gaps are running right through the middle of the (personal) sustainability discourse, for example between both the sustainability metanarratives of discon-nection and reconnection, Kaidi Tamm explained. Behind these we can find fundamental differences in the worldviews and the attitudes towards the world: either to control it (from an outer, prominent position) or to engage oneself as part of a whole (see for example Parodi, Veciana and Ottmar, Tamm).

The concept of sustainable development has grown out of the occidental, Christian cultural background and passes on its deeply rooted cultural motives like the special status of man or a linear, eschatological understanding of time. By following the new paradigm of reconnection (Tamm, Villido) sustainability activists all over the world try to live sustainable development in a more whole-some way, especially by adding a spiritual dimension to sustainable development. By doing so they mostly refer to non-Christian (particularly non-monotheistic) cultural motives or spiritual practices and philosophies, and try to integrate them. Perceiving the Christian god as not existing ('dead') or at least as a god who is disconnected from human being and everyday life they search for alternatives that are connected to a greater extent, and find them in the (ancient) natural religions ("mother earth") or non-theistic views and philosophies like Buddhism. With this, fundamental cultural differences are brought into the field of sustainable development – and make it obvious, that "sustainable development" is a Western invention and an approach that is dominated by the West till now.

In general, the call to include and bridge the gap to a spiritual dimension of sustainable development grows louder among sustainability researchers (e.g. Chapter 1 'Similar approaches'). Also in the chapters of this book, many authors refer to spiritual growth or practice, among them Reiner Manstetten, Stella Veciana and Kariin Ottmar, Ingvar Villido and Sabin Wendhack. In principle, within sustainable development personal sustainability would be the field that is able to address and comprise such demands and approaches.

Closely linked to the differences in the (cultural-religious) worldviews there are fundamental differences in the ways of accessing the world: in the occidental-Western a cognitive access to the world around us has been perfected and become predominant over the centuries, while in the orient a more integral access was handed-down, resting on human relationship in a strong way. Whereas in the Western cultural area dealing with the outer world is stressed in the Far Eastern, traditionally, self-awareness is (still) important, too.

These differences can be allegorically – but beyond that also physically – mirrored in the human body – as a gap between the head and the rest of it. In areas characterised by Western culture human access to the world takes place via the head above all, especially through the eyes and the brain. The rest of the body is mostly ignored. Among the senses the sense of sight (closely linked to the brain and thinking) is hauled out. In Far Eastern philosophies in contrast, the status of the head, the brain and the sense of sight is not emphasised as much.

Even if it is not possible to go deeper into the differences in the course of this book, personal sustainability generally opens up the possibility to complement a Western-dominated view and concept of sustainable development with elements from other cultural areas – in particular from the Far East. By the way, doing so, personal sustainability enormously helps to render sustainable development more culture-sensitive, too. To put it another way: if we are not looking on human, inner, spiritual and world view aspects of sustainable development there are no entry points for including such foreign and strange approaches and worldviews.

We, the authors of this chapter, appreciate and support these efforts to a more holistic, wholesome and human sustainable development in general (surely not in all ways that are checked out e.g. at the edges of the esoteric sustainability scene), and suppose that personal sustainability can help to integrate some of the differences by addressing the various approaches, making their differences clear and opening a discourse about them.

The gaps can be found also in the proposed solutions regarding sustainability challenges: for example along the line of 'inner' and 'outer' solutions. What helps us making our world more sustainable: outer technologies or inner technology (Sacks), economic and legal regulations or personal awareness (Villido), thinking and brainstorming or 'brainsilencing'? By means of personal sustainability these questions can be addressed and discussed.[2] By the way, the proposed 'outer' solutions generally correspond with inner human aspects, beliefs, worldviews and conceptions of man. However, normally the inner aspects are not transparent, explicit and in consequence not open for dialogue – nevertheless they are implicitly effective. Personal sustainability can bring them to light – and as such it clearly is an instrument of the enlightenment.

Freedom, responsibility and relationship

Sustainable development up to now adopts an objective, respectively inter-subjective perspective, it takes a view upon things from above and is directed to the outer and collective context. The approach to necessary change is shaped by this attitude: the latter influences the questions that are asked and the answers that are considered having the potential to lead on. Reflecting on sustainable development at the moment often leads to two questions: how to motivate people to engage in the issue and take over a new form of dealing with our common home and its resources and second, why they don't do so yet. If the contemplation is more self-reflective, the questions are slightly different: how can I contribute to sustainable development to a larger extent and why don't I do so yet. The traditional direction of the discussion of sustainable development is the spirit of the outer means: "How can we motivate people?", "How can I contribute?", in our minds there occur principles, potential or necessary change of behaviour, change of norms, perhaps the change of regulation.

The actual necessities sustainable development suggests contribute on top to the typical atmosphere created when discussing it: we have to need less, reduce our consumption which, as a result of the type of society we're living in (i.e. a society oriented towards material values) means to reduce our space and our lives. The atmosphere implied by this direction of thinking is one of scarcity, narrowness and anxiety. On top of that, the scenarios that threaten us in case we don't manage to achieve sustainable development are disastrous to an extent of creating additional fear connected to the issue. For people who care for and engage in sustainable development issues, it often is a real task not to be overwhelmed by the situation carrying that atmosphere and ending up in powerlessness and depression. On the other hand, people often behave as if the issue had nothing to do with them, their lives and the lives of their children, even those who are in fact concerned do that from time to time. Such a separation from the issue almost seems to be necessary (at least at times) regarding the narrowness the situation implies, the fear that is involved and has to be processed mentally and the risk of being overwhelmed by all this. Repression of the subject and the atmosphere it carries seemingly is necessary.

As the most surprising result of this book we consider the emergence of a space of potential evolution regarding sustainable development that completely contradicts the above-described approach towards change and the atmosphere that comes with it. It is a potential that opens up space for being, that allows growth, that promises expansion and life.

In his chapter, Reiner Manstetten emphasises that liberal society is an achievement we don't want to remain behind anymore and he stresses the importance of individual freedom as a basis of all development. However, in our present Western culture, we might take individual freedom for something different than what is meant by Manstetten. He underlines that what he refers to "should not be confused with arbitrariness and irresponsibility against fellow humans and nature" and explains: "Such confusion is, perhaps, one of the most serious reasons for unsustainable attitudes towards nature and society" (Manstetten, p. 24).

Marcel Hunecke points out that changes in behaviour "are to be achieved on a conscious and voluntary basis and not via strategies of manipulation", emphasising that the individual is to be taken seriously. Sabin Wendhack argues:

> Focusing on subjective body means expanding oneself into the world. This does not only mean taking more space for oneself and it does definitely not mean blocking this space for the others, isolating oneself against outer influence. On the contrary, it is supposed to come along with sharing the space with others and the world.
>
> (Wendhack, p. 91)

Thus, personal sustainability suggests that the development, evolution and, in the end, the growth of the person seems to be essential regarding sustainable development. It is important that growth here is not understood as we often understand it in our way of thinking nowadays, as a blocking and isolating type of growth, meaning more space for an ego-centred person, but as a non-blocking growth into space shared with others. In consequence, the desire for growth and development, which is a desire that is essential and necessary for human being and life, has not to be given up and denied. Instead its way and direction has to be changed, from quantitative to qualitative growth, from exclusive growth to growth allowing contact and relationship with the surroundings, other beings and the world. Even if we don't have to give up growth, it will become more dangerous and challenging than buying more and bigger things or developing better technologies: we'll have to engage with each other a greater deal, expose ourselves to each other, process the emotions and impressions coming along with that and commit ourselves to the respective inner work. In summary we'll have to invest a larger part of our forces in this field. However, on the other hand there is the potential that thereby it will be shown that qualitative growth and more and more intense relationships will satisfy us to a greater extent than the type of growth prevailing at the moment. It might be the case that the focus on material values and growth that is still present nowadays is a way of compensating for needs of an inner kind or of relationship anyway.

Shelley Sacks, also engaged with expanding inner worlds employed to connect and that way creating space to foster collective processes and ease to live together in a more fruitful manner, stresses that concentrating on this inner space, developing, refining, intensifying and extending it, might be a necessary means in order to balance the power laid on external institutions and technologies, where human responsibility has declined due to disconnection. She writes: "To balance the disproportionate emphasis on enhancing human beings from the outside I argue that it is time to take the inner space and the inner field seriously." The other side of these steps towards autonomy that is at least recognised if not reclaimed as a necessary precondition for sustainable development throughout the chapters, is responsibility, as Shelley Sacks underlines: if we don't engage in shaping the world but leave those fields to outer technologies, "humanity runs the risk of losing both the freedom to imagine and working toward a viable future, and the responsibility that is the other side of this freedom" (Sacks, p. 184).

This freedom implies that sustainable development needs to be more than a moral claim exterior to ourselves, aiming at reducing our scope of life. On the contrary, as it is connected to the evolution of the person, it does not go well together with claims, but with the reconquest of the inner space and the very own personality. This includes, as there are less gaps in connection or parts not developed, disposing of more proper resources, which is a basis for being able to adopt full responsibility. This might enable us to react in an appropriate way and fill the vacuum of responsibility created by consigning so much development of the world to institutions and outer processes.

Both Shelley Sacks and Oliver Parodi stress that developing the inner space and engaging in relationship might lead us to evolutions we cannot imagine up to now. Focusing on and attaching importance to personal sustainability means to allow and appreciate each individual to develop, together and in relationship with others. Needing to give up control from outside and trust in each other, it opens up possibilities not comprehensible within our scope and paradigm. Both authors argue that here lies the key to develop into forms of essentially different kind, Oliver Parodi for example speaks of "a new form of human being, relatedness and consciousness" (Parodi, p. 78), which might be able to contribute in a way to sustainable development that is not imaginable by now.

In all the chapters contained in this book it becomes apparent that the direction of development implied by personal sustainability, which in the first place is one into the inner world and depths of the individual, always goes along with extending and intensifying relationship. There is no chapter promoting an egocentric view, personal sustainability is always understood fostering common grounds in the end. That means, in a second step, engaging in the inner space of the individual, somehow seems to be a bridge to community (see for example Veciana and Ottmar). That corresponds to the requirement of sustainable development and the possible reason for transformation not taking place as it would be necessary: we will be able to meet the challenges we face only together. At the same time, the narrowness that we might feel at the moment will make it necessary to close ranks and rely on each other.

Even if it feels like that at the moment, it might be that this direction finally is not leading into more narrowness but to overcome narrowness and discover significantly more space to develop and to lead a more vital, intensive and reciprocally benefitting life. While the atmosphere surrounding sustainability issues at the moment is determined by anxiety and fear, it might be the case that this is not the end of the story. The fear we are confronted with also tends to impede our curiosity for ourselves and the world and our longing for a life that is more intense, more vital and more in touch with the others. It impedes our own and common development in direction to expansion allowing contact with the other and the world. In the end, if we are forced to stop repressing the situation and follow our curiosity for life, we will pay attention to this fear so that it loses its power on us. We will be able, as Shelley Sacks puts it: to "take a hard look at what is going on and reflect on its implications" (Sacks, p. 184). At that point we will have started to overcome fear and that will open up space for love, joy and the satisfaction arising from togetherness.

Concerns

Looking back at the different contributions and ideas and gathering the findings arising from that, at the same time we are aware of some possible shortcomings and dangers of this endeavour. First, the scene remains poorly tangible and some-how incomplete. What renders it difficult is that part of this situation seems to be owed to the nature of the topic itself. Classical (scientific) theory building might miss – or even worse – damage crucial points of the subjects investigated. Apart from that, dealing with personal sustainability opens up human being for further and deeper rationalisation and instrumentalisation, and in consequence, dragging these issues into the spotlight of attention and the public is indeed dangerous.

The concept of personal sustainability remains unclear, is too vague or overloaded

After this first step of pointing at a whole half of the sustainable development cosmos missing, which is a huge field, and trying to explore it from a multitude of perspectives, there is no consistent theory or overview formed and the field of personal sustainability has to remain unclear to a certain extent. However, this book is a first explorer's expedition and part of a starting bigger 'research move-ment'. Like in all (promising) research endeavours, more research will follow and a discourse will grow and hopefully clarify the scene. In this course, it might be necessary to differentiate and mark specific parts within the field of personal sustainability, for example to separate "inner transition" from an "anthropological dimension of sustainable development" or the "conceptions of man of personal sustainability" etc.

However, in future debates about personal sustainability it should become clear what the term "personal sustainability" is supposed to mean and in what function it is used. This chapter "Conclusions" and the Introduction hopefully will contain helpful ideas for this.

Part of the vagueness, at least seen from a scientific perspective or a perspective of mind, is owed to the particularity of personal sustainability: dealing with individual, inner issues, sensation, intuition, mental constitution, relationship to other human beings and group processes, it is on the one hand not tangible by common 'objectifying' scientific methods that are systematically blind for uniqueness, individuality and subjectivity. On the other hand it is even changed in its kind, damaged or destroyed by treating it with (such traditional) scientific methods. Partly it needs a different handling, a more tender one, one valuing life higher than concept, one being able to accept and endure contrast that cannot be solved within a perspective of mind.

At this point we suspect that theory building will – for the particularity of the subject described above – be possible only to a certain degree. In order to not fall into arbitrariness or just bad quality because of that, it is very important to make clear where and why it is not possible to represent specific subjects of personal sustainability in a consistent scientific theory, but also to make clear when safe and shared scientific ground is reached again and to put effort in differentiation and accuracy concerning the subject. Thus, a theory of personal sustainability will probably always remain incomplete.

With "personal sustainability" a huge field of varying subjects is addressed. Besides being unclear, the concept of personal sustainability might be overloaded with all kinds of content. As its topics are handled in many fields under many names but not in sustainable development discourse yet, and as this human half of sustainable development has been neglected so far, all kinds of things can be set in relation to personal sustainability. To prevent the term and concept from being overloaded it is crucial never to lose the context of sustainable development. All subjects treated within the concept of personal sustainability have to deal with sustainable development in a direct way. Losing the link to sustainable develop-ment, personal sustainability would be open to all kind of inner or human aspects without any focus or orientation and that way fall victim to arbitrariness.

Emphasising the importance of the link to sustainable development it becomes clear that the understanding of sustainable development itself, on which it is relied dealing with personal sustainability, is relevant and constitutive, too. Looking for example at the different concepts of sustainable development and their respective metanarratives of disconnection or reconnection mentioned by Kaidi Tamm, there would be major differences in the form and content of the corresponding approaches to personal sustainability. If you start from a strong or weak under-standing of sustainable development, from a strong anthropocentric or a broader ecocentric sustainable development approach, personal sustainability as a concept might differ blatantly. In consequence, to avoid confusion (by transparency of the assumptions) the understanding of sustainable development has to be explained each time dealing with personal sustainability.

Personal sustainability is impossible

Depending on what is meant and addressed by personal sustainability (see this chapter "Conclusions") people might notice different impossibilities. However, there's one we take seriously. It would be a big task to explore the fields of personal sustainability scientifically, as a huge multi-perspective and inter-disciplinary research endeavour. It would take time and a lot of effort, but given the current state of sciences it is possible. In contrast, exploring personal sustainability in a fundamental transdisciplinary manner, a way that we consider adequate and have already tried in the last years (as described in this chapter "Highlights") seems to be and might be impossible. Perhaps the gaps and gorges between the different approaches and worldviews clashing in the field of personal sustainability are too deep and wide to be bridged over. Perhaps the differences are too many and too fundamental to deal with beneath one title.

That could be the case. However, it depends on the aspiration and aims given to the approach "personal sustainability". Referring to this chapter "Conclusions", to open a field for all kind of approaches dealing with personal and human aspects is possible and worthwhile. Also theoretical work on personal sustainability and personal sustainability practices are possible and helpful even though they will probably remain incomplete and a universal approach, one 'unified theory of personal sustainability' is neither possible nor desirable in the near future.

Dealing with personal sustainability means bridging fundamental gaps, but not levelling the landscape. For us it is a worthwhile aim to create references and to show interplays between different subjects of and approaches to personal sustainability – but not to unify them and develop one consistent theoretical structure. In consequence, personal sustainability (research) for us is more an occasion and an instrument of understanding. Looking at the variety of topics involved and the gaps pervading the field of personal sustainability, it might take a long time and lots of (discursive) efforts to build a common understanding of personal sustainability.

Personal sustainability is dangerous

Personal sustainability involves the human being in the striving for and the considerations on sustainable development. Apart from that, it deals with personal and often private aspects of individuals and, what is more, it accesses and thereby opens up the inner structure of human being. Drawing attention to the human being and their inner lives involves certain dangers, respectively one danger on different levels and in different shapes. In general, it is the old biblical story: everything you put in words, you get a certain power and control over. And what is more, the modern (successful) re-edition of the story: everything you put to a rational discourse, you make ready for use. That includes abuse.[3] In consequence, in starting the discourse about personal sustainability topics they become accessible for potential use and abuse. That is a very normal process when entering a new field and not characteristic for personal sustainability. However, in the case of personal sustainability it might be specifically sensitive. Thus, we will have a look at some major issues we observe in this context.

a) Human issues as means for sustainable development

At first, there is the danger of instrumentalisation of human being. Human being or, more specific, individuals, can be regarded as means or tools for the purpose of a(n outer) sustainable development. Although it is a very well-known story to use and abuse people for a bigger goal, it is new and introduced by personal sustainability to the discourse of sustainable development. We have already stated in the introduction that this danger comes along with personal sustainability and proposed that personal sustainability should be considered an independent goal of sustainable development and a value in itself. This would avoid that the human being is instrumentalised and loses its autonomy and freedom in the name of sustainability. Additionally, debates on personal sustainability should include philosophical and ethical perspectives, addressing the danger of use, misuse and abuse of it, in order to prevent acting in inhumane ways when dealing with human aspects in the name of sustainable development.

b) Loss of privacy

Since modern times the human sphere has been separated into private and public life. While before there was no elaborated and protected private sphere, from then on the right to have one was approved and established for ever larger parts of the population. Since enlightenment and latest after the Second World War, after many hard lessons learned, the protection of private life against state or third party power is an essential value of modern Western culture and an integral part of human rights. The main motive of this conviction is to prevent the abuse of the private sphere and harm resulting from such abuse for the individual. Knowledge about the private sphere can be misused by others. Traditionally, such knowledge about a person's private life is accessible only to people that have a (close and private) relationship to this person and are trusted by her or him. However, personal sustainability research counteracts this situation by particularly addressing personal or inner aspects (which are most private) and bringing them to discussion and thereby to the public. Regarding personal sustainability itself, the ideas presented in this book often imply an opening up of the private sphere towards others.

In many places and contexts, sharing private issues beyond the traditional relationships already works nowadays, be it in communities (see Veciana and Ottmar) or in the exchange of knowledge on private subjects in order to change situations (e.g. in the course of psychotherapy). In such settings, a certain, extraordinary level of trust and sensitivity is offered by the sharing partners. A higher level of trust and sensitivity like that can prosper and be thriving for individuals and society only if there is an appreciation for it, expressed in the will to and in a common culture of respect for it.[4]

Personal sustainability as approached in the chapters seems to be connected with an orientation and an opening up towards each other (e.g. Veciana and Ottmar, Wendhack, Sacks). In order to build relationship, openness is required and honesty in dealing with others. As a basis for this, also in the context of personal sustainability, sensitivity and trust are crucial. As trust is something that is granted in advance and as there is no guarantee of respect for it, there is the danger of violation by the abuse of confidence, be it in severe cases by taking advantage of knowledge or in less severe cases for example by spreading it.

202 O. Parodi, S. Wendhack and K. Tamm

c) Trivialisation and devaluation

Not putting something into words and not discussing it in public, or at least addressing it with prudence and care instead of submitting it to comprehensibility, clarity and accuracy can express appreciation and respect for it, its variety and its not fully comprehensible nature. This can be observed for example with lyrics or the approach and style of Eastern philosophy in contrast to Western one (e.g. Jullien 2000). Dealing with a topic in a Western scientific context means analysing it and defining it accurately. Thereby it gets current and familiar, which might lead to a reduction of meaning regarding depth and richness of details and nuances.

By exposing a subject to scientific discussion people get accustomed to the terms employed and, perceiving these terms more and more as placeholders, they lose contact to what is meant by them. Losing contact here means not perceiving the subjects with the whole person anymore. In consequence, though they are increasingly applied, the terms might develop into superficiality, regarding the depth of a term as well as the degree a person is involved dealing with it.[5] In consequence, opening a scientific discourse on personal sustainability and carrying out personal sustainability research, there is the danger of trivialisation and devaluation – in two dimensions: First, personal sustainability research – acting in a common analytical-scientific manner – can remain superficial and might not catch the essential meanings and findings. That would mean that personal sustainability research fails as an epistemological endeavour. Second, by carrying out personal sustainability research, the subject, the human being and her or his inner world, can be devaluated. That would be a horrible consequence and exactly the opposite we are targeting at.

In order to counteract these dangers a more evolved capacity of the persons dealing with personal sustainability is needed: extended awareness of the nature of personal sustainability contents and their incomplete tangibility, as well as the knowledge of and a fine sense for the limits of scientific methods.

d) Commercialisation and exploitation

In the first place commercialisation and exploitation are issues regarding sustainable development itself. While the idea of sustainable development was developed as an independent goal, a value in itself, nowadays many perspectives of sustainable development have their orientation towards economic aspects or are designed from an economic point of view. In many cases such a perspective had been chosen in order to promote the subject: it is argued that it is easier to reach people via the economic way, within our highly economically oriented society it is easier to establish the subject if it is presented dressed like that. Nevertheless, even if often done this way for good motives, or just from habit, it is questionable if approaches considering sustainable development an economical good meet the point. The same deliberations are considerable for personal sustainability, to an even greater extent. As with personal sustainability, human beings and their inner lives are involved, there is the danger that they are put into a (capitalistic) logic of exploitation.

Some examples: big (top) companies offer or even push their employees to meditate, practice yoga or other stress reductive methods, apparently for them to become healthier and more stress resilient – but in the end to render their employees more efficient, creative and productive. Apart from that, more and more people take yoga or Mindful-Based Stress Reduction (MBSR) classes and meditate within their leisure time. Though many of them do so in order to cope with their overloaded daily lives, especially with the requirements and loads of their jobs. Or even worse: people enhance their personal abilities and capacities by taking psychiatric drugs – to be able to accomplish their jobs. These are examples for personal and inner human issues being directly put to the (capitalistic) value-added chain. In the name of "personal sustainability" something similar is conceivable: inner human matters being exploited via an economic approach – aiming for an outer sustainable development.

On the other side of the market, to satisfy these growing demands of personal development and enhancement, the number and variety of 'personal enhancement offers' is huge and growing. A big market of 'personal development' is growing. Personal development – and why not *sustainable* personal development – that way becomes a product and good. In consequence, personal sustainability as a good will probably be appreciated by proponents of a sustainable lifestyle and become a best seller – but not automatically contribute to a sustainable future.

e) Manipulation

Personal sustainability deals not only with the private but also with the inner sphere or the mental constitution of individuals (see Hunecke, Lass). The inner human structure, the intimate inner sphere of an individual, his or her mental constitution, strengths, competencies but also difficulties and injuries may be opened up for others in the name of sustainable development. In particular contexts where inner and mental structures are addressed and worked with, trust, respect and sensitivity are demanded and fostered by strong codes of conduct that have been established. For example, psychologists and psychiatrists are bound to a professional secrecy in order to protect private and intimate matters of clients. Furthermore they still follow the Hippocratic Oath to prevent abuse, violation and damage of their patients. In contrast, for other contexts dealing with human aspects, also for personal sustainability, no such codes of conduct are available up to now.

Access to the inner constitution of individuals means power over them. In the extreme case, one may get direct control over a person. In fields where there is no respective awareness and no corresponding codes of conduct are established, it is dangerous to open inner and mental structures to the public. Knowledge of these structures can mean access to them in a direct and manipulative way, which can be imagined comparatively harmless for example in case of influencing buying behaviour or extremely abusive considering psychological warfare or torture. Consequences of such (massive) manipulation can be the loss of freedom of action and autonomy, the loss of individuality or mental violation.

Also concerning this risk it becomes obvious that exploring new research fields means opening up knowledge, having a broader access to the human situation and the world and therefore increased power to use or misuse them: it is crucial and part of the learning process of humankind to evolve and achieve the necessary level of moral integrity, i.e. the maturity to be able to assume responsibility for handling this knowledge (see below).

Perspectives

What is needed regarding personal sustainability and personal sustainability research in the near future? What is crucial to be considered for it and what can the next steps be? Closing this book we want to present some future perspectives for personal sustainability.

Perspectives for the research and concept of personal sustainability

For the prosperity of personal sustainability research, further disciplines, scientific and non-scientific approaches have to be included. Beside the disciplines represented by the authors in this book and the disciplines and approaches already mentioned in the introduction (see Chapter 1 "Similar approaches" and "Aims and approaches of the book") it would be fruitful to integrate anthropology in order to get a broader fundament for personal sustainability dealing with human being and specific sociological theories and approaches like e.g. the Resonance Theory (Rosa 2016) to link personal sustainability to current societal analysis. Apart from that, ethnology and cultural studies would complement the field by rendering the discussion more global and multi-cultural, as well as theology as a discipline that can build bridges to spirituality and spiritual practices.

As mentioned above, in order to prevent personal sustainability from arbitrariness it is crucial to link the discourse about personal sustainability to the various sustainable development discourses, especially to the topic "transition to sustainability"/"transformation research" (see e.g. IST 2017) and the sustainability discourses dealing with topics on the micro- and meso-level, such as "sustainable consumption", "degrowth" or "sustainable lifestyles". We would like and hope that personal sustainability will not be discussed by an isolated community only but become a cross-topic throughout all sustainable development discourses. Integrating personal, inner aspects to all kinds of sustainable development topics could be a valuable supplement – even to topics such as climate change, energy consumption, biodiversity or water use: What are the personal, inner human aspects linked to these sustainability topics?

What we have tried and practiced to a small extent with this book is important for personal sustainability, and also for personal sustainability research: to link scientific approaches with non-scientific knowledge and practices, be it traditional philosophies and inner practices like Yoga or Zen, alternative movements like "Buen Vivir" or "Décroissance" or very individual inner or bodily experiences.

In each of these cases we have to leave the solid ground of scientific disciplines and even common scientific methods.

In consequence, for pursuing personal sustainability research seriously and in a responsible manner, a new methodology is needed and has to be developed in order to link the inter-subjective research and knowledge of sustainable development (as well as parts of personal sustainability) with the subjective, personal, inner research and unique insights of every individual. Orientation for this can be provided by the current methodology of transdisciplinary research, action research and transformative research, where scientists and practitioners corporately generate new knowledge (and competences) for sustainable development (e.g. Hirsch Hadorn *et al.* 2008, Stringer 2014). However, to integrate the inner dimension of human being and very unique experiences of individuals into personal sustainability research and theory is very special. It goes beyond the integration of non-scientific practical knowledge and literally means to integrate humane being. Therefore, the existing methods of transdisciplinary research have to be adjusted and extended, and probably additional, entirely new methods have to be developed.

And it might also work the other way round: personal sustainability research as an inter- and transdisciplinary endeavour could be very fruitful for the respective scientific disciplines as well as for the practitioners participating in this endeavour. Far beyond the sustainable development discourse stimuli to anthropology, philosophy, psychology, sociology, cultural studies, etc. are conceivable.

For the concept of personal sustainability it would be very interesting and fruitful to look at personal sustainability from a multi-cultural perspective. So spreading the concept of personal sustainability into the international discourse and involving scientists and practitioners from all continents is promising. Beside the danger of an overwhelming diversity of (scientific) approaches in the intercultural discourse there is the chance to recognise the own cultural blind spots dealing with personal sustainability.[6]

For personal sustainability as a programme as well as for a transition to sustainability and a lived culture of sustainability we aim at, besides scientific personal sustainability research, doing personal and inner research is very important. We as human individuals have to explore and recognise ourselves. Without "Know thyself" (Greek: "Gnothi Seautón"), without knowing ourselves much better than is common nowadays in Western societies, a sustainable development will finally fail (see Niehaus *et al.*, Lass, Parodi, Veciana and Ottmar, Villido).

For us, the editors, the next step regarding personal sustainability research will be – besides continuing our inner and outer research on personal sustainability – to have a closer look at the links and interdependencies between inner, personal aspects of sustainable development and the close surroundings of individuals. Personal sustainability and interpersonal and communal aspects, education and personal sustainability, communities and (sub-)cultures of sustainability are topics for the book planned next.

Perspectives for personal sustainability

Perhaps one of the most promising perspectives concerning personal sustainability and this book is that people will talk about inner sustainability and the link between an inner and outer as well as a personal and global sustainable development – and this not only in scientific discourses but also in education, business, organisational development and management, in civil society movements, municipalities, communities, the cultural sector and arts.

This includes the exploration of the own inner landscape and condition, that means personal experience, sensations, emotions, thinking, the connectedness to others or our environment and becoming aware of them (see Villido, Lass). Engaging in that exploration, the individual will increase his or her consciousness of themselves and their acting, be connected to a larger extent and thus more sensitive and stable.

In consequence, he or she will be able to know better how to pursue sustainable development and be more apt to put it into practice. The latter will be the case neither because of increased knowledge nor because of higher motivation but because the integration of the person will close the gap between knowledge and action and consequently there will be less difference between them.

To foster that process, training and practice is needed (see Niehaus *et al.*, Lass), and to bring it to society it is needed to integrate it in schools, universities, companies, governmental agencies and other sectors. A precondition for that is to promote and foster the topic "personal sustainability" and the dialogue on it beforehand.

For us, becoming personally more sustainable goes along with the expansion of autonomy of an individual as well as – the other side of the coin – her or his responsibility (see this chapter 'Highlights'). Therefore, developing personal sustainability with its new forms of togetherness implies an evolution regarding moral aspects, broadening the moral horizon.

An evolution regarding moral capacities here cannot refer to moral claims, established norms or regulation only. What is required cannot be complied by outer means of such kind. Personal sustainability will get rather refined, decentralised and complex, thus that outer means will not be sufficient to promote it. Inner commitment instead will constitute a part of it. In consequence, what will be required is the autonomy of the individual in a way that includes personal development, reflexivity, awareness, sensitivity and responsibility arising from the perception of connectedness. The respect for confidence that is paid on the other hand will not be one allowing to count on the fulfilment of regulation or the compliance with norms, but on proper sincerity.

Personal sustainability can be considered to broaden and settle personal autonomy for the individual by relying on inner aspects such as refined attitudes, intuition, the perception of subjective body, the relation to the world, including emotions and also comprising the possibility of developing these aspects and thereby oneself. In contrast to the movement of enlightenment that was based on reason alone, personal sustainability comprises less distinct (at least seen from a perspective of mind) and more 'tender', however not less powerful, ways to relate to the world. As it could be observed in enlightenment, with increased personal autonomy there comes a higher level of responsibility for oneself and the whole. Oliver Parodi writes that truth might be completed by love now. Comparable to enlightenment where it was started to regard truth higher than power, the current situation promotes or even demands to regard also love higher than power.

Thus, one of the key findings from dealing with personal sustainability in this book might be the following: it counteracts the exploitation and instrumentalisation of human beings. Taken seriously, and this is crucial here, it leads to free and autonomously acting persons, who are able to assume responsibility for themselves and their acting. They are able to do so not only on a rational but also on an emotional level, implying enhanced awareness. The link to sustainable development is that human beings are only able to protect other humans, nature and the planet from exploitation if they have the experience to be free from it themselves, if they know autonomy and therefore are capable of assuming responsibility. If that is true, it might lead to new and very different approaches for sustainable development. The transition to sustainability does not only require environmental technologies, legislation and market regulation but at least as necessarily: free, autonomous, self-reflexive, sensitive and connected people. In the end, or at the very beginning, sustainable development might not be a question of achieving the Sustainable Development Goals but of dignity and humanity.

Notes

1 For example: you often read or hear about "psycho*logical*" or "eco*logical* effects". But what is meant are mental effects or effects affecting the ecosystem. It is not the scientific discipline evocating these effects. The discipline only addresses the perspective and the distinctive way you look at these effects and contextualise them.
2 Or more strongly-worded: adding personal sustainability to the sustainable development discourse, we will no longer be able to avoid and bypass the inner and human aspects. We will have to recognise and deal with them.
3 It is important to remark that using things, nature and even persons is an essential part of human life. It is not the intent to speak in favour of abandoning this way of being in the world completely, that would be at least not adequate, at most ridiculous. The questions are *how* we use them and if we are free and responsible in our decisions, if we decide for or against a form of use in a conscious, autonomous way or not. We would tend to suggest that a large part of the exploitation we observe in the world is driven by own lack of inner freedom of the actors.
4 The movement towards sharing inner matters also generates strange or ugly effects as for example the afternoon talk shows or "Big Brother" and similar programmes, where people spread out their private lives without any connectedness and sensitivity.
5 The trend to replace connectedness and sensitivity by increased explicitness can – aside from science – also be observed in common culture, for example in nowadays' Disney films.
6 At this point we want to indicate that the concept of personal sustainability as well as the concept and programme of sustainable development are grown on a modern Western body of thought. As such they have a strong cultural bias. We presume that personal sustainability focuses on Western aspects of (non-)sustainable development. E.g. poverty and the lack of basic material needs, physical violence and oppression that are so widespread on earth are not addressed by personal sustainability by now.

We want to stress that personal sustainability must never be abused to bypass or relativise basic material needs (see this chapter 'Concerns').

References

Hirsch Hadorn, G.; Hoffmann-Riem, H.; Biber-Klemm, S.; Grossenbacher-Mansuy, W.; Joye, D.; Pohl, C.; Wiesmann, U.; Zemp, E. (Eds) (2008): *Handbook of Transdisciplinary Research*. Dordecht, the Netherlands: Springer Netherlands.

IST 2017: International Sustainability Transitions Conference 2017. Retrieved 7 September 2017, from http://ist2017.org/home/about/.

Jullien, F. (2000): *Detour and Access. Strategies of Meaning in China and Greece*. New York: Zone Books.

Rosa, H. (2016): *Resonance – A Sociology of the Relationship to the World*. Frankfurt, Germany: Suhrkamp.

Stringer, E.T. (2014): *Action Research: A Handbook for Practitioners*. 4th ed., Thousand Oaks, CA: SAGE.

Index

Locators in **bold** refer to tables and those in *italics* to figures.

academic context: alternative approaches
  8–10; historical context 6–7; the
  personal in sustainable development
  1–4, 5–6; terminology 6–7;
  transdisciplinary research 11–12
active listening 128
aesthetic, inner technologies 15, 175, 180
aesthetical education 30–31
alternative sustainable development:
  community practices 120–129,
  130–132; World Commission on
  Environment and Development 118
ancient civilisations 21–22, 23
anthropocene 171–172, 174
anthroposemiosis 151–152
anxiety disorder 107, 108
Aristotle 22, 26, 27, 30, 171, 175
art of life: Bildung 60–63; self-care 13,
  53–60; self-guidance 51–52
arts: aesthetical education 30–31; inner
  technologies 175; inspiration for
  personal sustainability 9
automatic complexes 107–109, 139
awareness: automation and disconnection
  138–140; change-making 142–143;
  community practices 120; different
  ways of knowing 137–138; human
  identity 146–148; meaning of 143–144;
  mental health 98–101, 102–104, 107,
  110–111; mental–emotional paradigm
  141–142; new paradigm 136–137,
  144–145; personal virtues 29; shared
  and individual reality 140–141;
  sustainability transition 145–146,
  148–149; *see also* self-awareness

Bacon, Francis 61, 75
behaviour therapy 86–87
Behrens, William 153

Berkowitz, Bill 8
Beuys, Joseph 171, 176
Bieri, Peter 61, 63
"Bildung" 13, 60–63, 93
body *see* subjective body
Brown, Brene 159
Brundtland report 4, 18–19, 118
Buber, Martin 84, 87–88

capacity building 164–166
Centre for Experimental Cultural Design
  (ZEGG) 121, 123–124
change-making: awareness 142–143;
  reflexivity 163–164
Chomsky, Noam 137, 138
Christianity: "Bildung" 60–63; human
  relationships to the world 75; nature
  154–155; self-care 55; sustainable
  development 193–194
civil society: community 45–46;
  metanarratives **157**, 157–158
Climate Summit 179
coaching, psychology of sustainability 43,
  44
collective side of sustainability 1; *see also*
  community practices
Collins, Rebecca 8
commercialisation 202–203
communication, community practices
  130–132
community, psychology of sustainability
  45–46
community building 8, 124–127, 130–132
Community Learning Incubator for
  Sustainability (CLIPS) 120
community practices 116–118, *117*,
  132–133; alternative sustainable
  development 120–129; comparative
  analysis 130–132; for personal

sustainability 120–129; personal sustainability barriers and drivers 118–120
companies, psychology of sustainability 45
conflict resolution, community practices 14, 118–120, 126, 127, 131
connective practice methodology 171, 176–177, 201
Conscious Discharge practice 127–129, 130–132
consciousness, intra-personal skills 103–104
constancy 25, 28
corporations, psychology of sustainability 45
counselling: Christianity 55; resource-oriented 35–36; *see also* therapy
Croft, John 120
cultural change: personal sustainability 9–10; sustainable development 3–4
cultural memory 27
culture: community practices 126–127, 128–129; the good life 22–23; groups 119–120, 125–126; liberty 23–24, 196; and nature 20–22; *see also* sustainable cultures

de Chardin, Teilhard 175–176
Deely, John 156, 164
deep ecology 9, 70, 154
degrowth movement 154
Descartes, Rene 75, 110
disconnection: awareness 138–140; reflexivity 153–155, 157–159
Dittmar, Vivian 127–129
downscaling-upscaling aspects 159–160
Dragon Dreaming 120
duplicity syndrome 162

Earth Forum methodology 177–184, **182**
ecological economics 26
ecological movement: human relationships to the world 77–78; personal sustainability 8, 9
ecological sustainability 7
economic sustainability 7; *see also* 'limits to growth'
ecopsychology 9
Ecovillage Design Education (EDE) 120
ecovillages 116–117
ecovillages, community practices *122*, 127–129

education: aesthetical 30–31; awareness 110–111; community practices 120; mental health awareness 98–101, 102; Plato 52; psychology of sustainability 44–45; Socrates 52
ego: self-identity 104–106; unconscious automatic complexes 109
Egyptian civilisation 22, 23
Ehrlich, Paul 153
emotions: community practices 129; intra-personal skills 106–107, 108–109, 111–112; mental-emotional paradigm 141–142
empowerment *see* self-empowerment
environment: disconnection 153–155; protection laws 19
environmental psychology 9, 34
Exchange Values project 178–179, 180
exploitation 202–203

fake news 27
fear, sustainable cultures 68–69, 197–198
firms, psychology of sustainability 45
forgiveness 28
Forum method, community practices 121–124, 130–132
Foucault, Michael 53, 56–57
freedom: inner technologies 184–185; liberty 18, 23–24, 25–26, 28, 196; responsibility 195–198
Freire, Paulo 179
Freud, Sigmund 84, 87
future generations 4, 18–19

Gauntlett-Gilbert, J. 110–111
Giddens, Anthony 158, 162–163
Global Ecovillage Network (GEN) 116–117
Goethe, J. W. 21, 76, 180, 183
good life: culture 22–23; *homo sustinens* 26–29; orientations to happiness 36–38, **38**; psychological resources 37–43; self-guidance 51
Goodwin, Brian 137, 138, 146, 161
governance, metanarratives **157**, 157–158
group culture 119–120, 125–126
Gudynas, Eduardo 116

Hadot, Pierre 53
happiness: psychological resources 37–43; psychology of sustainability 36–37, **38**, 47
Hardin, Garrett 153

Harro, J. 112
healing therapy 13–14, 84–87, 89–92
health promotion 43–44; *see also* mental health
hedonism, psychological resources 38–39
Heidegger 23
historical context, personal sustainability 6–7
Homburg, Shirli 13
homo mobilis 25
homo narrans 155–156, 166
homo non-sustinens 24–25, 26
homo oeconomicus 24–25, 26
homo semioticus 164, 166
homo sustinens 25–29
human capital 8
human identity 146–148
human signature strengths 36–37
Hunecke, Marcel 13, 40, 196

identity: being human 146–148; intra-personal skills 104–106, 112
imaginal practice 176–184
impartiality 28
individual reality 140–141
inner conflict resolution, community practices 14, 118–120, 126, 127, 131
inner technologies 15, 171–172; connective practice methodology 176–177; Earth Forum methodology 177–184; the field of freedom 184; imaginal practice 177–184; individuals' role 172–173; I-sense 171, 172, 184–185; sustainable development and sustainability 173–176
insight, personal virtues 26–27
intangible-tangible aspects 161
integration, subjective body 84
interdisciplinary research 9, 191
inter-personal skills, community 118–120
intra-personal skills 14, 95–96; community 118–120; conscious and unconscious 103–104; emotions 106–107, 108–109, 111–112; functions 96–97; future perspectives 111–112; identity confusion 104–106, 112; known and unknown 103; mental health awareness 14, 98–101, 102–104, 107, 110–111; mental health causes 98–101; mental health trends 97–98; problems of the current paradigm 101–102; unconscious automatic complexes 107–109
I-sense 171, 172, 184–185

Joubert, Kosha 120
Judaism, human relationships to the world 75
Jung, Carl Gustav 104–105, 106, 108–109

Kant, Immanuel 27, 30, 52
Kaplinski, Jaan 154
Karlsruhe Institute of Technology (KIT) 6, 11
knowledge: different ways of knowing 137–138; intra-personal skills 103; personal virtues 27; psychology of sustainability 34–36; self 51–52, 205; sustainable cultures 66–68; tangible-intangible aspects 161; Western culture 139–140, 202
Körpertherapie 88–89
Kriya Yoga 138, 143, 145, 147

Lass, Helena 14
leadership, personal sustainability 9, 120, 125–126, 130–131
legal context, environmental protection 19
Leopold, Aldo 154
liberty: culture 23–24, 196; *homo sustinens* 25–26; personal virtues 28; sustainable development 18
life satisfaction 46
lifestyles: community practices 116, 118, 121–122; health promotion 43–44; personal sustainability 204–207; psychology of sustainability 34–36, 37–40, 46–47; self-care 57–60; terminology 33
'limits to growth': disconnection 153–155; Malthus 3, 153; reflexivity 165; sustainable cultures 66, 68
love: sustainable cultures 69–72, 207
Luxemburg, Rosa 28

MacIntyre, Alasdair 155
Maiteny, Paul 136
Malthusian 'limits to growth' 3, 153
Manstetten, Reiner 12–13, 196
market, personal development 202–203
marketing-mode 35
Marx, Karl 163–164
Mead, Margaret 163–164
Meadows, Dennis and Donella 153
meaning construction: psychological resources **38**, 39–40, 41, 44–45; reflexivity 164

mental health: awareness 14, 98–101, 102–104, 107, 110–111; causes 98–101; conscious and unconscious 103–104; emotions 106–107; future perspectives 111–112; identity confusion 104–106; intra-personal skills 14, 95–102; known and unknown 103; manipulation 203–204; sustainability in crisis 83–87; therapy 96, 97, 102, 109, 111; trends 97–98; unconscious automatic complexes 107–109; *see also* psychology of sustainability
mental–emotional paradigm 141–142
Merchant, Caroline 158–159
metanarratives 14–15, 156–158, 164–166
Millennium Development Goals 69
Mindful-Based Stress Reduction (MBSR) 203
mindfulness: psychological resources **38**, 39, 41, 42, 44; psychology of sustainability 47; well-being 96
mindfulness-based cognitive therapy (MBCT) 111
Montaigne, Michel 55–56
morality 19, 26, 197, 206
mortality, self-care 59
motivations: psychological resources 40–41; psychology of sustainability 34–35, 47
Motz, Marilyn 137

Naess, Arne 9
narratives 14–15; metanarratives 14–15, 156–158, 164–166; reflexivity 155–156, 164–166; subjective body 89–90
National Institute for Health and Care Excellence (NICE) 111
nature: awareness 29; and culture 20–22; disconnection 153–155; human relationships to the world 73–78
Niehaus, Michael 13
non-profit organizations 45
noosphere 175–176

Oldemeyer, Ernst 73
Ottmar, Kariin 14
Our Common Future (Brundtland report) 4, 18–19, 118

Panksepp, Jaak 106, 107, 111–112
Parodi, Oliver 13, 197, 207
participation 162–163
Peck, Scott 124, 125, 126, 127, 131

personal development market 203
personal sustainability: alternative approaches 8–10; concerns 198–204; conclusions 189–192; contribution to sustainable development 1–4, 5–6; highlights 192–198; historical context 6–7; meaning of 1, 198–199; perspectives 204–207; terminology 6–7, 190–192; this volume 10–15
personal virtues: the good life 22–23; *homo sustinens* 26–29; sustainable development 18, 19–20
Plato 27, 52
pleasure capacity **38**, 38–39, 42
Pleasure-Accomplishment-Meaning theory 36–37, 42–43, 47
positive psychology 35–36
privacy 201
psychology of sustainability 13, 33–34, 46–47; coaching 44; community 45–46; companies 45; health promotion 43–44; knowledge sources 34–36; lifestyles 34–36, 37–40; non-profit organizations 45; orientations to happiness 36–37, **38**, 47; resources for 38–43, *41*, **43**; school 44–45; subjective well-being 37–38

Randers, Jörgen 153
reality, awareness of 140–141
receptivity: aesthetical education 30–31; personal virtues 28–29; self-care 57
reconnection 157–159, 193
reflexivity 151–152, 166–167; capacity building 164–166; change-making 163–164; disconnection 153–155, 157–159; individuals' role 162–163; metanarratives 156–158; narratives 155–156, 164–166; reconnection 157–159; sustainable development and sustainability 152–153; tangible-intangible 161; upscaling–downscaling 159–160; *see also* self-reflectivity
Reich, William 88–89
religion: aesthetical education 30–31; "Bildung" 60–63; human relationships to the world 75; self-care 55
resilience 14, 112
resource-oriented counselling 35–36
responsibility, sustainable development 195–198, 206–207
Richter, D. 122, 123
Roman civilisation 22

Sacks, Shelley 15, 196–197, 198
Saiva Siddhanta tradition 138
scale 1–2, 159–160
Schiller, F. 30
Schloss Tempelhof community 124, 126
Schmidt, Dick 13
Schmitz, Herman 88, 89
school, psychology of sustainability 44–45; *see also* education
School of Sustainability (SoS) 6
Schumacher, E. M. 15
scientific knowledge 202
self-acceptance **38**, 39, 40–41, 44
self-actualisation 162–163
self-awareness: change-making 142–143; community practices 120; personal virtues 29
self-care: art of living 13, 53–60; "Bildung" 60–63; exercises in 57–60
self-control 27–28, 103, 109
self-cultivation 60–63
self-efficacy **38**, 39, 40–41, 44–45
self-empowerment, community practices 14, 118–120, 122–123, 126, 128–129, 131–132
self-governance 120
self-identity 104–106, 112
selfishness 24–25, 26
self-knowledge 51–52, 205
self-productivity 58
self-receptivity 57
self-reflectivity 57–58; *see also* reflexivity
self-representation method 121
self-talk 119
self-writing 119
Seligman, M. E. P. 35, 36–37
shared reality 140–141
Sieben Linden ecovillage *122*, 127–129
social context, self-care 59–60; *see also* community practices; intra-personal skills
social movements 162–163
social sculpture-connective practice 171, 178–179
social-ecological research 34
Socrates 51–52, 53–54, 56–57, 62
solidarity **38**, 40, 41, 44–45
South Africa, Earth Forum 178–179, 180, 181
spiritual practice, aesthetical education 30–31

Stage Model of Self-regulated Behavioural Change 34
Stahl, S. 111
Steiner, Rudolf 171
Stoic philosophy 54–55
subjective body 13–14, 83, 92–93; implications of shift 90–92; as missing perspective 87–90; rationality 71; sustainability in crisis 83–87
subjective well-being 37–38
sustainability in crisis: awareness 136, 148; subjective body 83–87; *see also* 'limits to growth'
sustainability transition 72, 85–87, 145–146, 148–149
sustainable cultures 19–24; creation of 65–66, 78–80; fear 68–69, 197–198; human relationships to the world 72–78; love 69–72; truth 66–68; *see also* culture
Sustainable Development Goals 69
sustainable development/sustainability: inclusion of personal sustainability 1–4, 5–6, 192–193; inner technologies 173–176; meaning of 4, 18–19, 31, 177–178; reflexivity 152–153; types of 1–2

Tamm, Kaidi 14–15, 193, 199
tangible–intangible aspects 161
technological development: sustainable cultures 67; sustainable development 1–2; *see also* inner technologies
technosphere 175–176
therapy: community practices 127–129, 130; healing 13–14, 84–87, 89–92; mental health 96, 97, 102, 109, 111; self-care 58–59; subjective body 87–92; sustainability in crisis 83–87; *see also* counselling
Thompson, M. 110–111
transdisciplinary research 11, 12, 191, 192–193
trivialisation 202
truth, sustainable cultures 66–68

unconscious automatic complexes 107–109
unconsciousness, intra-personal skills 103–104
upscaling–downscaling aspects 159–160
utilitarianism 8

Value–Belief–Norm model 34
Veciana, Stella 14
Vernadsky, Vladimir 175–176
Villido, Ingvar 14, 103, 105, 108, 109
virtues *see* personal virtues

well-being: and mental health 95–96;
    psychology of sustainability 37–38,
    43–44, 47; *see also* mental health
Wendhack, Sabin 13–14, 196
Western culture: automatic complexes
    139–140; *homo oeconomicus* 24–25;
    knowledge 139–140; liberty 25; nature
    154–155; scientific knowledge 202;

self-care 55–56; sustainable
    development 193–194
White, Hayden 154
White, Lynn Townsend 154
will, personal virtues 27–28
World Commission on Environment
    and Development (WCED) 4, 18–19,
    118
World Health Organization (WHO),
    mental health 97–98

yoga 6, 89, 94, 138, 140–145, 147,
    203–204
Yogananda, P. 106